Disneyland and Culture

D0117799

Disneyland and Culture

Essays on the Parks and Their Influence

edited by KATHY MERLOCK JACKSON
and MARK I. WEST

McFarland & Company, Inc., Publishers
Jefferson, North Carolina, and London

The chapter by Robert Neuman first appeared in *The Journal of American Culture* 31:1 (March 2008): 83–97, and is © Wiley-Blackwell Publishing; reprinted by permission.

The chapter by Richard V. Francaviglia first appeared as "Walt Disney's Frontierland as an Allegorical Map of the American West," *Western Historical Quarterly* 30 (Summer 1999): 155–182, and is © Western History Association; reprinted by permission.

A shorter version of the chapter by Suzanne Rahn appeared as "Snow White's Dark Ride" in *Bookbird* 38.1 (2000): 19–24.

This book makes reference to various Disney copyrighted characters, trademarks, marks and registered marks owned by The Walt Disney Company and Disney Enterprises, Inc.

LIBRARY OF CONGRESS CATALOGUING-IN-PUBLICATION DATA

Disneyland and culture : essays on the parks and their influence / edited by Kathy Merlock Jackson and Mark I. West.
    p.   cm.
    Includes bibliographical references and index.

    ISBN 978-0-7864-4372-7
    softcover : 50# alkaline paper ∞

    1. Disneyland (Calif.)— Social aspects.   2. Disneyland Paris (Marne-la-Vallé, France)— Social aspects.   3. Celebration (Fla.)— Social aspects.   4. Amusement parks— Social aspects.   5. Walt Disney Enterprises.   I. Jackson, Kathy Merlock, 1955–   II. West, Mark I.
GV1853.3.C22.D57311   2011
791.06'879496— dc22   2010045771

British Library cataloguing data are available

Cover design by Kelly Elliott; Mickey Ears logo is © Disney Enterprises, Inc.

Manufactured in the United States of America

McFarland & Company, Inc., Publishers
  Box 611, Jefferson, North Carolina 28640
  www.mcfarlandpub.com

To the memory of Ray Browne
and to Pat Browne,
whose enduring work in popular culture
changed the way we look at the world,
enriching and inspiring generations of scholars

Table of Contents

Disneyland's Variations

Disneyland's Influence

Introduction

On July 17, 1955, Walt Disney unveiled to the masses the project that had consumed him for the previous several years: a theme park in Anaheim, California, that he called Disneyland. Now over a half a century old, the park and what it wrought have no doubt exceeded Disney's wildest dreams. Not only was Disneyland a success that drew hundreds of thousands of visitors and spawned various Disney-themed parks worldwide, but it also had a pronounced cultural effect in areas as diverse as the uses of public space; trends of architecture, entertainment and tourism; identification of heroes; interpretation of history; and modes of celebration. That is what this book is about. It is not so much a chronicle of Disneyland, for that story has been told many times over, but rather an exploration of the cultural impact of what may have been the greatest leap of imagination from one of the twentieth century's most creative and whimsical futurists.

Disneyland opened at the height of the post–World War II baby-boom era, and it was baby boomers and their parents who first caught theme-park fever, embarking on what later came to be regarded as the essential vacation, one's childhood pilgrimage. When visiting Disneyland, and later Walt Disney World in central Florida, families entered a place already familiar and comfortable due to the popularization of Disney characters and storylines via Disney's prodigious use of televison. Debuting in 1954, *Disneyland* on ABC showcased the four realms of Disney's theme park: Fantasyland, Adventureland, Frontierland, and Tomorrowland. Relying on a large archive of classic animated films and combined with new material, *Disneyland* won over viewers, making Mickey Mouse, Donald Duck, Snow White and the Seven Dwarfs, Peter Pan, Tinker Bell, and Davy Crockett as recognizable to American families as their next door neighbors. The following year *The Mickey Mouse Club* began, confirming Disney's understanding of the link between television, movies, beloved characters and stories, and the need for a place to celebrate them. Disney vowed that his park would be clean and safe, and within this sanitized environment, visitors felt protected, entertained, and open to new ideas, sensations, and images. Innovative landscaping, architecture, transportation and business practices enhanced the Disney experience, creating what company executives called "Disney magic."

The magic spread, too powerful to be self contained. Disney masterminded not only media products and recreational facilities but also ways of looking at the world, making sense of our environment, interpreting history, and finding connections. Disney strategies of "themeing" and corporate synergy permeated American culture. Today the children and grandchildren of the postwar baby boomers have embraced elements of Disney's theme park concept and transformed them in new ways.

The essays in this book speak to this transformation.

The Disneyland Concept

The Theme Park
The Art of Time and Space

Margaret J. King *and*
J. G. O'Boyle

> [Walt Disney World] was not just an amusement park, but an environment stimulating new ideas.
>
> Francois Barre, director
> Parc La Villette Museum, Paris
> [qtd. in Schooner 39]

Defining the Genre

Walt Disney did not invent the theme park. He did not even create the name. To Disney and his team of designers — his *Imagineers*— Disneyland was simply "the park." The term "theme park" came into public usage several years after Disneyland's opening, coined by a journalist at the *Los Angeles Times* when it became obvious that Disney's creation could not be faithfully described with the terminology of the traditional amusement park (Blake 439).

But naming something is not the same thing as understanding it. Popular confusion of the two media is still the rule rather than the exception, complicated by the fact that many amusement parks added themed elements or themed areas to their amusement cores, then retitled themselves theme parks. Today the terms "theme park" and "amusement park" are used interchangeably but in origins, design, intent, and effect the theme park is as different from the amusement park as a performance of the Brandenburg Concerto is from a punk rock concert.

5

For Walt Disney and those who worked on the prototype model in the early 1950s, it was enough to talk about what the parks do, and how they do it — what's inside, what it looks like, and what sort of experience it creates. The tradition of saying "There's no way to explain it: you've just got to see it for yourself" (Blake 425) was enough for the first generation of Imagineers when there were no other contenders for the theme park title. Today, however, the evolution of the theme park as a major cultural and commercial force, along with the contemporaneous and interconnected revival of the amusement park as a high-tech industry, makes it both necessary and possible to compare and contrast the two institutions and develop the following working definition of a theme park.

> Theme Park: A social artwork designed as a four-dimensional symbolic landscape to evoke impressions of places and times, real or imaginary [King 837].

The theme park/amusement park dichotomy runs much deeper than terminology. Amusement parks are limited experiences. They are, by definition, places of amusement. Their attraction lies in the immediate physical gratification of the thrill ride — what the late Disney President Frank Wells called "soft adventures"— the apparent defiance of Newtonian laws of action and reaction, the exhilaration of speed, the push and pull of gravity, the rush of adrenaline response to the illusion of potential bodily harm. The theme park, on the other hand, is an environmental art form, one that owes far more to film than physics.

Unlike amusement parks which can grow by accretion, adding a roller coaster here or a carrousel there as the capital budget allows, a theme park, or each themed area within an expanding theme park, must be planned, built, integrated, and unveiled as a unified design in order to preserve its thematic integrity. This detailed holistic evocation of a place in time is one of the major elements that distinguishes the theme park from its distant cousin the amusement park.

Theme parks are cultural mind maps — symbolic landscapes built as storyboards of psychological narratives. They are the multi-dimensional descendant of the book, film, and epic rather than the spawn of the roller coaster and Tilt-A-Whirl. In the theme park, rides are mechanisms designed to position the visitor's point of view, much as a camera lens is aligned, moving riders past a series of meticulously focused vignettes to advance the narrative (Finch 392).

Rides also offer the opportunity to expand the experience with physical sensations appropriate to the narrative: the disorientation of flashing lights and smoke, the evocative smell of charcoal, appropriate temperature changes, the rush of wind, and the confirmatory sensory input associated with floating or soaring. Rides are but one of many communications media integrated into the body of the theme park, acting as "executive summaries" to underline the principal themes of the overall theme park experience—an experience that averages eight hours. Time spent on rides comprises a small fraction of the total theme park experience—as little as ten or fifteen minutes.

Unlike the amusement park patron, a theme park visitor can fully engage in the theme experience without ever setting foot on a ride. There are many other features to engage and hold attention: architecture, design, animated and live performance, video, sound and music, light and water technics and the simple fulfillment of pedestrian movement within and among the artfully landscaped themed "worlds." The theme park is not ride-dependent, while rides are the raison d'être of the amusement park. A theme park without rides is still a theme park; an amusement park without rides is a parking lot with popcorn.

The Evolution of the Medium

> Walt Disney has built a Versailles of the twentieth century—but it was a Versailles designed for the pleasure of the people.
>
> Christopher Finch
> *The Art of Walt Disney* [392]

Theme parks had life in spirit and essence long before Walt Disney expanded his vision to the orange groves of Anaheim. As any tourist to Bavaria can attest, Neuschwanstein, Prince Ludwig's mountaintop palace whose wedding-cake architecture inspired Disneyland's Sleeping Beauty Castle, is certainly a theme park. Obsessed with the work of composer Richard Wagner, Ludwig ordered Neuschwanstein's fantastic interiors designed as stage sets to dramatize the themes of Wagner's operas, particularly *Lohengrin*, the Germanic interpretation of the Arthurian Grail quest. In the best theme park tradition of imagineered decor, Ludwig's castle even boasts an indoor lake with artificial caves and grottoes, a throne room that never held a real throne, and a minstrels' gallery where no minstrel ever played. In this total fantasy environment, the Mad Prince could fully immerse himself in the role of Wagner's mythic hero.

The Imperial Summer Palace of China's Manchu dynasty would also have qualified as a theme park. Destroyed by the British in 1860, the Summer Palace was not an edifice, but eight miles of gardens, artificial lakes, pavilioned islands, parks, and Imperial dwellings crafted over centuries and so intricately designed to blend nature, art, and architecture in a harmonious whole that contemporary observers marveled that it was impossible to tell where nature left off and artifice began. Likewise Versailles, where royal engineers used light, mirrors, and hydraulics to raise a palace-and-fountain complex where the Sun King could exercise complete control over the nature of light and water, and for another French creation, Marie Antoinette's toy farm, where neatly-groomed and perfumed animals stood in spotless stalls to simulate the "farm experience"—albeit one deemed fit for a queen.

In this country, publisher and film magnate William Randolph Hearst's "castle" at San Simeon, America's most publicized lavish estate, also fills the bill. Hearst's movie craft shops both created and reproduced "period" architectural details to augment original artifacts imported from Europe, designers and architects commingled reality and illusion with abandon, and landscapers literally moved mountains to integrate the main building, surrounding guest cottages, and outbuildings into an American interpretation of a baronial fiefdom.

These constructions were far more than mere amusements or diversions for the elite — as embodied in the more typical private menagerie, folly, maze, formal garden, or even Catharine the Great's tobogganing hill, which was nothing less than a straight-line wooden roller coaster. Each was something more important and arresting — the attempt to construct a total alternate universe, an enclosed environment physically separate and therefore psychologically autonomous with respect to the surrounding world.

The Disney Transformation

Walt Disney invented the *American* theme park, not just in geographical location, but American in its egalitarian spirit. The personal playlands of royalty were themed upon the elite's vision of themselves as lords of nature as well as man — places where princes and potentates could be, quite literally, masters of all they surveyed. In the same cultural vein, Disney's egalitarian park celebrated the accomplishments and aspirations of the audience for whom it was designed — the American people. Just as Wagner reinterpreted Germanic folk legends into operas celebrating teutonic superiority and destiny, Disney reinterpreted and adapted the folk legends, stories, and myths of our own myriad ancestral homelands focused through the American lens.

The Disney Studios reinterpreted and retold our old world myths with our new, bold, American accent. The result was a showcase of American versus European sensibilities: optimism over cynicism, light over darkness, transformation over resignation, fair play over influence, and enthusiasm over fatalism. Just as the European and Asian elite reveled in the reflection they cast in the mirror of their private pleasure parks, the American public flocked to Disneyland because it reflects and celebrates the virtues we most admire and cultivate in ourselves.

Instruction and Delight

Walt Disney reincarnated the theme park as a place of entertainment and delight as well as education. Previous American theme park models geared to the general public were predicated on an educational or inspirational mission mandated by their founders. The 1893 Columbian Exhibition in Chicago (where Walt's father, Elias Disney, is said to have worked as a contract carpenter) celebrated American achievement in terms of the Old World, particularly in the almost exclusive use of European-inspired neo-classical architecture (Larsen 375–376). Promoters touted a white-clad "celestial city of men, set upon a hill for all the world to behold," an ethereal "city beautiful," and exercised total control over photographs distributed to the media in order to project a public image of upper-class dress and manners. In fact, the Exposition's slim profit margin came primarily from the socially embarrassing "Midway Plaisance," where the rubes were gulled by games of chance and awed by "anthropological tours" of the world's exotic places: Cairo, Blarney Castle, Old Vienna, and even a fully-populated Dahomey village. Given the high tone of official descriptions of the "White City" it is ironic that the only popular reference that remains today is the term "midway" as a synonym for the tawdry carnival pitch.

Frederic Thompson and Skip Dundy's Luna Park (1903) and William H. Reynolds' Dreamland (1904) were Coney Island's contribution to the theme park genre. Unlike the better-known Steeplechase Park which featured thrill rides like the Ferris wheel and roller coaster, Luna Park and Dreamland used the "experiential" powers of the theme park medium to recreate other times, places, and worlds.

Along with the thrill rides, visitors could take "A Trip to The Moon," emerging from their space capsules to stroll the lunar landscape and be accosted by "moonmen" (giants and dwarfs) and "moon maidens" handing out samples of green cheese. They could voyage "20,000 Leagues Beneath the Sea," experience the eruption of Vesuvius and destruction of Pompeii, view the Creation, The End of the World, or even, literally, go to Hell — complete with fluttering tissue-paper flames and menacing demons. A 12,000-seat stadium could accommodate the Boer War as re-enacted by 600 actual veterans fresh from Johannesburg, 300 midgets populated Liliputia, and scores of firemen bravely battled the flames pouring from an entire city block of asbestos-covered tenement buildings — twice a day (Snow).

On hot summer days, visitors could ride a mountain railway through the Swiss Alps soothed by blasts of cooled air or watch Galveston disappear beneath the waves in a recreation of the great flood of 1900. These were the immediate ancestors, in both spirit and technology, of attractions such as Disneyland's Matterhorn Bobsleds, Disney's Hollywood Studios "Catastrophe Canyon," "Star Tours," and Universal Studios "Earthquake: The Big One."

Using the flexibility of temporary "carnival architecture" built of wood covered with a mixture of pliable plaster staff, Thompson, Dundy, and Reynolds looked to the Mysterious East and other exotic climes for their themes and designed their parks as exotic "Electric Baghdads" of phantasmagoric towers festooned with one million incandescent bulbs. Luna Park and Dreamland were collaborations of technology, scale, and spectacle that were American in spirit, but not in theme. Like the Columbian Exhibition, they drew their technology from America, but most of their inspiration from foreign shores and exotic or mythic locales (Kasson 6–8).

John D. Rockefeller, Jr.'s sponsorship of Colonial Williamsburg (1927) helped set the terms for the "improving" model of theme park in which the word "entertainment" is still reluctantly uttered. At Greenfield Village (1933), automaker Henry Ford assembled a collection of buildings including Thomas Edison's Menlo Park workshop and Fort Myers laboratory, Noah Webster's birthplace, Stephen Foster's home, Luther Burbank's home and office, and the Wright brothers' home and bicycle shop — all shipped in from their original sites and reassembled in Dearborn, Michigan for the inspiration and edification of the masses. Such high-mindedness is in itself an American archetype, a byproduct of the Protestant work ethic. In fact, Walt Disney's first impulse was to follow in the steps of Ford and Rockefeller with a series of traveling dioramas to animate great moments in American history and folklore in the classroom.

But Disney was a Missouri farm boy, his own childhood spent in a variety of backbreaking jobs. His most fondly recalled youthful moments were those lost in another world — that of the storybook. Later, as a communicator constantly pushing the frontiers of animation and film, he saw the possibilities in creating a new type of three-dimensional movie for a new kind of "audience" — one that moves around, interacts, and reads its own personal plots and subplots into the script.[1]

Finally, Walt Disney also invented the first permanent commercial theme park. This was possible because of the emergence of the twentieth-century middle class. This is an audience unprecedented in history: a numerically dominant working population with a host of advantages formerly reserved solely for the elite: general education, knowledge of other options and the freedom to pursue them, geographic and class (cultural) mobility, leisure time, and discretionary income.

As important is the equalizing nature of television, which enabled a continent-wide ethnically-diverse population to share a common set of values, memories, and cultural benchmarks. Whereas previous theme parks were possible only with the massive resources of an autocrat, a nation/state, or a pre-income tax industrial baron, the rise of the new mobile television-raised middle class with a shared cultural experience made a permanent pay-as-you-go theme park feasible for the first time in history.

Breaking into the Fourth Dimension

The theme park is a physical creation in three dimensions. Psychologically, however, the environmental matrix of the theme park is a four-dimensional one, the fourth dimension being time.

The theme park, in essence, temporarily suspends physicist H. A. Lorentz's theory of space-time interdependency. The mechanism of themeing makes it possible to transmute time into physical space. Visitors step out of Einstein's four-dimensional space-time continuum. They can literally walk the unpaved streets of Colonial Williamsburg, the boardwalk of a turn-of-the-century small town, or the tanbark of a 1943 Army Air Corps flying field. As a total-immersion artform whose every programmed detail evokes images of other times, people, and places, the theme park can transport us into a hyperreality of past or future. The theme park, in many of its incarnations, could more correctly be defined as a "time park."

In one respect, the theme park offers something less than the traditional "reality." Visitors are still encapsulated in the protective bubble of the present, immunized from such period unpleasantries as yellow fever, smallpox, dysentery, sweat-shop labor, child marriage, death of old age at thirty-three, or Nazi shrapnel. While these are customarily referenced, they are edited out of the physical narrative — slavery at Colonial Williamsburg, for instance. In an historically-accurate environment, three out of four costumed docents would be portraying Black slaves.

Hyperreality and Memory

The theme park, then, offers us not reality, but *hyperreality*—a tightly edited, stylized, and focused version of reality, shaped to advance a specific narrative. Theme parks are not intended as reconstructions; they are symbolic communications. The technology of the parks: altered scale, re-engineered perspective, color, harmonics, texture, lighting, sound, and iconography, all combine to produce an effect "more real than real." Hyperreality springboards off our preconceptions—which come from film, paintings, and books, but rarely from memories of the real thing—until the visitor reaches a state of what historians call "sensibility," the feeling of actually "being there," totally immersed in another time and place.

The psychic echo of our memory plays a central role in the modern theme park visit. We all bring to the parks the eidetic imagery and iconography of other times and places, sorted and codified in our memories from myriad sources. Well-traveled visitors may remember the campanile in Florence or China's Temple of Heaven from personal experience. Most, however, bring "mediated" memories from popular sources — eclectic images from advertising, photographs, television, movies. In either case, these memories, imperfect and derivative to begin with, are colored by time and emotion. The woman who stands in Epcot's World Showcase and reports, "I've been to Florence, and it looks just like this" is being perfectly truthful. Disney's campanile, its colors burnished, physical space compressed, contemporary anomalies edited out, and perspective exaggerated, is faithful to the *memory* of her experience in a way that the real thing can never be.

Theme-park buildings are to architecture as matte paintings are to cinema. When viewed in narrative context on film and paintings appear to be completely detailed cityscapes, castles, or other worlds. When viewed as paintings, they often turn out to be detailed only at the point of focus. The background is a rudimentary "mind sketch" or concept map relying on our unconscious expectations and memory associations to fill in the details.

Memory also plays a crucial role in the social architecture of the theme park; the interaction between the park audience and the created environment, the docents, cast members, guides, and employees, and their fellow park visitors. Memory contains not only images of place and people, but of associated modes of behavior. The theme cues visitors to the standards of appropriate behavior within each environment.

Visitors to a traditional art museum adopt an air of reverence, speaking in the hushed tones of churchgoers (a behavior pattern frequently out of synch with the vibrant exuberance and life-affirming elan of the subject matter) because the architectural style of the museum, with high vaulted ceilings and marble halls, echoes the consciously awe-inspiring monumental architecture of the church and state.

Similarly, visitors to Disney's Magic Kingdom, no matter what their social or behavioral norm outside the park, soon adopt an air of natural, even exaggerated politeness. Disney designers made a conscious decision to make only one entrance and exit to that park — one that led directly up Main Street, U.S.A., an evocation of a small midwestern town of the early 1900s.

No sign identified this locale. Instead, the sensory symbolics of the thematic language form — the town square, the music of a brass band, the clang of a trolley bell, the hiss of steam from the wood-burning locomotive, the American flag flying above gabled rooftops, the gingerbread detailing on the shopfronts — subconsciously but instantly cues visitors to their own position in space and time. Collective popular memory then responds by matching the sensory input with a behavior mode appropriate for the setting: that of a more leisurely era when everyone on the street was a neighbor and friend (Goldberger 40).

The fragility of cultural coding is highlighted by the very different audience responses to each Disney Park. Of those visitors who have experienced Main Street, U.S.A. in both Anaheim's Disneyland and Florida's Magic Kingdom, the almost universal preference is for Anaheim's muted ¾ scale version over the more overwhelming full-scale recreation at the Magic Kingdom.

While Disneyland's forced perspective of the upper stories makes them appear taller than they are, the three-fourths-scale at ground level exactly replicates the feeling of returning to childhood haunts as an adult when "everything looks so much smaller." The full-scale Walt Disney World Main Street, set along a broader avenue, is less successful in evoking welcoming "childhood" memories and cultural behavior patterns.

This contrast is even more pointed at Epcot. Both Disneyland and the Magic Kingdom have an instantly identifiable narrative quality, beginning with a "title page" or opening scene — the town square. From this visitors are led naturally up Main Street by the beckoning vista of the castle, which draws them into the heart of the park with its central hub. Both parks have a natural progression of pathways and plotlines which invite exploration, with the central icon of castle as the visual bookmark.

Epcot has no such entryway, just a short stretch of parallel pathways flowing from the ticket booths under Spaceship Earth. There is no welcoming sense of "arrival," no immediately obvious storyline to create mental pathways. Unlike the friendly and welcoming architecture of the past, the "futuristic" architecture of Epcot's Future World is designed to awe and impress. Epcot is best viewed at a distance — the promenade around the Seven Seas Lagoon between Future World and World Showcase gives a panoramic view of the pavilions on both sides; just the opposite of the intricate, step-by-step networking design of the first-generation park.

The sheer scale of Epcot (it is, in fact, two parks; Future World and World Showcase) with a central lake that must be circumnavigated, instead of a quickly traversed central hub, makes it the most physically exhausting of all Disney parks. This lack of a welcoming and cultural-coding "main street" is currently being addressed in the form of Innoventions, an attraction which, in the design stage, evokes images of an electronic town square and traditional market fair, centered around a fountain plaza.

Like the first-generation grandparent, Disney's Hollywood Studios returned to the notion of an entryway down a nostalgically-scaled Hollywood Boulevard of the 1930s. Originally designed as a half-day park, it proved so unexpectedly popular that a 1940s-themed Sunset Boulevard has now been added. This is not so much a third-generation park as a return to the lessons of scale and human dynamics learned in Anaheim. Disney's Hollywood Studios makes elegant use of limited space, the architecture is familiar, whimsical, and welcoming, and the narrative pathways enticing and obvious.

Evoking behavior cues through themeing calls for a careful choice of theme. Willow Grove Park, just north of Philadelphia, was one of the original "destination" parks built by the street car companies in the 1890s to encourage ridership. In its heyday it featured not only the traditional amusement park attractions such as carrousel and roller coaster, but band concerts directed by John Philip Sousa that routinely drew audiences of thousands.

By the 1960s, Willow Grove Park had fallen on hard times. New management decided to keep the by-now-classic wooden coaster, but restructure the park in the new theme-park mold. The theme decided upon was the Wild West, and the park was renamed Six-Gun Territory. It was an unfortunate choice. The park drew urban gangs who understood too well the behavior patterns appropriate for a lawless frontier environment. The park responded with armed, uniformed paramilitary guards who then evoked their own response patterns. Violent confrontations, including real shootings, quickly sealed the fate of the park. The site is now a shopping center (Cox).

Reduction of Chaos

Learning, thinking, interpretation, and problem-solving can be as tiring as physical exertion. "Museum fatigue" is a common syndrome — too much sensory input in a short period and both brain and body will demand rest — which is the principle reason the average visit to a North American museum is under an hour (MacDonald).

Likewise, the Disney theme parks are constantly bombarding the visitor with sensory input. In addition, the logistic demands of a visit to the parks simulate, even exceed, those outside it. Like our cities, theme parks are crowded, competitive, decision-laden environments requiring considerable pre-planning and re-planning as contingencies, chance, and fresh opportunities arise, involving repeated negotiation within the visitor's group.

A theme park visit, unlike a beach or spa vacation, demands almost continuous decision-making and problem-solving. One unofficial guidebook even compared the complexity of the experience to the logistics of an amphibious landing. The visitor is constantly engaged in the process of learning, because learning is how we adapt to our environment. Finally, Walt Disney World Resort is built in what can only be described as a physically abusive environment — glaring sun, high temperatures, muggy environment punctuated by sudden thundershowers, and is traversed almost entirely on foot. And yet, in dramatic contrast to the museum, the average visit to a Disney park is eight hours.

Studies on the cognitive processes of thinking, learning, and memory, show that thinking is dependent on the manipulation and interpretation of symbols. The ability to create and use symbols in order to understand, store, and recall information is the defining feature of intelligence. The numeral "5" is an example of a symbol that expresses a single specific value. A flag, a sculpture, a building, or a religious icon is a symbol that "carries" multiple concepts.

Themeing communicates by use of "carrier" symbols as a shorthand system. This system reduces both the time and strain of interpretive processing. In addition, themeing simultaneously bombards us with multiple and complementary symbols, calling upon the full range of senses — vision, hearing, touch, and to a lesser extent, smell and taste. In the hyperreality of a themed environment, this barrage of input is confirmatory rather than confusing because even the most minor theme-breaking dissonant elements — which visitors would have to mentally isolate, code, compare, identify, and fold into the narrative — have been edited out. Themeing eases the mental chaos of the interpretive process.

In addition, the theme park may present a series of interrelated themed areas, each contributing a subplot to the overall narrative. Through the arts of landscape and architecture, transition zones are incorporated into the park design in order to ease dissonance, creating a smooth mental segue from subtheme to subtheme. These transitions are so subtle — as they must be — in order to escape conscious notice.

One transition zone between Walt Disney World Resort's Fantasyland and Frontierland, for instance, is a curving street that progresses from cobblestones to gravel to dirt, the architecture metamorphosing from medieval stone facades, through stone and half-timber and Tudor daub and wattle, to the comparable hues and textures of the rough timber and adobe of the American frontier — all in the space of a hundred yards. Transition zones make it possible for visitors to time-shift several centuries and travel thousands of miles in the interval of a few moments without ever losing their psychic equilibrium — their sense of time and place and their role in it.

Compare the effectiveness of this gradation technique to the visual chaos of the World's Fair, each national and corporate pavilion competing for attention. Visitors are expected to engage and interpret myriad unrelated ideas and concepts — some of them quite complex — coded in diverse design styles and presented in rapid succession. Visitors no sooner absorb and "file" one concept than they are forced to undergo the process again and again throughout the entire World's Fair experience. The results are often — literally — mind-numbing.

To understand theme parks it is helpful to understand moviemaking. The first Disney park was designed by filmmakers. Thus transition zones are the equivalent of the movie fade — the slow dissolve of one scene into another rather than the intellectually-jarring jump cut. The narrative structure is the plot — Disney park designers work initially from a script and storyboard rather than architectural drawings.

This accounts for the lack of reliance on print in the parks themselves. Directional signage in a theme park is an indicator of a lack of continuity in the visual narrative. Film is concerned with images, not dialogue the average film script can be read in thirty minutes. There is minimal signage in a well-designed theme park simply because the symbolic landscape projects the message with more immediacy, power, and clarity than could be accomplished with text, no matter how well-written.

Referencing the Past

[Visitors to Walt Disney World Resort] rediscover their own memories, even fantasies. They are immersed in a universe there everything was at once true and false; false because it consisted only of background and illusion, but true because it existed in everyone's heart and dreams.

Francois Barre

A triumph of historical imagination.
                                    Richard Snow, editor
                                American Heritage Magazine
                            on Disney's Main Street, U.S.A. [22]

Theme parks echo our lives. We live in the moment, then in the remembered moment. Except for the immediate instant, our lives consist entirely of the past. We learn from past experience in order to make sense of the present and future. Even in places themed to the future — Tomorrowland, Epcot — the attractions are, by necessity, grounded in the historical past.

Disneyland and Walt Disney World have been referencing history since their inception. The time-shift mechanism presents the past as it was — as someone else's present. By allowing visitors to step into the alternative present, the theme park enables them to make connections and locate themselves on the continuum.

Themeing relies on grounding the visitor with identifiable benchmarks of a shared culture. In the twentieth century that shared culture is not ethnic, religious, or tribal, but technological. Modern communications medium, particularly television, inculcates a mental inventory of cultural archetypes on a national, and increasingly global, scale. By starting from these archetypes — not to be confused with the more limiting stereotype — the themed environment embraces the visitor with a sense of familiarity, of "being there before," which simultaneously reduces stress and opens the mind by providing recognizable reference points from which the theme park designers can then introduce new concepts and ideas.

Theme parks, particularly the Disney theme parks, have a high return visitation rate because they are firmly grounded in our collective cultural memory. Even to the first-time visitor, Disneyland and Walt Disney World impart a sense of *deja vu* — a feeling of homecoming. Disneyland's Main Street, U.S.A. and Disney's Hollywood Studio's Hollywood Boulevard — both evocatively scaled and memory-hued — evoke mediated images of a childhood when the world was human-scaled and embracing.

Theme parks are exempt from Thomas Wolfe's dictum that "You can't go home again." The symbolic landscape of the theme park endures just as we remember — its colors undimmed, its music eternally gay, its streets and pathways forever beckoning — because it was designed to reflect a collective memory to begin with.

Note

1. This is, in fact, the announced goal of computer-programmed ride design: to give each rider a customized experience, never the same twice. It is the closest we can come today to *Star Trek: The Next Generation's* Holodeck or Ray Bradbury's more sinister Nursery — personal theme parks whose content, through advanced computer programming, is completely customized to reflect the fantasies of the user.

Works Cited

Blake, Peter. "The Lessons of the Parks." In *The Art of Walt Disney: From Mickey Mouse to the Magic Kingdoms*, by Christopher Finch, 425–439. New York: Harry N. Abrams, 1973.

Cox, Harold E. "Rise and Decline of Willow Grove Park." Presented at the Old York Road Historical Society. 19 March 1963.

Finch, Christopher. *The Art of Walt Disney: From Mickey Mouse to the Magic Kingdoms.* New York: Harry N. Abrams, 1973.

Goldberger, Paul. "Mickey Mouse Teaches the Architects." *New York Times Magazine.* 22 October 1972: 40–41, 92–99.

Kasson, John F. *Amusing the Million: Coney Island at the Turn of the Century.* New York: Hill and Wang, 1978.

King, Margaret J. "Theme Park." In *The Guide to United States Popular Culture*, edited by Ray B. Browne and Pat Browne, 837. Bowling Green, OH: Bowling Green State University Popular Press, 2007.

Larson, Erik. *The Devil in the White City.* New York: Vintage, 2004.

MacDonald, George F. "Museum of the Future." Cultural Olympics. Barcelona, Spain, May 1989.

Schooner, Allon. "Can Museums Learn from Mickey and Friends?" *New York Times.* 30 October 1988: 39.

Snow, Richard F. (writer).*Coney Island,* film based on *Coney Island: A Postcard Journey to the City of Fire.* American Experience, PBS. Boston: WGBH, 1991.

_____. *Coney Island: A Postcard Journey to the City of Fire.* New York: Brightwaters, 1984.

_____. "Disney: Coast to Coast." *American Heritage Magazine.* 38:2 (February/March 1987): 22.

Synergystic Disney
New Directions for Mickey and Media in 1954–1955

KATHY MERLOCK JACKSON

The cover of The Walt Disney Company's 2004 annual report features the words "Disneyland 50" written in sparkling letters above an image of Cinderella Castle surrounded by dozens of Disney characters from Mickey Mouse to the Incredibles. Inside the issue, the company's then Chief Executive Officer, Michael Eisner, in his letter to shareholders, writes,

> It was on July 17, 1955 that Walt Disney unveiled something called Disneyland. No one had ever seen anything quite like it, and it created an entirely new category of entertainment, called the "theme park."
> It also transformed this Company and proved in an incredibly dramatic way how great creative content can lead to other great creative content. Suddenly, there was a place where people could meet Mickey Mouse, could fly with Peter Pan and could visit Davy Crockett's wilderness frontier. Disneyland, in turn, led to even more creative success and growth with Walt Disney World, Tokyo Disney Resort, Disneyland Resort Paris, and Hong Kong Disneyland [5–6].

Today, more than fifty years after the opening of Disneyland, The Walt Disney Company serves as a textbook example of "synergy," defined by mass communication theorists Werner Severin and James Tankard as "the notion that cooperative interaction among acquired subsidiaries of merged parts of a corporation creates an enhanced combined effect ... companies can spend the least and make the most profit" (358). Janet Wasko, in her critical analysis of the Disney empire called *Understanding Disney: The Manufacture of Fantasy*, writes,

> Disney created strong brands and characters that were marketed in various forms (mostly through films and merchandise) throughout the world. However, the

company's synergystic strategies accelerated dramatically in the 1950s, when the company opened Disneyland, the theme park that used previously created stories, characters, and images as the basis for its attractions [71].

Walt Disney's use of television during the crucial years, 1954 and 1955, sparked the synergystic process that fueled the popularity and growth of what would become one of the world's largest media conglomerates.

In 1953, Walt Disney had one thing on his mind: the completion of his theme park Disneyland, which fell under the business of WED Enterprises, the personal corporation that he established for his projects outside the studio. However, Disney had exhausted all of his financial resources, both corporate and personal, and still fell short of the funds he needed. One morning he woke up with the answer. "Television!" Walt told his brother [and business manager] Roy [Disney].... "That's how we'll finance the park-television!" (qtd. in Thomas 244). Disney met with the board of directors of Walt Disney Productions and convinced them that television programming, which could be produced quickly and cheaply by drawing on the archival material the studio already owned, would go a long way in providing visibility for the company's movies. Thus, board members gave their go ahead, despite their reluctance to embark on two new risky ventures — Disneyland and television — simultaneously. Walt Disney then sent Roy to New York to work out a deal. He would do a weekly prime-time television show for whichever network agreed to give him the loan that he wanted in order to put the finishing touches on the theme park in Anaheim, California, bearing his name.

For years, Disney had been persuaded by television executives to embrace the fledgling medium but, except for two Christmas specials, in 1950 and 1951, he had not committed. Nevertheless, his limited experience proved promising, serving to promote his studio's upcoming animated releases, *Alice in Wonderland* and *Peter Pan* respectively. As one reviewer predicted after his first special, "That telecast should be worth $1,000,000 at the box office to *Alice in Wonderland*. I think Disney has found the answer to using television both to entertain and to sell" (qtd. in Cotter 4). Indeed he had. Jay Telotte notes that Disney's early television specials strengthened the company's reputation for quality, already evidenced by its twenty-five Academy Awards for animated cartoons, documentaries, and technical achievements, concluding, "As Walt and Roy Disney had learned through these one-shot productions, their studio could create programs that would draw a large audience, and those efforts could help build an audience for their other projects" (Telotte xvi). Early on, Disney understood the profitability of branching out into new media forms. For example, when he moved into live-action film, he said,

I knew I must diversify.... I knew the diversifying of the business would be the salvation of it. I tried that in the beginning, because I didn't want to be stuck with the Mouse. So I went into the Silly Symphonies. It did work out. The Symphonies led to the features; without the work I did on the Symphonies, I'd never have been prepared to even tackle *Snow White*. A lot of the things I did in the Symphonies led to what I did in *Fantasia*. I took care of talents I couldn't use any other way. Now I wanted to go beyond even that; I wanted to go beyond the cartoon [qtd. in Thomas 204].

Despite Disney's openness to television, he was a movie man at heart who discovered a new set of rules governing the way business was done in television. When he first proposed a television version of the story of Zorro, for example, network executives advised him that he would have to submit a pilot. "Look, I've been in the picture business for thirty years," Disney replied. "Don't you think I know how to make a film?" (qtd. in Thomas 242). "But this is different; this is television," he was told (qtd. in Thomas 242). Disney, whose studio had already argued that entertainment was the same in any medium, but the industry thinking was consistent: "No pilot, no series" (Thomas 242).

By 1953, however, Disney needed television and was willing to be flexible in adapting to the industry's agenda. After speaking with executives from the three networks, Roy Disney worked out a deal with ABC, which had only had two hit series to its credit, *The Lone Ranger* and *Stop the Music*, was ranked last in the Nielsen ratings, and was anxious to get a quality series produced by a prestigious movie studio in its prime-time line-up (Telotte 6–7). Thus, ABC and Disney signed a contract which stipulated Disney's agreement to produce a weekly one-hour television show in exchange for ABC's $500,000 investment in Disneyland; furthermore, ABC agreed to become a 35-percent owner of Disneyland and to guarantee loans up to $4.5 million (Thomas 260; Telotte xxii). Disney was paid $2,000,000 for the first season, renewable for up to seven seasons for a show called *Disneyland* (Telotte 8). It was scheduled to premiere in October 1954 and Disney's theme park bearing the same name to open in July 1955. All went according to plan.

The first episode of *Disneyland* aired on ABC on Sunday evening, October 27. In his television series, Disney used the same four divisions — Fantasyland, Adventureland, Frontierland, and Tomorrowland — that categorized the realms of his theme park, corresponding with the studio's cinematic genres: its signature animation, as well as action-adventure, the Western, and science-fiction. Although initially reluctant, Disney also appeared himself as a warm, friendly, enthusiastic host in opening segment of each show, linking his image with not only the program the audience was about to see, but also with his theme park reaching the final stages of construction. (He was even nominated for an Emmy Award for Most Outstanding New Personality but lost to George Gobel.) He provided, as Bob Thomas notes, "continuity and identification" (225). Thus, Disney used his company's new television division to popularize his theme park and movies, becoming one of the first of the major studio heads to effectively practice synergy.

While many of his contemporaries boycotted television, considering it to be either substandard or a threat to the film industry, Disney felt otherwise. "I thought we movie makers ought to get into television ourselves and make it work for us," he said (qtd. in Miller 206). He also noted, "Through television I can reach my audience. I can talk to my audience. They are the audience that wants to see my pictures" (qtd. in *Walt* 46). They were also the audience that would attend his theme park. As Disney reflected, "Every time I'd get to thinking of television I would think of this Park. And I knew that if I did anything like the Park, that I would have to have some kind of medium like television to let people know about it" (*Walt* 45).

Disney was right. His Sunday night series, which gave ABC its highest rating ever and ranked sixth on the Nielsen scale, was an immediate hit, proving to be an important promotional device for his other ventures (Telotte 9). The first episode, titled *Disneyland Story*, showcased attractions being planned for his theme park as well as the direction the television series would take. Additional shows during the first season provided reports on the park's progress. According to J.P. Telotte, "From its opening, ... *Disneyland* sought to situate its audience within an entertainment universe that was endlessly self-referential and that would build its audience on an understanding of and even eagerness for such self-referentiality" (10).

Two particular episodes of *Disneyland* that aired in its first season succeeded beyond even Disney's wildest dreams. On December 8, 1954, *Operation Undersea*, a documentary on the making of the Disney live-action film *20,000 Leagues Under the Sea*, appeared and immediately gained the nickname "the long, long trailer." Although it was criticized by some for being nothing more than a huge promotional piece for Disney's upcoming film, it was good enough to win an Emmy Award for being the best show of the year and to lure holiday audiences into the theaters, a godsend for Disney, who had spent $4.5 million on the feature. When the movie was released on December 23, 1954, it became a popular and critical success, as audiences delighted in its climatic battle scene between a giant squid and a submariner. It also proved to be a springboard for a future Disney theme park attraction. On June 14, 1959, the Submarine Voyage was unveiled in Fantasyland, giving visitors the experience of boarding a submarine and exploring lost undersea worlds.

On December 15, 1954, the first installment of the three-part story of Davy Crockett ran on the *Disneyland* television show. Originally, there were problems with the trilogy because there was not enough material to fill three television hours. To remedy the problem, Disney asked a new studio composer George Bruns to write a little song as filler. A half hour later, Bruns had something, and Disney arranged for a demo recording. "The Ballad of Davy Crockett," as the song became known, was to be featured in all three installments of the show. The first glimpse into the song's popularity appeared when snippets of it were played in a preview of the first *Disneyland* show, and when *Davy Crockett, Indian Fighter*, the first installment of the series, aired, it became a colossal hit. "The Ballad of Davy Crockett" ranked number one of the Hit Parade for thirteen weeks and sold ten million copies (Thomas 257), propelling Disney's music division.

Disney was unprepared for the unprecedented popularity of the Davy Crockett story and its star, Fess Parker. "We had no idea what was going to happen with 'Crockett,'" he recalled. "Why, by the time the show finally got on the air, we were already shooting the third one and calmly killing Davy off at the Alamo. It became one of the biggest overnight hits in TV history, and there we were with three films and a dead hero" (qtd. in Maltin 122). Wanting to capitalize on the phenomenon of the television series, Disney pieced together the three episodes, including George Bruns' by then famous song, into a feature film, *Davy Crockett, King of the Wild Frontier*, which was released on May 25, 1955. By that time, the sale of Davy Crockett products, especially coonskin hats, had created a lucrative revenue stream for the Disney merchandising department, resulting in a $300 million industry. All told, ten million coonskin hats were sold, in addition to toy rifles, costumes, coloring books, and other items bearing the Disneyland Frontierland imprint.

The impact of the *Disneyland* Davy Crockett trilogy was monumental. Although the shows cost $700,000 and Disney was only assured of $300,000 from television, he made far more from merchandising. The popularity of the series solidified *Disneyland* as the number one television show in America and created a bankable star, Fess Parker, who played a key role in the opening of Disneyland and starred in many of the studio's live-action films, including *The Great Locomotive Chase* (1956), *Westward Ho the Wagons!* (1956), *Old Yeller* (1957), and *Light in the Forest* (1958). Parker, and Buddy Ebsen, who also starred in the Crockett series, became linked with Disney in the popular imagination, promoting the studio's image and products. Also, the Walt Disney Music Company, which was formed in 1949 for sheet music sales, thrived for the first time, and Disney established a new subsidiary for phonograph records (Thomas 258). Disney was unsure if audiences would go to the theaters to see a spliced together version of what they had already seen on television, but surprisingly they did. *Davy Crockett, King of the Wild Frontier* earned $2,500,000 at the box office and whetted people's appetites for the Frontierland experience at Disney's soon-to-be-opened theme park.

The month after Davy Crockett hit movie theaters, Disney released another feature, the animated fantasy *Lady and the Tramp*, which premiered on June 16, 1955. Disney promoted this, too, on his *Disneyland* television show, and it proved crucial to the film's good reception. Disney had grown weary of animating familiar fairy tales because audiences were difficult to satisfy, given their expectations based on what they read in books. However, it was even more risky to release an expensive animated feature that no one had ever heard of. Through his use of television, Disney was able to popularize the original story of Lady and the Tramp so that by the time that the movie appeared, filmgoers recognized it and wanted to bring their children. Thus, television opened a new door for Disney by enabling him to familiarize audiences with unknown property before a film version was released. Lady and the Tramp would also be featured in the Fantasyland realm of the theme park.

Disney's television fare during the first season of *Disneyland* consisted mostly of items from the studio archives, especially cartoons that featured characters who would become the stars of Disneyland's Fantasyland, as in "A Tribute to Mickey Mouse." It also included feature-length animated films, such as *Alice in Wonderland*, live-action films, such as *Treasure Island*, and nature documentaries, such as *Seal Island*. Although it was cost effective to use archival material, the studio also produced original shows, often exceeding the $100,000 budget necessary to ensure a profit. The *Man in Space* series, for example, was an expensive three-episode venture produced by Ward Kimball on the history and future of space travel with technical commentary by NASA rocket scientists, including Wernher von Braun. Like *Davy Crockett*, it turned out to be good enough to be released in theaters, and it dovetailed nicely with Disney's theme park realm of Futureland, which had a cornerstone attraction titled Rocket to the Moon.

When Disney's $17 million Disneyland opened in Anaheim, California, on July 17, 1955, everything went wrong, prompting Disney to dub the day "Black Sunday." Despite intense heat, thirty-five thousand people swarmed through the gates to the park. Many of them had obtained counterfeit tickets to the invitation-only event designed exclusively for the press, dignitaries, and those who had worked on the park and their families. Throughout the day, rides broke down, restaurants ran out of food and drink, and lines to attractions ran long, causing people — especially children — to become irritable and impatient. A gas leak in Fantasyland necessitated that the area be closed. The entire event was captured on live television, with Ronald Reagan, Bob Cummings and Art Linkletter serving as a master of ceremonies. Despite the bad reviews, however, Disneyland attracted a million visitors in its first seven weeks, and predictions of attendance were exceeded by fifty percent (Thomas 290). The best explanation for this is that by the time the park opened, Disney, through his prodigious use of television, had created an audience for the park, and people were excited to see it for themselves despite what the reviewers said. In essence, Disney received income, a guaranteed loan, and merchandising residuals for the opportunity to promote Disneyland on television. The success of the television show fueled the success of the park and the films, signaling the effects of synergy.

Disney used television once again in 1955 when the *Mickey Mouse Club* premiered on ABC on October 3. By this time, Mickey Mouse, whose career in movies was waning, had been established as the host of Disneyland, and the show, with its familiar M-I-C-K-E-Y M-O-U-S-E chant served to further promote the Mouse, the park, and other Disney properties. While the Wednesday evening *Disneyland* show attracted families, the 5:00 P.M. after-school *Mickey Mouse Club* was a variety show of cartoons, singing, dancing, and newsreels geared to children and teens at a time when the post–World War II baby boom was reaching its highest point and contributing to America's becoming a child-centered culture. "Children," said one woman in 1955, "give life new meaning, a new focal point, a new frame of reference, a new perspective" (qtd. in Mintz 277). At its height of fame, the *Mickey Mouse Club* attracted seventy-five percent of the nation's televisions and created a market for Disney byproducts, especially Mickey Mouse ears. It also popularized, especially for teens, not only a group of cool youths called the Mouseketeers but everything associated with the Mouse and Disney. Given the show's ability to attract youth, it had no difficulty attracting advertisers, especially Mattel, whose Burp Gun and Barbie dolls became among the first toy phenomena of the television era. Cy Schneider, who worked for Mattel, describes the effect of the first Burp Gun advertisements aired during the *Mickey Mouse Club*:

> Before Christmas 1955, Mattel had shipped more than one million Burp Guns at $4.00 each. Considering the company's previous annual sales volume for their entire line of products was only $4 million, this was unheard of success. They had more than doubled their sales volume. The demand for the Burp Gun was so great, there wasn't even a part to be found in stores ... we even received a letter from President Eisenhower asking us to find a Burp Gun for his grandson David. The Burp Gun had fired shots heard around the world [22].

Thus Disney's relationship with Mattel Toys was cemented, and in subsequent years Mattel products were made for and sold throughout Disneyland.

The years 1954 and 1955 proved pivotal for television as well as for The Walt Disney Company, as it set into motion many of the synergystic practices that would characterize the company, and the media industry in general, in subsequent years (see Appendix A). In the mid–1950s, Walt Disney believed this was the right thing to do in order to build his company and achieve his goals. As Jay Telotte asserts,

> More than simply establishing another source for capital ... this accentuation on combining entertainment and merchandising also helped spur the worldwide popularity of Disney's films and affected the company's entire production process. Certainly, this thrust marked the beginning of a fruitful symbiosis — of product and marketing, of mass entertainment and personal consumer experience — that would increasingly come to identify the company, to mark its singular place in American culture as the primary and most successful example of the entertainment-marketing conglomerate, and later to script the terms for the company's entry into television and other mass media" [xi].

However, today, in a vastly different media landscape, critics like Sam Craig, director of the Entertainment, Media and Technology program at New York University, disagree. "Synergy has proved more elusive than a lot of people imagined," said Craig (qtd. in Sutel D3). The Walt Disney Company, which replaced Michael Eisner with Robert Iger as chief executive officer, has expressed no plans to downsize, as other companies, such as Viacom, have. However, as Associated Press writer Seth Sutel observes, "After many years of getting bigger, major media companies are trying something new: getting smaller" (D3).

In the more than five decades following Disney's foray into television and the opening of Disneyland, corporate synergy has created what some regard as a media monster, consuming resources, choices, and opportunities. This metaphor recalls a scene in *Jurassic Park* (1993), a cinematic blockbuster inspired by Disney's theme park phenomenon. In the film, an exchange occurs between John Hammond, the park's owner, and Ian Malcolm, a scientist who espouses chaos theory. "All major theme parks have delays," says Hammond. "When they opened Disneyland in 1956 [sic], nothing worked."

"But, John," Malcolm replies, "when the Pirates of the Caribbean breaks down, the pirates don't eat people."

Disneyland may not have been quite ready for prime-time on opening day, but due to a prime-time television show which popularized Disney's animated characters and the theme park concept, the public had already embraced it, demonstrating to Disney how different corporate entities could mutually benefit one another. In subsequent years, the Disney empire grew, and as Janet Wasko outlines in *Understanding Disney*, today encompasses theatrical films, home video, cable television, network television, theatrical productions, audio products and music publishing, children's products, art and collectibles, online business, consumer product marketing, publications, theme parks worldwide, resorts and hotels, regional entertainment, a cruise line, a prototype community, a sports franchise, a research and development arm, and radio (43–61). Some may regard this highly synergystic model as a corporate monster; however, for Disney in 1954 and 1955, its early inception served a purpose: promoting Disneyland so that the risky venture paid off, establishing a blueprint for the company's business practices and, most importantly, signaling new directions for the media and entertainment industries.

Appendix: 1954–55 Disney Timeline

October 27, 1954   *Disneyland*, the first Disney television series, premieres on Wednesday nights on ABC. The first episode, *The Disneyland Story*, describes future episodes of the series as well as the Disneyland theme park. Walt Disney appears as the host of the show and is nominated for an Emmy Award for Best New Television Personality.

December 8, 1954   *Operation Undersea*, a documentary on the making of the Disney live-action feature *20,000 Leagues Under the Sea*, runs on *Disneyland*. Although it is dubbed "The long, long trailer," it wins an Emmy Award for Best Show of the Year.

December 15, 1954   *Davy Crockett, Indian Fighter*, the first episode of the Davy Crockett trilogy, airs on *Disneyland*. The show stars Fess Parker and is an immediate hit, as is its theme song "The Ballad of Davy Crockett" by George Bruns.

December 23, 1954   The live-action feature *20,000 Leagues Under the Sea* is released.

January 26, 1955   *Davy Crockett Goes to Congress*, the second episode in the Davy Crockett trilogy, airs on *Disneyland*.

February 23, 1955   *Davy Crockett at the Alamo*, the last of the Davy Crockett trilogy, airs on *Disneyland*.

May 25, 1955   The live-action feature *Davy Crockett, King of the Wild Frontier* is released in theaters. It is an edited version of Disney's three television episodes.

June 16, 1955   The animated feature *Lady and the Tramp*, the first animated feature filmed in Cinemascope premiers.

July 17, 1955   Disneyland, Walt Disney's $17 million theme park, opens in Anaheim, California.

October 3, 1955   *Mickey Mouse Club* television series airs its first show at 5:00 P.M. on ABC.

Works Cited

Cotter, Bill, *The Wonderful World of Disney Television: A Complete History*. New York: Hyperion, 1997.
Maltin, Leonard. *The Disney Films*, 3d ed. New York: Hyperion, 1995.
Miller, Diane Disney, as told to Pete Martin. *The Story of Walt Disney*. New York: Dell, 1956.

Mintz, Steven. *Huck's Raft: A History of American Childhood.* Cambridge, MA: Belknap Press of Harvard University Press, 2004.

Schneider, Cy. *Children's Television: How It Works and Its Influence on Children.* Lincolnwood, IL: NTC Business, 1989.

Severin, Werner J., and James W. Tankard, Jr. *Communication Theories: Origins, Methods, and Uses in the Mass Media*, 5th ed. New York: Addison Wesley, 2001.

Sutel, Seth. "Viacom Is Scaling Back as Synergy Dreams Fade." *Virginian-Pilot*, 19 March 2005, D3.

Telotte, J. P. *Disney TV.* Detroit: Wayne State University Press, 2004.

Thomas, Bob. *Walt Disney: An American Original.* New York: Hyperion, 1994.

Walt. This collection of Walt Disney's quotations is available at the Walt Disney Archives, Burbank, CA. [There is a published volume: Smith, Dave, ed. *The Quotable Walt Disney.* New York: Disney, 2001.]

Walt Disney Company. Annual Report 2004.

Wasko, Janet. *Understanding Disney: The Manufacture of Fantasy.* Malden, MA: Blackwell, 2001.

Animator as Architect

Disney's Role in the Creation of Children's Architecture

MARK I. WEST

Children's culture, meaning, in this case, all cultural elements that are associated with children's play and entertainment, has no fixed boundaries. Over the years, it has expanded to include children's films, children's television, and, with the opening of Disneyland in 1955, children's architecture. However, the significance of Walt Disney's decision to construct buildings designed to entertain children has been largely overlooked, even by those who have seriously studied Disney's revolutionary amusement parks. This oversight is unfortunate because the creation of children's architecture was one of Disney's most original contributions to American children's culture.

When Disney began thinking about building an amusement park, he deliberately ignored the examples set by parks which were already in existence. In his opinion, these establishments were "dirty, phoney places, run by tough-looking people" (qtd. in Schickel 310). He also felt that when families went to these parks, "the grownups were bored" (qtd. in Menen 106). He, therefore, did not rely on the advice of traditional amusement parks' owners and designers. Instead, he turned to his employees for assistance. In 1952, he brought together a group of art directors, animators, and other people associated with his film studios and set them to work on his amusement park. He called this group WED Enterprises, after his own initials, and he referred to its members as "Imagineers" (Schickel 310).

Disney and his assistants did not know much about roller coasters or Ferris wheels, but they were familiar with filmmaking, and they relied heavily on this background when planning Disneyland. They knew that films were

29

popular, in part, because they allowed filmgoers to escape from reality for a few hours. This same principle, they reasoned, could be applied to Disneyland. Thus, they decided to design the park in such a way that its visitors would, as Disney put it, "feel they are in another world" (qtd. in De Roos 192). Because of their film background, they tended to view Disneyland as a sort of glorified movie lot. The success of the park, as they saw it, depended upon their ability to duplicate the controlled environments found in motion picture studios. Hence, even though they planned to include rides in Disneyland, they were primarily concerned with the general atmosphere of the park (Finch 393–411).

After much deliberation, Disney and the WED staff decided to divide Disneyland into five sections: Main Street, Frontierland, Adventureland, Tomorrowland, and Fantasyland. The park's designers made sure that the buildings, attractions, and transportation in each section related to that area's particular theme. In so doing, they introduced the concept of theme parks to American society (Kyriazi 167).

Since Disneyland's designers intended that each section's theme be conveyed primarily through its buildings, they were very concerned with the external appearances of all of the park's structures. This type of symbolic architecture required that the WED designers not follow conventional architectural procedures. Paul Goldberg elaborates on this point in an article on Disney's approach to architecture:

> WED staffers point with pride to the fact that in the Disney scheme of things the architects and designers have the last say, not the engineers. The standard practice is for a WED project designer to prepare a set of renderings showing how the completed building should look. These are passed along to an engineer who is instructed to devise a means for making the design workable without changing its appearance — exactly the opposite of traditional architectural practice [96].

In keeping with Disney's desire that Disneyland should appeal to all ages, only Fantasyland was designed specifically for children. Oddly enough, this was Disney's least favorite section, and he would sometimes show signs of impatience when reporters questioned him about it. While he did not become as involved with the planning of Fantasyland as he did with the other four sections, he still directed its overall development (Menen 106).

In attempting to formulate an architectural style for Fantasyland, the park's designers fell back on Disney's feature-length animated films for guidance. Since these films were already widely associated with children, it seemed logical to use them as a basis for Fantasyland's buildings and other attractions. Also, since many members of WED had worked on these films, this approach enabled them to make use of their film backgrounds. By associating buildings with films, Disney added a narrative element to the architecture of Disneyland. Beth Dunlop comments on this aspect of Disneyland in her book titled *Building a Dream: The Art of Disney Architecture*:

> At Disney, every architect must turn storyteller, and the results range from the wryly whimsical to the almost abstrusely intellectual. Disney's architecture can be silly, sentimental, profound, enchanting, or challenging — sometimes all in one building. And whichever, it is always somehow cinematic, architecture with the pace and cadence of a film [13].

WED's designers translated this conceptual approach to children's architecture into a reality with the construction of Storybook Land, one of Fantasyland's chief attractions. The buildings in Storybook Land were based on several of Disney's films including: *Pinocchio*, one of Disney's earliest and most successful feature-length films; *Cinderella*, a 1950 release; and *The Adventures of Ichabod and Mr. Toad*, a 1949 release that was partially based on Kenneth Grahame's *The Wind in the Willows*. WED's designers intended for Storybook Land to provide three-dimensional representations of scenes from these films. Thus, the buildings were designed in the style of Disney's cartoons. All of the buildings were built on the scale of one inch to one foot. WED's designers realized that the illusion they were trying to create would be disrupted if visitors walked among these miniature buildings. Therefore, the buildings were situated on a lakeshore so that visitors could view them from aboard a boat. In Aubrey Menen's article, "Dazzled in Disneyland," he provides the following description of the boat ride and the miniature buildings:

> I boarded a painted barge, sitting down close to the water level. The barge waddled slowly round the shores of the lake, which was planted with miniature trees. From among these trees, scattered around the lake's margin, emerged a house, a castle and a village. As we passed the house, an automobile horn sounded furiously. It was Toad Hall from *The Wind in the Willows*. Cinderella Castle came next, with a fantastic array of turrets and balconies that hung in the air. Then came the village, with its leaning houses and church steeples from which, as we passed, bells rang in a silvery carillon. This was where Pinocchio was born [72].

The castle in Storybook Land is only one of the castles in Disneyland; the other, Sleeping Beauty Castle, is much larger and better known than its miniature sister. Sleeping Beauty Castle serves as the entrance to Fantasyland. Although it is named after Disney's film version of the classic fairy tale, the castle was actually completed four years before the film was released. Apparently, Disney began working on the film in 1950, but he laid it aside while Disneyland was under construction (Maltin 152–54).

Sleeping Beauty Castle, in all probability, is more commonly associated with children's culture than any other single building in America. This is because for years it served as the backdrop for the introduction to Disney's television program. For the millions of children who have watched this program, the image of Tinker Bell waving her wand in front of Sleeping Beauty Castle is a very familiar sight. In fact, for years Disneyland employed an aerialist to re-enact this scene in front of the castle every night throughout the summer (De Roos 199).

With the opening of Walt Disney World Resort in October 1971, Walt Disney Productions introduced America to Cinderella Castle, WED's most impressive example of children's architecture. The castle serves as the park's focal point, and it towers above all of the other buildings in the park. It is eighteen stories high, making it much larger than Sleeping Beauty Castle. Cinderella Castle was not patterned after any particular castle; instead, WED's designers attempted to duplicate as closely as possible the dream castles found in several of Disney's animated films. In describing the effect WED's designers were trying to convey through the castle's design, a Disney spokesperson said:

> Imagine a full-sized fairy-tale castle rivaling Europe's finest and all of the dream castles of literary history in space-age America: a castle without age-crusted floors and drafty hallways; a royal home grander than anything Cinderella could have imagined; an ancient castle that looks brand-new [Goldberger 96].

From an architectural point of view, the castles at Disneyland, Walt Disney World, and the Disney theme parks in Tokyo, Hong Kong, and Paris are Disney's most influential buildings. As Erika Doss points out in her essay "Making Imagination Safe in the 1950s: Disneyland's Fantasy Art and Architecture," "Each of the Disney theme parks has a castle as its central landmark" (182). Not only do these castles provide the parks with their focal points, but they also represent the culmination of Disney's efforts to design buildings that resonate with children's imaginations and aesthetic sensibilities. In her discussion of Disney's castles, Beth Dunlop writes:

> The castles of Disney's several kingdoms don't strive for authenticity; they were born in a world of fairy tales and fantasy, and that is where they've stayed. These castle "belong" to Sleeping Beauty or Cinderella, not a long-forgotten baron or princess. They are candy-coated castles, gilded confections, and they have become the enduring architectural symbols of Disney's theme parks [99].

When Disneyland became a commercial success, a number of people attempted to imitate it. Small theme parks were soon built across the country, and many of them utilized elements of Disney's children's architecture. However, instead of using Disney films as the basis for their buildings, the owners of these parks had their buildings designed around nursery rhymes, fairy tales, Biblical stories, and Christmas themes. Story Book Forest in Ligonier, Pennsylvania, for instance, contains buildings that represent "Little Red Riding Hood" and "The Old Woman in the Shoe," while Noah's Ark Amusement Park in Wisconsin Dells, Wisconsin, features a large ark.

If Disney's castles and miniature buildings are viewed in conjunction with the buildings found in these various small theme parks, certain similarities become apparent. By noting these similarities, it is possible to arrive at some of the defining characteristics of children's architecture. Nearly all of the buildings are associated with children's stories of one kind or another. They are intended to be looked at or played in, and they usually do not serve any practical function. Many of them do not follow standard rules of proportion — some are built on a miniature scale while others are abnormally large. They are frequently brightly colored and are usually quite ornate. Also, medieval architectural motifs are often incorporated into the buildings' designs. Lastly, a number of them are deliberately constructed to look out of kilter.

Children's architecture, as Disney developed it in the 1950s and '60s, foreshadowed the rise of Post-modern architecture in the mid–1970s. Like Disney's designers and architects, Robert Venturi, Charles Moore, Frank Gehry, and other leading Post-Modernists have turned away from Modern architecture's abhorrence of "elaborate coloration, variegated materials, ornamentation, an decorative systems" (Hollander 412). Post-modern architecture, although not intended specifically for children, shares many characteristics with Disney's children's architecture. Both make use of illogical designs, bold colors, and ornate facades. Both also involve "reinventing the past" (Dunlop 123). Thus, in addition to being a leading figure in the realm of children's culture, Disney can also be seen as a prophet of Post-modernism.

Works Cited

De Roos, Robert. "The Magic Worlds of Walt Disney." *National Geographic.* August 1963: 159–207.

Doss, Erika. "Making Imagination Safe in the 1950s: Disneyland's Fantasy Art and Architecture." In *Designing Disney's Theme Parks: The Architecture of Reassurance,* edited by Karal Ann Marling, 179–189. Paris and New York: Flammarion, 1997.

Dunlop, Beth. *Building a Dream: The Art of Disney Architecture.* New York: Harry Abrams,1996.

Finch, Christopher. *The Art of Walt Disney: From Mickey Mouse to the Magic Kingdoms.* New York: Harry Abrams, 1973.

Goldberger, Paul. "Mickey Mouse Teaches the Architects." *New York Times Magazine.* 22 October 1972: 40–41+.

Hollander, Michael. "Attitudes of Modern Architecture in Post-Modern Criticism." *Yale Review* 69 (1980): 411–426.

Kyriazi, Gary. *The Great American Amusement Parks: A Pictorial History.* Secaucus, NJ: Citadel, 1976.

Maltin, Leonard. *The Disney Films.* New York: Crown, 1973.

Menen, Aubrey. "Dazzled in Disneyland." *Holiday,* July 1963, 68–75+.

Schickel, Richard. *The Disney Version: The Life, Times, Art and Commerce of Walt Disney.* New York: Simon and Schuster, 1968.

Disneyland
Attractions

Disneyland's Main Street, U.S.A., and Its Sources in Hollywood, U.S.A.

ROBERT NEUMAN

Much critical commentary has been devoted to examining Disneyland's Main Street, U.S.A., a picturesque streetscape built in the style of American commercial architecture of the years 1890 to 1910 (the park opened on 17 July 1955). In particular, the search by historians and cultural critics for sources of inspiration has led to earlier amusement parks and fairs, as well as specific towns, from Fort Collins, Colorado, to Marceline, Missouri, Walt Disney's boyhood home. The result of such analysis, however, has been an overemphasis on the autobiographical aspect of Main Street as a replica of Marceline's principal thoroughfare. Simultaneously, another mode of interpretation has regarded Main Street as a "movie set" in the limited sense of an imaginary world scripted like a movie or TV show in which the visitor is an actor. It may be useful at this point in the discourse to recall that Main Street was a uniquely American symbol that Disney shared but did not invent, and that the idea of Main Street was widespread in literature, the theater, and film in the years prior to Disneyland's creation. Indeed, its representation in the movies produced on Disney's turf in "Hollywood, U.S.A.," as part of the genre of the small-town film of the 1930s and '40s, offers a new avenue of inquiry. Consideration of how Main Street functions in long shot, close-up, and social context in several representative movies from these years helps to illuminate the design choices made by Disney's artists. In addition, a detailed look at the typical Hollywood back lot reveals various visual tricks borrowed by the designers of Main Street from the repertoire of set-design techniques.

An August 1958 view of Main Street, U.S.A., Disneyland in Anaheim, California. The view is southward toward the Main Street Station. The Swift Market House and a horseless carriage are on the left (courtesy Michael Sumrell).

Finally, an investigation of four fully realized street sets built on Hollywood back lots in the years preceding Disney's theme-park street provides a new framework for understanding it.

Disneyland's Main Street deserves ongoing analysis because of its perceived status as "one of the most successfully designed streetscapes in human history" and its extraordinary impact on urban planning and the preservation movement over the last half century (Francaviglia, "Main Street U.S.A." 148). Its situation and function as the pathway into what is generally regarded as the first theme park is remarkable. Visitors arriving from the main gate during the initial year of operation walked under the Victorian station of the Santa Fe and Disneyland Railroad and entered the Town Square flanked on the west side by the Police Station, Town Hall, Fire Station, and Bekins Van and Storage, and on the east by the Bank of America, Town Square Realty, the Opera House, and Maxwell House Coffee House. The square merges with an axial corridor bordered by replicas of small-town American commercial buildings and broken into two blocks by an intersection, Center Street, comprising short blocks on either side.

Most of the early shops were operated by outside lessees and sponsors, thus providing much-needed funding for the park (Mason 17–18). The build-

Detail of west storefronts, including the Upjohn Pharmacy and Carnation Ice Cream Parlor, from August 1958 (courtesy Michael Sumrell).

ings on the west side, starting at Town Square, originally housed in sequence the following: the Emporium, Crystal Arcade, Upjohn Pharmacy, Carnation Ice Cream Parlor, Sunnyview Farms, Puffin Bake Shop, Penny Arcade, Candy Palace, and Coca Cola Refreshment Corner. On the east side stood: the Wurlitzer Music Hall, Wonderland Music Company, Fine Tabacco, Main Street Cinema, Jewelry Store, Yale and Towne Lock Shop, Swift Market House, Gibson Greeting Card Shop, Ellen's Gift Shop, Blue Bird Shoes, Kodak Camera Center, Timex Clock Shop, Grandma's Baby Shop, Intimate Apparel, Ruggles China and Glass, and the (fictive) Plaza Hotel and Apartments (Janzen 26–33; Koenig 32–39). The resulting community of businesses was surprisingly akin to a real Main Street.

The merchants, in cooperation with WED (the Disneyland design organization), strove to create a vintage atmosphere on the interiors. For example, the Upjohn Pharmacy was a veritable museum, allotting minimal space to the company's current products. According to an early promotional brochure, "Well over 1000 antiques were collected by the personnel of the Upjohn Company, in a search that took them to auctions, attics, old pharmacies, dealers, and historians in New Orleans, Chicago, New York City, South Carolina, Michigan and New Jersey. The showcases, fans, counters and other equipment were designed by experts and faithfully reproduced." The only historical ele-

Detail of west storefronts, with the Upjohn Pharmacy, and Center Street, from August 1958 (courtesy Michael Sumrell).

An April 1957 view toward the southwest with horsedrawn streetcars, the Crystal Arcade, and the Upjohn Pharmacy.

ment lacking was a soda fountain, an amenity provided by the neighboring Carnation Ice Cream Parlor.

Although primarily designed for pedestrians, over the years the street has accommodated light traffic ranging from such horse-drawn vehicles as trolleys, surreys, and the fire wagon, to horseless carriages and a double-tiered omnibus. At certain times of day costumed performers enliven the buildings in the form of an organ grinder, brass band, or barbershop quartet, while the alluring aroma of fresh pastries and cookies wafts from the bakeshop. At the end of the street lies another public square, the Plaza, in effect the park's hub, from which the themed "lands" radiate. The vista culminates in the storybook towers of Sleeping Beauty Castle.

Employing Main Street as a point of transition between the real world outside the berm and the fantastic and exotic lands within, Disney located the architecture of this spine in a peaceful period of American history both familiar and comforting. The façades connote small-town America in a general way — hence the name "Main Street, U.S.A." — in opposition to the declining urban centers and suburban sprawl of the 1950s (Longstreth 24–35). In the words of Francaviglia, this choice of time and place, between the end of the gaslight era and the start of the age of electricity, is "archetypal and shared," satisfying a deep "nostalgic longing" ("Main Street, U.S.A." 143). Symbol of a less-troubled bygone era, Main Street reaffirms basic American ideals for each new generation of visitors.

Early Concepts

Where did Walt Disney get the idea for Main Street? It is well known that he had his artists research a broad scope of amusement parks and recreated historical towns nationwide, from Knott's Berry Farm in Buena Park, California, to Coney Island, New York. A few buildings were very loosely based on specific prototypes, as when Harper Goff, designing the City Hall, cast a glance at photos of the City Hall in his home town, Fort Collins, Colorado (Francaviglia, *Main Street Revisited* 147–51). The single most-discussed source is the principle commercial thoroughfare, Kansas Street, of Marceline, Missouri, where Disney lived from ages four to eight (1906–10). Thus Francaviglia calls Main Street "an autobiographical statement by Disney himself" ("Main Street, U.S.A." 156), and Karal Ann Marling posits that "[a]ll of Disneyland is Walt Disney, but the most personal, idiosyncratic part of the autobiography written there in buildings, streets, and sidewalks is Main Street, U.S.A." ("Imagineering" 89–90). Steven Watts describes it as "nearly a replica, although highly idealized, of Marceline's main street, as photographs of the latter make clear" (22). But in truth old photographs of the town portray a very different, gritty reality of a broad, muddy road with cluttered telephone poles, raised wooden sidewalks, and plain street fronts (Burnes et al. 24).

The Marceline connection dates back to the inaugural days of the park in July 1955, when a *Look* magazine writer, already defining Disneyland as autobiographical, commented, "Here is a replica of Main Street in a small American town as Walt remembers it from his childhood" (Gordon 29). One year later Diane Disney, in the serialized biography, "My Dad, Walt Disney," in the *Saturday Evening Post*, intuited the same relationship, based on his fond accounts of the family's Missouri farm (Miller 70). Early guide books to Disneyland, however, such as the one published in 1964, two years before his death, make no mention of the town (Disney n.p.). In 1989 senior designer John Hench alleged in an interview that Disney, in considering shop types for Disneyland in 1953, recalled businesses in Marceline (Marling 60). The current guidebook to Marceline builds on this idea by claiming that Disney researched the town during his trip back in 1946, but he in truth was not actively engaged in planning Disneyland until a couple of years later (*Tour Guide of Marceline* 6, 26). The idea that Main Street in some fashion emulates

Marceline is debunked by designer Goff: "Well, that's a good story" ("Interview with Harper Goff" 7).

Without denying the role played by these much-discussed sources, it is useful to search for Main Street's origins by returning to Disney's earliest projects for a theme park. The initial written evidence for an amusement park, an internal memo drawn up on 31 August 1948 for a "Mickey Mouse Park," shortly after his trip with Ward Kimball to the Chicago Railroad Fair and Henry Ford's Greenfield Village in Michigan, calls for a Main Village, a Western Village, and a Carnival Section. The first of these was described as a small town built around a village green, close to a rail station, with civic monuments like a town hall, fire and police stations, a post office, and a combined movie/opera house. Disney also included a list of potential stores, such as a pharmacy with a soda fountain, clothing, music, and magic shops, and a restaurant (Jackson 48–49; Broggie 88–91).

The earliest conceptual drawings, dating from 1951, for a park located on a parcel of land across Riverside Drive from the Disney Burbank studio, include a small town with a main street adjacent to a train depot, the whole rendered in a modest, clapboard style (Marling, "Imagineering" 39–42, 52–54). Seeking approval from the Burbank Board of Parks and Recreation in March 1952, Disney referred to this part of the park as "a small midwestern town at the turn of the century." But in a detail largely overlooked by historians, the *Burbank Daily Review* indicated that the planned park would also incorporate "a complete television center, with theater, stages, sets, and technical equipment" ("Walt Disney Make-Believe Land Project"; Barrier 233–34). In short, early in the development process the park was conceived along the lines of a studio back lot. Significantly, whereas other major Hollywood studios already had working back lots, some on occasion open to the public in the form of a guided tour, as in the case of Universal Studios, Disney was not yet producing live-action films on the Burbank lot, and the animation facility was not considered a viable tourist attraction.

The aspect of a back-lot tour continued to be operative once the Burbank site was rejected in favor of the clandestine Anaheim location in August 1953. The prospectus for a new park, shown by Roy Disney to television executives in New York in September 1953 in a bid for financial support, included plans for three production facilities: the Opera House on Town Square for the *Disneyland* TV series; Treasure Island in Frontierland for the *Mickey Mouse Club* show; and Tomorrowland, home of the futuristic *World of Tomorrow Television Show*. When Disney joined forces with the fledgling ABC television network in March 1954 to produce the *Disneyland* TV series in exchange for assistance with park funding, together they informed the public that "The Disneyland amusement park is an ambitious project, which would serve two purposes — as a film production center and as a tourist attraction for which admission would be charged" (Pryor, "Disney to Enter"; Marling, "Disneyland 1955" 188, 203). Disney even characterized the *Disneyland* program as a back-lot experience: "Everybody appears to be curious about how movies are made. I hope that we can be entertaining in showing some of the things which go on here from day to day" (Pryor, "Hollywood Double Entente"). When the Anaheim site was revealed on 2 May 1954, the *New York Times* reported that the future park "will resemble a giant motion-picture set" and would function as "the principle center of the weekly one-hour TV show" (Pryor, "Land of Fantasia"). Similarly, *Woman's Home Companion* called the park "a living set for television…. When it's finished, you'll be able to visit this TV set. You will enter on 'Mainstreet' [sic]" (Wirsig). Disney reiterated this idea during the first *Disneyland* TV broadcast on 27 October 1954 by telling his audience, "Next year our television show will be coming from this Disneyland." As it turned out, three months after the park's opening, ABC announced that it would broadcast a daily half-hour radio show, "Walt Disney's Magic Kingdom," from the park, but it was only in 1962 that a production facility was constructed behind the Opera House façade ("New Disney Show"; Gordon and Mumford, *Disneyland Nickel Tour* 102–03).

While the park was being touted as a kind of back lot, the little town remained a constant in the projects for the Anaheim site. Indeed, for some time during the planning stage Disney envisioned as the entrance to Disneyland a small town comprising three elements encountered in succession — the railway station, Main Street, and a residential district. This aggregate would have simulated a familiar pattern experienced during the first half of the twentieth century by a majority of Americans, for whom travel to a small town consisted of arrival by train, movement through the downtown, and reception at the home of a relative or friend.

Perhaps because train travel has ceased to be the most prevalent mode of long-distance transport in this country, recent discussion of the Main Street Station has tended to focus on its position as the park's frontispiece, experienced chiefly upon arrival from the outside and as a stopping-off point on the peripheral berm, rather than as an integral part of Main Street itself. However, before the era of highway and air travel American small towns were accessible primarily by train, and many such towns (including Marceline) were built as service points for the railways (Gabler 12). In considering Disneyland's rail line, writers invariably focus on Walt's hobby of model railroading, but it is equally important to regard the Main Street Station as an integral part of the street, formally, spatially, and conceptually.

The same goes for the planned residential neighborhood, even though it was ultimately not built. Concept drawings of 1953 by Dale Hennesy and Bruce Goff show a neighborhood at the end of Main Street with grand houses conceived in the Second-Empire style (illustrated in Kurtti and Gordon 9; "Main Gate" 3). Moreover, it has not been previously observed that four of these houses, with their fancy mansard roofs, face the hub in the famous aerial view of the park drawn by Herb Ryman in September 1953 to accompany the prospectus shown in New York by Roy Disney (illustrated in Gordon and Mumford, *Brush with Disney* 144–45). Other than as an integral part of Disney's small town, it is not clear how these houses might have functioned — brief consideration was given to the idea of guest accommodations (Marling, *Behind the Magic* 40–41) — with the exception of one, designated in a Goff drawing as a Haunted House (Marling, "Imagineering" 59). Although these homes were not constructed on the hub, the Haunted Mansion later reappeared at Disneyland in New Orleans Square (planning for which began in 1957; additionally, a project conceived in 1957, Edison Square, a turn-of-the-century cul-de-sac of urban row houses to be located off Main Street, went unrealized). In short, by reuniting conceptually the three elements comprising the path into the park as originally conceived, one can demonstrate relationships between Main Street and Hollywood's portrayal of small towns in terms of both the particulars of set design and broader issues of content.

The Small-Town Film

The present consideration of Disney's "small town" derives from analogies with set design that are already embedded in the literature on Disneyland. For example, Marling has written, "Main Street is a movie set, a section of backlot foolery." Her emphasis, however, is on the idea that the visitor enters a fictitious place scripted like a movie or a TV show, and it is "The Walt Disney Story" that is playing ("Imagineering" 89; also Francaviglia, "Main Street, U.S.A." 147, 152; Finch 63). Indeed, among authors, the connections with cinema are usually phrased in terms of Main Street being "like a movie" through the use of devices such as narration, continuity, and cross-dissolves (Watts 437; Gabler 497). Yet writers have paid scant attention to Main Street's relationship to the small-town film.

To begin, Disney's choice of the little town as an American archetype was by no means original. His interest is related to Hollywood's depiction of small towns in the movies, called by Emanuel Levy "a permanent staple of the American cinema from the very beginning. Their preeminence has derived from their prevalence in other cultural forms: books, short stories, and stage plays" (16). Like Disney, producers and directors chose this subject as the locus of essential American values symbolized by the flag on the village green, the family home, the civic center, and places of business (Marling, "Behind the Magic" 38). From over 160 movies of the 1930s and '40s that incorporate aspects of the genre, four representative examples will demonstrate how Main Street typically functions in film, both in isolation and in conjunction with the train station and residential neighborhood (Levy 265–70; MacKinnon 191–98). The street appears in a variety of ways: constructed on a back-lot set, painted as a backdrop on a sound stage, or as an actual downtown street. Sometimes it is not visible at all but is emphasized through dialogue. The point is that, as might be expected, Main Street was a common feature of Hollywood films, and its various forms would later reverberate during the creation of Disneyland's little town.

The classic small-town film, *Our Town* of 1940, directed by Sam Wood (art directors, William Cameron Menzies and Lewis J. Rachmil) was shot on a sound stage to maintain the abstract and universal content of Thorton Wilder's play (1938). The principal thoroughfare of the fictional Grover's Corners, New Hampshire, is little more than a backdrop painting seen in an extreme long shot in the opening moments of the movie. But its importance to the town and its relationship to the railway and residential neighborhoods is immediately indicated by the Stage Manager/Mr. Morgan (Frank Craven), addressing the audience directly: "Running right through the middle of town is Main Street. Cutting across Main Street on the left is the railroad tracks...." He makes the point that the residents can tell the time by the arrival of the trains. "Next to the post office is the town hall; jail's in the basement.... It's a nice town, 'know what I mean?' ... Along Main Street there's a row of stores with hitching posts and horse blocks in front of 'em. The first automobile is going to come along in about five years." In other words, the film covers roughly the same idyllic period, 1901 to 1913, as that represented at Disneyland's Main Street, when both horse-drawn and motorized vehicles existed side by side.

In *Our Town* Main Street also appears in close-up, notably in the form of the drugstore, where George and Emily (William Holden and Martha Scott) drink strawberry ice-cream sodas while Mr. Morgan laments the arrival of the new gas-powered traffic: "I'm telling you, you have to look both ways before crossing Main Street these days.... I can remember a day when a dog could [lie] on Main Street all day long without anything to disturb him." Typically in small-town films, the drugstore is the chief socializing locus for people of all ages, and thus represents the American ideal of community (AlSayyad 57).

In the opening monologue the Stage Manager also points out the steeples of all the churches of various denominations. By way of contrast, this emphasis on churches in the description of *Our Town* points up the fact that at Disneyland the one building *missing* from Main Street is the church. However, in the planning stage such a structure was in fact proposed in an early concept sketch by Goff (c. 1952–53; illustrated in Marling, "Imagineering" 59), and a church appears at the end of the crossing street in Ryman's 1953 schematic aerial view — it is named the Little Church around the Corner in the accompanying prospectus. But Disney, characterized by one historian as "something of a secular humanist," evidently decided on the separation of Church and State in his magic kingdom (Francaviglia, *Main Street Revisited* 176)!

In the Katherine Hepburn vehicle of 1935, *Alice Adams* (director, George Stevens; art director, Van Nest Polglase), two key scenes take place on main street (the street name is not designated). Instead of an establishing shot as in *Our Town*, the street is shown in a succession of close-up details of shop fronts. Specifically, the filmmakers use street signage in a highly effective way to convey information to the audience, quickly and silently, regarding the setting and the conflict faced by the title character. In the opening shot of the film the banner draped across the street announces the name and age of the small town: "75th Jubilee Year: South Renford, the Town with a Future." Next, the camera pans in close-up from left to right across the names of three main-street businesses: "South Renford News, Circulation 5000," "Vogue Smart Shop," and "Samuels 5 —10—15 ¢ Store." The following medium shot encapsulates Alice's desire for upward mobility as she exits through the open glass doors of the dime store, whose cheap trinkets are all she can afford, to the closed, forbidding front of the Vogue dress shop, representing the elite but restricted world to which she aspires. The camera pans further to the left to Nashio Florist, where the flowers are too expensive (the word "corsages" on the front acts as a verbal cue to the narrative).

Later, when Alice sneaks back to main street to find a job at Frincke's Business College, the flight of eighteen steps emblazoned with names of blue-collar occupations contrasts with the front of the nearby barber shop and shoe-shine chair occupied by Arthur (Fred MacMurray), emblematic of his position in leisured society. Class restrictions notwithstanding, the special character of the American downtown is its embrace of all social levels. A short stroll from the street takes the couple to the ̣residential neighborhood, past large, elegant homes to her "little place." In *Alice Adams* even the smallest details of Main Street, as Disney would later understand, comprise a meaningful and expressive vehicle for conveying aspects of the American experience.

Alfred Hitchcock shot his favorite among his own films, *Shadow of a Doubt* of 1943 — co-written by Thornton Wilder — in a real small town, Santa Rosa, California (art director, John B. Goodman). Employing the big city vs. small town dichotomy that is common within the genre, the movie opens with a sequence in a grey, seedy rooming house in Philadelphia but then shifts to the sunlit imagery of Santa Rosa's charming downtown, accompanied by a sweet musical theme and showcasing the traffic cop, whose repeated appearance in the movie (three times) symbolizes small-town stability. Santa Rosa is cast as the center of good invaded by evil that arrives from the city early in the story at the train station in the form of Uncle Charlie (Joseph Cotton). The rail station appears again at the end of the film, with Uncle Charlie's forced exit from town and the climactic struggle on the train itself. Thus the station is a pivotal element within the small town, operating as the point of connection between the closed world of the home and the larger world outside. The importance of the residential district is underlined by Uncle Charley in his farewell speech: "But I want you all to know that I will always think of this lovely town. It's a place of hospitality, kindness, and homes — *homes*." Like Disney in his early vision for the park, Hitchcock integrates the three essential elements of the small town so that they play complementary roles in the film.

At times Main Street is physically absent from a small-town film, but a line of dialogue conjures up its essence. In Frank Capra's *Mr. Deeds Goes to Town* of 1936, Deeds and Babe (Gary Cooper and Jean Arthur) commiserate on a park bench in the midst of a corrupt New York City, talking of how they miss their respective birthplaces. "I'm from a small town too, you know," she says. "Probably as small as Mandrake Falls. Oh, it's a beautiful little town too. A row of poplar trees right along Main Street. Always smells as if it just had a bath. I've often thought of going back." The only views of Deeds's hometown, Mandrake Falls, that we see are of his house and the train station, the latter again denoting the juncture between the big city and the country. It is the point of arrival for the urban shysters and the point of departure for Deeds, who never had a reason to be away from the little town ("I don't think we have any suitcases!"). In other words, this movie and others of the period, being produced on Disney's own turf in Hollywood, used images of the small town to depict the same American cultural values that Disney, child of the Victorian age and survivor of the Great Depression, sought to affirm at his theme park.

The Hollywood Back Lot

While Disney, as a Hollywood producer, was familiar with the ideal of small-town American life that had become a genre in American movies, he also knew the many studio back lots where fictitious Main Streets stood along-side Western and medieval sets. These lots comprised a kind of proto-Disneyland. Their false fronts and assorted exotic locations, packed into a single site, offered him a ready-made vision of what he hoped to achieve in Anaheim. Disney's back-lot mentality is evident not only in his aim to broad-cast television shows from the park but also in his naive desire to build the attractions cheaply, like stage sets — not realizing that public-building codes would drive up the cost of construction (Bright 68).

It should be remembered that in the era before cameras and sound equipment became small and portable, it was easier, less costly, and more effective to build a false city street out of wood, plaster, canvas, and paint than to film on location. There were ten major studio back lots and six studio ranches in the L.A. area. For example, the financial success enjoyed by MGM in the '30s and '40s allowed the studio's Culver City studio to grow to 183 acres. This property included offices, sound stages, and the famous lots where European villages, Western towns, and Parisian boulevards stood side by side. MGM purportedly built the most elaborate of all urban sets encompassing the architecture of some forty well-known sections of various American towns and cities (Ramirez 104). Lot 3 at MGM was the location of Carvel, the hometown of Andy Hardy (Mickey Rooney) and centerpiece of one of the most successful series of small-town movies, comprising seventeen films in all. A movie like *Love Finds Andy Hardy* (1938; director, George B. Seitz) focuses on the domestic interaction of the characters filmed in houses on the Andy Hardy street, but conflicts and plot developments take place on main street, typically in the Carvel Drug Company, where Andy and Betsy (Judy Garland) enjoy chocolate sodas with vanilla ice cream.

These back-lot sets were assembled according to an established system. For many decades the key production designers for movies were illustrators, not architects (Heisner 25–40; Ramirez 26–53). Trained as painters, they first scoured books, photographs, and old prints for inspiration, with the goal of achieving the semblance of authenticity, if not exact historical accuracy. They then set out to draw illusionistic views of interiors and exteriors that incorporated the characters and took into account various positions of the camera. Such concept drawings consisted of both large-scale color paintings and hundreds of small sketches. These in turn were transformed into scale models made of cardboard that were worked up by draftsmen into blueprints for construction.

This is precisely the way in which Main Street was put together. The designers were illustrators and continuity sketch artists formerly working at other movie studios: Harper Goff (Warner Bros.), Herb Ryman, Marvin

Davis, Dick Irvine, and Sam McKim (20th Century–Fox), and Wade Rubottom and Harry McAfee (MGM) (Janzen 30–31; "Visualizing Disneyland" 8–11, Barrier 226–27). The initial stage comprised research comparable to that for a movie, with the help of the studio library, as described in the 1965 Disneyland guide book: "Hundreds of books, pictures and historical items were studied to get the feel of the interior and exterior of stores and shops of the 1900 era" (Disney n.p.). Their concept drawings resulted in the creation of a scale model. In fact, the first three-dimensional glimpse of the Disneyland theme park — shown to the world during the premiere of the *Disneyland* TV program eight months before the park's opening — was of the model of Main Street, photographed close-up in a tracking shot accompanied by sound effects to convey the sensation of moving down the street ("Planning the First Parks" 10–13).

From the realm of set design these artists borrowed numerous tricks (Ramirez 54–66, 81–96). Until now forced perspective is the single technique used at Disneyland to receive much comment from writers. The scale of architectural sets in movies was rarely realistic. For reasons of economy, fake buildings were usually constructed smaller than in real life, with the understanding that on film such differences were not noticeable. Upper floors were shorter in scale than lower floors, an effect that registers on film as greater height. Like a movie set, therefore, Main Street is smaller than in real life, and the upper floors are proportionally shorter than those below, approximately to the following degree: lower floors are nine-tenths their true size, the second floors eight-tenths, and the third floors seven-tenths (Gabler 533).

Furthermore, stage sets for movies are invariably fragmentary — only that which will be filmed by the camera is actually finished. This was partly the result of space and budgetary limitations. Likewise on Main Street, only those areas that are visible to the spectator are finished in period style. Roofs, second floors, and so-called backstage areas are not. Some of the doors are fixed and cannot be opened, and upper-floor window trimmings disguise storage areas. Once inside a storefront, the visitor can move from one shop to the next without going outside. Inner walls have been eliminated, similar to the way that on a film set moveable walls allow the camera to shoot the actors with greater freedom. Just as the materials used for sets, like plaster and canvas, are often inexpensive but visually convincing alternatives to masonry and brick, on Main Street a new substance, fiberglass — strong, cheap, and lightweight — fools the eye in much of the detailing (Francaviglia, *Main Street Revisited* 147).

Movie architecture is an exaggeration of reality. Unlike the human eye, the camera lens cannot differentiate between what is important and what is not, and being monocular, it tends to flatten things. The creators of Main

Street took a cue from the set designer, who emphasizes certain elements, like the edges of windows and doors, to give a more accurate impression, and heightens textures for the sake of contrast. As the celebrated art director William Cameron Menzies stipulated, "If, for example, you film a romantic place [on location] like a picturesque European street, you can achieve an exact reproduction — but that will still be minus the atmosphere, texture, and color. So it is always better to replace it with a set [erected in the studio] which gives the *impression* of the street as it exists in your mind, slightly romanticized, simplified, and overly textured" (Ramirez 86).

Architectural detailing in movie sets, which includes doors, window surrounds, columns, balustrades, and railings, is normally composed of recycled materials rather than newly built elements, for financial reasons but also in the interest of authenticity. The same was true at Main Street, where much of the detailing consists of "props" salvaged from other places. According to the 1965 guide to Disneyland, "A treasure hunt ranged across the country into antique shops, private homes and out-of-the-way junk shops in small villages. The searchers tracked down relics of the past ranging from old lighting fixtures to ... hitching posts.... There were 100-year-old gas lamp posts from Baltimore and Philadelphia, cresting and railing from old plantations in Nashville and Memphis, small park benches from San Francisco" (Disney n.p.).

Color is another element of set design that tended to be unnaturalistic in order to compensate for distortions imposed by lighting and the camera. Lighter colors on the upper stories give the illusion of height. Designers also used a subjective palette to enhance the mood of a scene. The shades used on Main Street, reportedly a palette of over two hundred custom colors overseen by Disney himself, were stronger and more varied than that of any real Main Street of 1900 (Hench 108–10; Comfort 145).

Finally, signage is a set-design technique borrowed by the Disney art directors and based on the real use of public signs in the urban context. As in the example of *Alice Adams,* Disneyland's Main Street signage served primarily the purpose of identifying businesses and corporate sponsors and, over time, celebrating Disney Company employees through the names stenciled on upper-floor windows. Disney's designers credit him with an acute sensitivity to the potential impact of words, type fonts, and graphics, and they claim that he was familiar with every sign, large or small, throughout the park (Imagineers 100). In sum, the architecture of the movies is functional insofar as it supports the narrative, enhances the actions of the characters, and evokes the emotional response intended by the script. The architecture of the back lot was rarely "real" but was usually "dramatic." In the same way Disney's designers rearranged the particularities of the small-town street to produce an idealized version of a Main Street that never existed in order to evoke nostalgia and encourage strolling and shopping.

Back-Lot Streets

Although writers have commented in passing on the stage-set-like character of Disney's Main Street, there has been no consideration of small-town street sets that preceded it. Examination of four in particular will illuminate later design decisions at Disneyland.

One of the more identifiable Main Streets in the movies was built as part of a small-town set on the Paramount Ranch, located northwest of Los Angeles. Although used primarily for its varied outdoor locations and frontier town, the ranch also provided space for American and European urban backdrops. The small-town set was the locale for two Preston Sturges films released in 1944, *The Miracle of Morgan's Creek* (art directors, Hans Dreier and Ernst Fegté) and *Hail the Conquering Hero* (art directors, Haldane Douglas and Hans Dreier). According to legend, Sturges wrote the script for *Morgan's Creek* specifically to save the charming set from demolition (Curtis 178; among other films, the set earlier represented the mythical town of Rivers End in *Meet Dr. Christian*, 1939). The same downtown buildings and their defining signage can be recognized in both Sturges films, despite the differing town names, Morgan's Creek and Oakridge. The most elaborately counterfeited front is the Regent movie theater, with its neon marquee, while the building most laden with signage is the pharmacy, whose awning, neon sign, and wooden placards advertise everything from drug prescriptions and cigars to sodas and candies. Although the narrative takes place in the present, *The Miracle of Morgan's Creek* derives much of its small-town ambience from the presence of both horse-drawn and fuel-powered vehicles on the street.

The Main Street set was one block in length, with six to eight businesses on each side. Transverse streets blocked the axis at the ends. Thus in *The Miracle of Morgan's Creek* the Bugle newspaper office and adjacent fire department terminate one vista, as may be witnessed in the scene where Trudy drives Norville's car over the curb in front of the Regent Theater on Main Street (Betty Hutton and Eddie Bracken). For *Hail the Conquering Hero* these buildings were replaced by the façade of a large white clapboard church forming the backdrop of the march of the citizenry down Main Street in the movie's climax. Their destination is the train station lining the cross street on the opposite end, similar to the transverse position of the Main Street Station at Disneyland. It is at the station that the Marines, who alter the life of the little town, arrive early in *Conquering Hero* and depart at the end.

Significantly, Sturges employs long tracking shots to reveal the relationship between Main Street and the residential sectors on either side. For example, in *Morgan's Creek* Trudy and Norville converse while strolling from a picturesque neighborhood of middle-class homes to the downtown cinema in an uninterrupted shot lasting four minutes — a technical feat at the time. In *Hail the Conquering Hero* Libby and Forrest (Ella Raines and Bill Edwards) walk in reverse direction from downtown to her house in a lengthy two-minute shot. The director uses the fluid camera movement across the set to present an integrated picture of the characters' hometown environment, and he characterizes the town as small enough to be traversed on foot. The fact that it is the same set in both movies is unimportant. Like Disney, Sturges's goal is to create an illusion of the typical American town whose size allows all of the inhabitants to know each other, resulting in a strong sense of community. The extraordinary, comic events that beset the protagonists are played against the good humor and eccentric behavior of the small-town citizens.

A particularly influential set was St. Louis Street, built at MGM on lot 3 for Vincente Minnelli's picture of 1944, *Meet Me in St. Louis*, based on the *New Yorker* stories by Sally Benson, a co-writer for *Shadow of a Doubt* (art directors, Lemuel Ayers, Cedric Gibbons, and Jack Martin Smith). Despite St. Louis's status as a city, the director emphasized that he treated the setting as a slice of small-town Americana (MacKinnon 19): the main conflict revolves around the question of whether the Smith family must leave its quiet, provincial existence and move to New York, where everybody is "cooped up in a tenement." In fact, whereas almost all previous movie musicals glamorized the big city or the theater, only a handful had focused on small-town life. The original plan was to dress up the Andy Hardy street on the lot, but Minnelli's vision called for creating from scratch a spectacular street graced with grandiose Victorian houses better suited to the time period of 1903 (Fordin 95–96). He considered the Smith house and Kensington Avenue to be characters in the movie of equal import to those played by the actors (Genné 252). Within a few opening seconds of the film, the requisite contrast between horse-drawn vehicles and automobiles makes its appearance on the street.

The Second-Empire style of the Smith house, with its steep mansard roofs, blocky towers, asymmetrical massing, and ironwork cresting, had been used for domestic buildings in earlier films. But Minnelli showcased the style as never before, partly through the set-design tricks of exaggerated color and scale, for which he is justifiably famous. Shot in Technicolor, *Meet Me in St. Louis* was Minnelli's first color film, and it defined the palette of the movie musical in the same way that Disney had done for the first color cartoon, likewise using Technicolor (*Flowers and Trees*, 1932). Each of the four seasonal sections of the movie opens with a view of the house and street transformed from a black-and-white photograph into a dazzlingly colorful moving image, particularly vivid with the contrast of the white clapboard and red roof tile repeated in the candy-cane-striped awnings. As mentioned above, Disney's artists would later choose the Second-Empire style for the large private houses proposed adjacent to Main Street facing the hub in the early concept drawings of 1953. The style gives magnificence, authority, and a touch of French sophistication to those structures actually built at Disneyland, like the Main Street Station, City Hall, and the Emporium. Additionally, the original ornate Main Street interiors, with their sparkling crystal and ornamental brickabrac, were conceived in the same Gilded-Age mode as the detailed interiors of *Meet Me in St. Louis*.

In the late 1940s Disney had only begun a career in live-action movies, but the film often cited as a personal favorite, *So Dear to My Heart* of 1949, includes an early version of Main Street, U.S.A., set in the year 1903 (director, Harold Schuster; art director, John Ewing). The movie's fictive locale, a small Midwestern town called Fulton Corners, was built on location near Porterville, California, north of Los Angeles. The view from the train station encompasses a dirt street leading to the main street bordered by Grundy's Mercantile Store, the Feed Store, a blacksmith shop, and a structure whose bell tower signals a schoolhouse or, more likely, a church. The characters never inhabit this street — it was primarily a simple mock-up serving as a background. They do, however, enter the Grundy shop: because of limited space at the studio, the store interior was constructed behind the façade. The later shops at Disneyland would similarly consist of real spaces behind false fronts. Amazingly, the set designers found an old, closed-up hardware store in Porterville and purchased its entire inventory for use as historic props (Maltin 88–89). Disney hoped to reuse in Disneyland the rail-station set, patterned after a real depot back east and given after filming to animator and train buff Ward Kimball to use as his Grizzly Flats Depot; ultimately its design provided the basis for the Frontierland Station (Broggie 266–68).

The best-known Hollywood Main Street is Genesee Street, with its tree-lined parkway, in Frank Capra's *It's a Wonderful Life* of 1946, built on the RKO ranch in Encino, California (art director, Jack Okey). Shown, like Minnelli's St. Louis Street, through all four seasons, the street is the centerpiece of the utopian town of Bedford Falls, a symbol of traditional American values (AlSayyad 45–70). Other scenes take place at the train station and in a charming residential neighborhood. The film opens in 1919, with the usual visual cue of the horse-drawn carriage vs. the automobile moving down the street in the first minute. Stretching three blocks, Genesee Street was comparable to Disneyland's Main Street in length and use of forced perspective. Seventeen of the twenty-seven businesses and institutions facing the street (reconstructed by Willian, 9) — from the bank and police station to the bakery and emporium — would also line Disney's Main Street. Some of the shops, such as Gower Drugs and the World Luggage and Sporting Goods Store, were fully outfitted and filmed behind the façades. Like Minnelli, Capra treated the street as one of the characters, especially in the transformation from the welcoming thoroughfare of Bedford Falls to the main drag of Pottersville, a dystopian nightmare of bars, dance halls, and strip joints lit by menacing neon signage.

Few Hollywood directors resembled Disney as much as Capra, sharing a populist point of view and an old-fashioned code of behavior. Capra paid homage to Disney in several movies. In *It Happened One Night* (1934) Clark Gable sings "Who's Afraid of the Big Bad Wolf?"; in *You Can't Take It with You* (1938) Jimmy Stewart evokes a fantasy world by referencing Walt Disney's name, and the basement inventors toil to the sound of "Whistle While You Work." Their friendship became a partnership when Disney, deeply engaged in creating propaganda films for the war effort, provided animated footage for Capra's *Why We Fight* series in 1942–43 (Shale 38–40). Capra spent time on the Disney Studios lot, and it is tempting to think that a few years later Disney could have visited the Bedford Falls set. Perhaps that is why the marquee of the Bijou Theater on Genesee street heralds a Donald Duck cartoon!

In 1989 The Walt Disney Company opened a new theme park in Florida dedicated to the golden age of movies, Disney–MGM Studios, whose point of entry, Hollywood Boulevard, is based on the prototype of Main Street, U.S.A. Explaining the symbolism underlying this streetscape, architecture critic Beth Dunlop made an observation regarding the impact of Hollywood on the national psyche before the age of television: "Disney's Imagineers saw parallels between the roles that Main Street and Hollywood have played in the national mythology. Indeed Hollywood — or the idea of Hollywood — eventually became a kind of symbolic national Main Street for Americans. The world of movies and moviemaking was a focus of America's optimistic hopes, especially in the dreary years of the Great Depression when the best antidote to the blues was a trip downtown to a picture palace to see a Hollywood extravaganza" (124). As a corollary to this myth-making, it was the medium of film that in the 1930s and '40s indelibly established the idea of the quintessential small town, with its train station, main street, and residences, thus reinforcing, invigorating, and giving meaning to the hometown experiences of millions of Americans. Walt Disney's method and purpose in visualizing the little town at the entrance to Disneyland through the collaborative efforts of his creative team was not only analogous to but influenced by these movies. In the last analysis, they both had as their purpose the affirmation of "the ideals, the dreams, and the hard facts that have created America," to quote Disneyland's dedication plaque in Town Square.

As for Disney's pronouncements on the matter, a comment that he made during the planning of Disneyland in March 1954, recently brought to light by Neal Gabler, says much about Disney's own conception of the park. In order to explain the idea of Disneyland as it was taking shape four months before construction began on the Anaheim site, he summed up his pet project in just a few words: "A cute movie set is what it really is" (533). In light of the evidence coming from Hollywood, U.S.A., these words ring particularly true for his vision of Main Street, U.S.A.

Note: Thanks are due to Loretta Lorance and Derham Groves for their perceptive comments on an early version of this paper presented at the 2007 meeting of the ACA/PCA. I also wish to express my gratitude to Karal Ann Marling, Michael Barrier, Didier Ghez, and Chris Newcomb for their generous assistance in tracking down primary documents.

Works Cited

AlSayyad, Nezar. *Cinematic Urbanism: A History of the Modern from Reel to Real.* New York: Routledge, 2006.

Barrier, Michael. *The Animated Man: A Life of Walt Disney.* Berkeley: University of California Press, 2007.

Bright, Randy. *Disneyland: Inside Story.* New York: Abrams, 1987.

Burnes, Brian, Robert W. Butler, and Dan Viets. *Walt Disney's Missouri: The Roots of a Creative Genius.* Kansas City: Kansas City Star, 2002.

Comfort, Mildred H. *Walt Disney, Master of Fantasy.* Minneapolis: Denison, 1968.

Disney, Walt. *Disneyland.* Verona: Mondadori, 1964.

Disneyland: Dreams, Traditions and Transitions. Anaheim, CA: Disney's Kingdom Editions, n.d.

Dunlop, Beth. *Building a Dream: The Art of Disney Architecture.* New York, 1996.

Finch, Christopher. *Walt Disney's America.* New York: Abbeville, 1978.

Fordin, Hugh. *The Movies' Greatest Musicals: Produced in Hollywood USA by the Freed Unit.* New York: Frederick Unger, 1984.

Francaviglia, Richard V. *Main Street Revisited: Time, Space, and Image-Building in Small-Town America.* Iowa City: University of Iowa Press, 1996.

_____. "Main Street, U.S.A.: A Comparison/Contrast of Streetscapes in Walt Disney World." *Journal of Popular Culture* 15 (Summer 1981): 141–56.

Gabler, Neal. *Walt Disney: The Triumph of the American Imagination.* New York: Alfred A. Knopf, 2006.

Genné, Beth. "Vincente Minnelli's Style in Microcosm: The Establishing Sequence of 'Meet Me in St. Louis.'" *Art Journal* 43:3 (Fall 1983): 247–54.

Gordon, Arthur. "Walt Disney." *Look* (26 July 1955): 29–35.

Gordon, Bruce, and David Mumford. *A Brush with Disney: An Artist's Journey.* Santa Clarita, CA: Camphor Tree, 2000.

_____. *Disneyland: The Nickel Tour.* 2d ed. Santa Clarita, CA: Camphor Tree, 2000.

Heisner, Beverly. *Hollywood Art: Art Direction in the Days of the Great Studios.* Jefferson, NC: McFarland, 1990.

Hench, John. *Designing Disney: Imagineering and the Art of the Show.* New York: Disney, 2003.

The Imagineers. *Walt Disney Imagineering.* New York: Hyperion, 1996.

"An Interview with Harper Goff." *The "E" Ticket* no. 14 (Winter 1992–93): 4–11.

Jackson, Kathy Merlock. *Walt Disney: A Bio-Bibliography.* Westport, CT: Greenwood, 1993.

Janzen, Jack E. "Main Street ... Walt's Perfect Introduction to Disneyland." *The "E" Ticket* no. 14 (Winter 1992–93): 24–33.

Koenig, David. *Mouse Tales: A Behind-the-Ears Look at Disneyland.* Golden Anniversary Special Edition. Irvine, CA: Bonaventure, 2005.

Kurtti, Jeff, and Bruce Gordon. *The Art of Disneyland.* New York: Disney, 2006.

Levy, Emanuel. *Small-Town America in Film: The Decline and Fall of Community.* New York: Continuum, 1991.

Longstreth, Richard W. *The Buildings of Main Street: A Guide to American Commercial Architecture.* Rev. ed. Walnut Creek, CA: AltaMira, 2000.

MacKinnon, Kenneth. *Hollywood's Small Towns: An Introduction to the American Small-Town Movie.* Metuchen, NJ: Scarecrow, 1984.

"Main Gate." *The "E" Ticket* no. 14 (Winter 1992–93): 2–3.

Maltin, Leonard. *The Disney Films.* 3d ed. New York: Hyperion, 1995.

Marling, Karal Ann. "Disneyland, 1955: Just Take the Santa Ana Freeway to the American Dream." *American Art* 5 (Winter-Spring 1991): 168–207.

_____. "Imagineering the Disney Theme Parks." In *Designing Disney's Theme Parks: The Architecture of Reassurance,* edited by Karl Ann Marling, 29–177. Montreal: Canadian Centre for Architecture, 1997.

_____, with Donna R. Braden. *Behind the Magic: 50 Years of Disneyland.* Dearborn, MI: Henry Ford, 2005.

Mason, Dave. "The Merchants of Main Street." *Frontier Magazine* 5:4 (July-August 2003): 16–27+.

Miller, Diane Disney. "My Dad, Walt Disney." Part Two: "Hard Times in Kansas City." *Saturday Evening Post* 229: 21 (24 November 1956): 26–27, 70–71, 78–79.

Mordden, Ethan. *The Hollywood Studios: House Style in the Golden Age of the Movies.* New York: A.A. Knopf, 1988.

"New Disney Show Listed for Radio." *New York Times.* 25 November 1955, 55.

"Planning the First Disney Parks ... A Talk with Marvin Davis." *The "E" Ticket* no. 28 (Winter 1997): 8–19.

Pryor, Thomas M. "Disney To Enter TV Field in Fall." *New York Times,* 30 March 1954, 24.

_____. "Hollywood Double Entente." *New York Times,* 11 April 1954, X5.

_____. "Land of Fantasia Is Rising on Coast." *New York Times,* 2 May 1954, 86.

Ramirez, Juan Antonio. *Architecture for the Screen: A Critical Study of Set Design in Hollywood's Golden Age.* Trans. John F. Moffitt. Jefferson, NC: McFarland, 2004.

Shale, Richard. *Donald Duck Joins Up: The Walt Disney Studio during World War II.* Ann Arbor, MI: UMI Research Press, 1982.

Thomas, Bob. *Walt Disney, An American Original.* New York: Hyperion, 1994.

Tour Guide of Marceline, Missouri, Walt Disney's Home Town. Kansas City, MO: Eisterhold, 2001.

"Visualizing Disneyland with ... Sam McKim." *The "E" Ticket* no. 18 (Spring 1994): 8–21.

"Walt Disney Make-Believe Land Project Planned Here." *Burbank Daily Review.* 27 March 1952: A.1.

Watts, Steven. *The Magic Kingdom: Walt Disney and the American Way of Life.* Boston: Houghton Mifflin, 1997.

Willian, Michael. *The Essential* It's a Wonderful Life*: A Scene-by-Scene Guide to the Classic Film.* Chicago: Chicago Review, 2006.

Wirsig, Woodrow. "Companionably Yours: Disneyland." *Woman's Home Companion* 81 (June 1954): 12.

Frontierland as an Allegorical Map of the American West

RICHARD FRANCAVIGLIA

> Now when I was a little chap I had a passion for maps.... At that time there
> were many blank spaces on the earth and when I found one that looked
> particularly inviting on a map (but they all look that) I would put my
> finger on it and say: When I grow up I will go there.
>
> —Joseph Conrad
> *Heart of Darkness* (1902)

Many people are fascinated by maps, especially those maps of continents
that show empty spaces suggesting unknown peoples and places. Cartographers draw maps that have the power to both inform and beguile their users
(Wood). On one level, maps perform the mundane task of depicting places
well enough so that we can locate them, and, hopefully, travel there. Resulting
from centuries of artistic refinement and scientific thought, maps are essential
in describing the world and places on it.[1] To do so, they rely on some ground
rules. Cartographers usually recite a litany of features that make maps effective:
they should be drawn with reference to geographic coordinates (latitude/lon-
gitude), use recognized projections, be drawn to scale, and be clearly oriented
(north customarily being "up") (Robinson). Maps, moreover, always have
contexts. Cartographic historians interpret maps in light of their sponsors,
map makers, society, and other earlier maps that often serve as their inspiration.[2] Maps, in other words, serve as barometers of geographic knowledge
(Thrower). Through them, for example, the western portion of North America
was first defined by Spanish cartographers, and later refined by Mexican and
American military and scientific expeditions.

At another level, however, maps transcend their claims to scientific objectivity. We have a passion for maps because they possess the power to inspire the imagination. At this level, maps are tools of the spirited mind — the empire builder and the storyteller: they fuel the desire to experience, even claim, the geographic area that they represent. Cartography in this context becomes motivational (or invitational), for it empowers the mapreader to experience place vicariously. Read collectively, maps may thus represent broadly shared aspirations, fantasies, and beliefs about places. This explains why cartography and expansion are inextricably linked. The beautiful historic maps of western North America seen in catalogs and archives represent not only the geographic knowledge, but also the geographic objectives, of the time. Through them, the frontier was delineated — given spatial form in reference to that which was known and settled, versus that which was unknown and conquerable. In reality, the places mapped were known by other (Native) peoples, and their input even found its way into the explorers' maps, but the voices of these Native peoples were not credited in the final product. Maps are powerful tools of appropriation.

As definitions of cartography broaden to embrace all representations of place, including mental maps, so too has the definition of a map expanded to include more than drawings of places on flat paper or parchment. Just as non–Western peoples used pictographs and objects such as sticks to represent places, we now recognize that maps can take many forms. Consider, for example, an accepted three-dimensional artifact — the globe — that signifies the shape of the earth. It, too, is a map, but one shaped more like the sphere it represents. But what about maps that take great liberties in depicting places, such as the whimsical cartograms or cartoons that show Texas stretching from coast to coast, or even ashtrays in the shape of Texas?[3] These, too, are maps, but their purpose is as iconic as it is informational.

At yet another level, even shaped environments may be maps. A farmer's pond excavated, or a grove of trees planted, in the shape of Texas come to mind, but an even better example is an imperial Chinese city that also serves as a map of the cosmos. In these cases, maps become metaphors and artifacts (Downs 287–93). When studied carefully, large scale features such as miniature golf courses or theme parks often embody visions of places — either places on earth or utopian places conceived in the mind of their creators and designers. These are also three-dimensional topographic representations of places real or imagined, and are thus maps.

Using the definition of cartography in this broadest of senses — as iconography of the geographic imagination — allows us to explore the vision of the West held by Walt Disney (1901–1966). Although no one can delineate precisely

Disney's mental map of the West, he did configure a portion of Disneyland, his theme park in Anaheim, California, to represent it, and the shape of his creations suggests its general contours. The historian and geographer may thus interpret this portion of his park, Frontierland, much like they do real places — deciphering, as it were, what Disney placed on his three dimensional map. Doing so involves considerable speculation, for as will be seen, Disney was circumspect about the actual design process involved in the creation of Frontierland. That, however, simply adds to the challenge of understanding his creations as environments that invite interpretation both as material culture and as symbols.

This essay focuses on Fronticrland, one portion of Disneyland, and one of Disney's most popular environments. To facilitate this interpretation, this essay uses a cartographic metaphor to identify the historical and geographic themes that appear to inspire Disney's western frontier vision. It is not coincidental that the theme park he created is called the "Magic Kingdom," for Disneyland builds upon images of places associated with history and fantasy. It is especially significant that Frontierland was specifically designed to represent a particular geographic locale — the American West. By interpreting Frontierland as a cartographic manifestation of a real place, it becomes apparent that this three-dimensional mental map of the West, like its paper counterparts, is closely tied to empire building and cultural identity formation.

So powerful is the name "Frontierland" that its mere mention evokes images of "the West" to most people. Those images are derived from television and novels rather than serious historical research. They are, nevertheless, valid representations of the frontier in popular culture. Although the name Frontierland appears contrived, it reaffirms an axiom of perceptual geography: places, by definition, must be named in order to enter our consciousness. Words serve as the basis for all place names (Basso). It is impossible to conceive of a place without using words to describe it (Tuan 684–96). Stated another way, place names are very short stories that summarize a lengthy narrative. Consider, for example, the names Wounded Knee, Virginia City, Bakersfield, or Austin — they resonate with cultural and biographical history because they are stories of origins and subsequent events. The names of these individual locations — which is to say stories abbreviated in place — are woven into a larger narrative when they are placed on a map. Thus, although it is tempting to think of a map as a purely *graphic* device, maps, like the places they represent, could not exist without *language*. Maps, in fact, occupy a unique interface between images and narratives.

Following the geographers' and anthropologists' advice, let us begin with the name: Frontierland. Turning to a dictionary for help in defining the place name, we immediately recognize its dual roots in two separate nouns —*frontier* and *land*. *Frontier* is defined either as (1) "a border between two countries," or (2) "a region that forms the margin of settled or developed territory," while *land* is defined as "a portion of the earth's solid surface distinguishable by boundaries or ownership." Note that frontier is also used as an adjective: it tells us about the *condition* of that particular land. The word *land* also works to describe the frontier as a realm. Note too that both words *frontier* and *land* are inextricably tied to *ownership*, either geopolitical, individual, or both. This is especially significant, for Disney's Frontierland works metaphorically at several levels, namely political, cultural, and geographic. Its importance, moreover, is best understood cartographically, that is, as a material manifestation of Disney's — and, broadly speaking, America's — mental map of the national experience. A closer look at the history and geography of Frontierland is in order, for a dispassionate study of it reveals its association with American mythology.

Viewed comprehensively, Frontierland fits into a continuous tradition of storytelling about American frontiers, that is, lands at the periphery of the settled and appropriated world. From Columbus to John Wesley Powell, four centuries separate "the unselfconsciously late-medieval discoverer from the self-consciously modern explorer" (Pagden 1). These discoverers and imperial explorers operated from about 1500 to 1900. They often wrote extensive reports about their exploits for future generations. To these chroniclers we may add twentieth-century interpreters like Walt Disney, who ultra-self-consciously portrayed the process of exploration and discovery in order to both educate and entertain. In Frontierland, Disney encouraged visitors to vicariously experience the unknown, turning theme park visitors into latter-day explorers far removed from the original time and place of exploration. In doing so, Disney also built on celluloid experiences and historically themed docu-dramas, such as his 1960 film *Ten Who Dared*, which portrayed John Wesley Powell's discoveries in the Grand Canyon. These vehicles of literature, film, and theme park helped build upon the nation's enduring popular fascination with frontiers, notably the interior American West. Through them new generations could still "discover" wondrous peoples and landscapes, albeit vicariously.

What Columbus triggered as an irrepressible *westward* quest for new lands continued unabated through centuries of exploration and discovery until military surveyors and geologists essentially completed the process by about 1900 (Allen). They cleared a path for those who would not be satisfied merely claiming and settling the periphery, that is, the more accessible coastal margins of the new continents. They directed their quests toward the interior — the very heart — and to what lay beyond. Significantly, Disney was born at just the time (1901) the era of American expansion on the continent was ending, and the United States became a world power to be reckoned with. This essay suggests that the frontier of westward expansion is held in the collective consciousness as a signifier of the search for many frontiers, including individual freedom, economic growth, and cultural/social development. If all westerns are morality plays reenacted at the margins of established society, then the locale of this action — the western frontier — is rich in contextual meaning. Frontierland is, above all, a historical, geographical, and ultimately mythical story given form by Disney.

That this energetic westward colonization drama continues to have broad public appeal is evidenced by the enduring popularity of the taming of the West in song, movies, cartoons, and theme parks. Consider the westward move as interpreted by shapers of popular culture in the animated film *An American Tail* (1986) produced and directed by Don Bluth shortly after he left The Walt Disney Company. Building on Disney's tradition of anthropomorphizing, *An American Tail* featured an immigrant family of mice (named, appropriately, Mousekewitz) who arrive in the United States from Russia after many trials and tribulations. In the popular sequel, *An American Tail: Fievel Goes West* (1991), still under the influence of the original, the mice remain restless. Finding their opportunity limited in the grimy cities of the East, they naturally look farther westward for opportunity. After hearing glowing descriptions of the region, the Mousekewitz family travels westward to the Wyoming frontier, where they triumph over adversity. Their son Fievel becomes a hero in the process of moving West. In popular stories of this genre, the frontier serves as a crucible in which tenacity and valor are regarded by success and possession. That the genre is flexible is verified in *An American Tail: Fievel Goes West*, for the mice appear to be cast as ethnically Jewish (not Anglo American) characters, and the message of their exploits is decidedly anti-corporate. However, this frontier fable still works as a tale of liberation from oppression. There is another theme operative in the genre of frontier stories, and that is re-generation. Horace Greeley's admonition to "Go West Young Man" suggests that youth would prosper, but it also suggests the West's ability to sustain youthful vigor and initiative. Even though he discovered the West in the 1920s, several generations after the "real" pioneers, Walt Disney sensed new opportunities there. Perhaps he also sensed its regenerative powers. It is important to remember that Walt Disney's brother Roy (who would play a major role in the development and financial management of the Disney enterprises) moved to California for health reasons in the 1920s. It was this move that first brought Walt Disney to the Golden State for a visit, but the move ultimately regenerated both brothers (Duchemin).

The belief in the regenerative powers inherent in the westward "American" migration is deeply embedded in our popular culture, and Disney capitalized on it. In doing so, he built on the sweeping literary generalizations about the West that would outlive Disney himself. Published a year before Disney's death, the popular 1965 novel, *The Ordways*, by Texas writer William Humphrey, captured the essence of the ethnocentric cause-effect quality of the West as youth and new beginnings:

> When a man decides to pull up his roots and set off in search of a new life, he instinctively heads west. No other point of the compass exerts that powerful pull. The West is the true magnetic pole. Ever since his expulsion from the garden to a place east of Eden, man has yearned westward as towards a state of remembered innocence, and human history is one long westward migration [Humphrey 54].

It is easy to dismiss such novels, films, and cartoons about the frontier as drivel, but they endure despite sustained withering criticism from academicians. Why? This essay suggests an answer: such seemingly trite stories have deeper significance. As historians of the West, we can study The Walt Disney Company and Disney's conception of the West to gain insights into the broader role of the West in Western/American culture. Disney was a remarkably successful purveyor of western icons, stories, and memorabilia. He used media and technology to tell, and retell, the engaging story of the frontier. The company took form with Walt Disney's animated films, beginning in the 1920s and 1930s (One of the earliest, *Steamboat Willie*, featured Mickey Mouse aboard a steamboat on the western rivers). Disney's feature films in the 1950s and 1960s, and his masterful use of television and theme parks beginning in the same period, earned him a reputation as America's premier shaper of popular culture in the mid–twentieth century. Although it is now commonplace to debate the significance of the "Disney version" of history, that vision continues to be conveyed through cartoons, films, products, and theme parks.[4] And it continues to have broad popular appeal. Recent scholarship confirms that historians in general — and western historians in particular — can profitably study Disney's creations for their deeper content and meaning, and for the multi-layered messages that resonate from them.[5] As historians, we are most effective when interpreting Disney neither as a villain nor saint, but rather as a biographical figure who ably captured America's nearly mythical fascination with the westering experience. One thing about Disney is undeniable: he is an immensely important — perhaps *the* most important — representative and shaper of twentieth-century American culture (Watts).

Disneyland, too, is of vast importance as an environment of popular culture that shapes worldviews. That magic kingdom is dialectically complex; it is traditional in that it built on popular mainstream values, but it is radical in that it helped revolutionize the way most people conceptualize and interpret the American experience. Understanding how the park functioned in this ambivalent role requires putting Disneyland in its historic context: as a phenomenon in time and space, Disneyland represented the decentralized, automobile-oriented entrepreneurism of Southern California in the early 1950s. When Walt Disney and his designers wrested Disneyland from the rectangular grid landscape of orange groves near Anaheim in 1954–1955, the park's design and small size necessarily represented both the genius of its creators and the compromises that they made in order to accommodate large numbers of visitors. But Disneyland definitely shaped, and was shaped by, the American psyche of the times. Disneyland's design even influenced the recent urban and suburban settlement of the real West (Findlay).

View from the air, Disneyland presents a non–Euclidean, but beautifully geometric, design that suggests a sense of cosmic order and symmetry. The design is simple enough at first blush; visitors to Disneyland enter the park through Main Street, U.S.A. that serves, metaphorically speaking, as a key by which the contents of the theme park are unlocked. Upon reaching the end of Main Street, U.S.A., at the park's center, visitors make a taxing decision: here at the plaza hub, they must decide which land to enter first. To the southwest is Adventureland, to the east Tomorrowland, to the north Fantasyland, and — significantly — to the west and northwest lies Frontierland. Hinting at the theme park's overall cartographic design, Walt Disney himself noted that Frontierland is located "to the west, of course," of the central plaza hub (Disney 10–11). This confirms that Disney conceptualized his creations geographically; like our culture, he constructed a mental map that was likely based on actual maps of the American West.

Although the word "west" is not used in its name (as it was in *Westworld*, a masterful 1973 film parody about theme parks), Frontierland, in this theme park, is obviously the American West. We can tell this by the clues Disney provided: simulated cacti, false front buildings, and colorful characters. It is noteworthy that even the Main Street, U.S.A., by which visitors reach Frontierland also hints of the West, for it was based in part on real streetscapes in the towns of Marceline, Missouri, and Fort Collins, Colorado (Francaviglia, *Main Street Revisited* 142–51). Disney believed that his railroad-straddling, market-oriented hometown of Marceline was not very far removed from the western frontier of the nineteenth century (Disney 10–11). It was in Marceline that Disney developed his love of the Missouri countryside that so enchanted him with its legends, railroads, steamboats, frontier characters, and Indian peoples. Of all the lands in Disneyland, however, Disney himself revealed that "Frontierland evokes a special response" and "occupied a great deal of my thought" (Disney 11). Significantly, it is the largest part of the 95-acre theme park.

A Disney interpreter wrote, "The Disney vision was clear. Scale meant everything, whether it was the fairy-tale size of the railroad, or the nostalgic foreshortening of Main Street, or the romanticism of Frontierland." If this is so, then Disneyland itself must be viewed as a stylized model of the world (if not the entire universe) and Frontierland a microcosm of that larger universe — the West (Thomas 266). Like most of Disney's creations, however, Frontierland is richly layered with meanings derived from both American folklore and literature. Disney's representation of the West involved linking a vivid narrative about the region to a design that could sustain the story line. Each part of the story was carefully conceived, named, and arranged in space to create a representation of a place. This makes Frontierland a cartographic manifestation of reality — a map — by which people may also collectively get their bearings on the landscape of imagination. Continuing the cartographic metaphor, Frontierland is actually a historical, or antiquarian, map. It represents Disney's vision of what the West was like in the time period that ended just before this birth. This golden time that Disney immortalized ended in the 1890s, the same decade during which Frederick Jackson Turner wrote his provocative frontier thesis. Using this era suggests that Disney called upon late-nineteenth-century sentiments from his parents' time. Thanks to Disney and others, such sentiments about the frontier lingered well into the twentieth century.

In contrast to literary writers who cast doubt on the indefatigability of the western spirit in the late nineteenth and early twentieth century, Disney's belief in the value of American society and technology was unshakable. If Frank Norris castigated western railroads in novels like *The Octopus* (1901), Disney later vindicated these same corporations in his theme park. Disney's faith persisted, despite his fatigue and mental breakdown in 1931, and his refusal to yield to the numerous setbacks that threatened him and his family with financial ruin. Disneyland, in fact, represented the blueprint of an obsession (euphemistically called a "dream") that Disney refused to give up despite its seeming impossibility. Frontiersman that he was, Disney mortgaged everything that he had to build the theme park. But if Disney was tenacious, he was also surprisingly naive. Many observers claim that Disneyland represents Disney's childlike vision of the world, if not universe, a fact often attributed to its appealing to the child in all of us. That being the case, some see Disney as a man who never matured, a man who retained his child-like innocence. This attitude, however, was not simply impotent innocence; it was the innocence of youth envisioning new empires. If Disney never lost his youthful, even naive, fascination with both the vanishing frontier and the peoples and machines that transformed it, then that naiveté or faith became his strength or asset. It clearly distinguished Disney from the cynics of his age. Thus, as Sinclair Lewis wrote *Main Street* (1920) to share his discontent with the pettiness of small town life in America, Disney countered by "imagineering" Main Street, U.S.A. as a paean to it. By his actions, Disney created a simplified American West in Frontierland that, like literature and film, had undeniable power to shape popular perceptions.

Despite his appreciation of popular American literature, Disney wrote surprisingly little. He did, however, write an occasional article for popular magazines. Of special interest to students of the West is Disney's 1958 article in *True West* magazine. In it, he used the travelogue format to advantage by taking readers on an imaginary tour of Frontierland from its portal at the log stockade, through Frontier Village, and then farther into the wilderness. Disney's appreciation of the topography, flora, and fauna of the West is evident in the features that he depicted and described: colorful Rainbow Canyon, mysterious Devil's Paint Pots (mud geysers), rugged Rock Gorge, stylized Coyote Rock, peculiar Elephant Rock, and the realistically-prickly Cactus Gardens. Note that these names are all Euro-American; there is no hint of other cultures in these ostensibly English names. These names reflect Disney's fascination with the region's unique natural history as immortalized in his popular early 1950s nature films, *The Living Desert* and *The Vanishing Prairie* (King, Audience 60–68).

As experienced in Disney's words and in the theme park, Frontierland unfolds much like a cyclorama, that is, a sweeping panoptic vision of American expansion. Disney packaged this frontier as a series of memorable physical or scenic features into which human activity was placed. He intuitively recognized the significance of geography in American history and in the American imagination. Stated another way, the West's "distinctive and unfamiliar landscapes," that "defied notions about utility and beauty" also helped to "shape the culture and character of the United States" (Hyde 351). Disney was well in tune with popular historic sentiment about the role of nature in the nation's destiny. Taken together, Disney's *True West* travelogue-style article and Frontierland itself reveal a deeply conflicted vision of the region as possessing incredible natural beauty that should both be exploited and preserved.

Disney laid out the parameters of Frontierland much like a cartographer draws a map. Of all of the sections of lands in the theme park, Frontierland's "Rivers of America" (the largest single geographic feature in the entire theme park) truly enchanted him. Disney wrote that "one of the biggest joys of my life is sitting on the levee in the Frontierland section of our park ... watching the steamboat *Mark Twain* belching smoke and skirting along toward the tip of Tom Sawyer Island" (Disney 10). Disney adored this part of Frontierland, with its pirates, keelboats, *Mark Twain* steamboat, "Indian Village," and the wilderness. He described Tom Sawyer Island in nearly mystical terms in the *True West* article. To him, its caves and harbors resonated with Indian and frontier lore. On Tom Sawyer Island, Disney constructed the mythical Fort Wilderness. Crowning a bluff overlooking the river, the fort served as headquarters for Davy Crockett and George Russel, who, Disney noted, "reported to Major General Andrew Jackson in the Indian campaign of 1813" (Disney 13).

To the public, Frontierland presented living history based on actual historical events and the Disney films in which these events were depicted. Disney wrote his *True West* article on Frontierland as an introduction to what he hoped to accomplish there, adding that it "isn't the end of the story," for, "as with all the park, I want to keep adding new features to Frontierland, new exhibits that will show today's youth the America of our great-grandparents day — and before" (13). Continuing the cartographic metaphor, Disney realized that the map of Frontierland, too, would change through time. This, of course, was progress. Disney, as master cartographer, empowered himself and his designers to change the map from time to time.

Designed to be expanded and improved, Frontierland has indeed changed over the years.[6] Although those four decades are fascinating, Frontierland in its first decade (1955–1965) stayed under Disney's close supervision, that is, remained closest to the ideals of its creator. Significantly, as Michael Steiner recently observed, Disney's Tomorrowland quickly became passé as it was impossible to keep futuristic. Frontierland, however, was prophetic in that it sustained a popular vision that led to the creation of the "New West" where the designer log cabin and computer coexist (Steiner 2–17). In other words, Disney intuitively sensed the strong role that the past would play in America's postmodern and post-industrial future. His romanticizing of the "Old West" helped lay the groundwork for the "New West" of amenity tourism and chic residence.

Disney's writings and reminiscences reveal a Turnerian view of the frontier. Like historian Frederick Jackson Turner (1861–1932), Disney felt that both his own life and that of the nation had been affected, even forged, by the frontier experience. He suggested as much in the *True West* article when he alluded to the pluck, grit, and character of the pioneers. As if taking cues from Turner's essay, the works of Disney help enshrine the frontier and sustain the dialogue about its validity that continues into the twenty-first century.

As western historians, we debate the importance (even the existence) of a singular frontier, but for a generation of political conservatives like Walter Knott, creator of Knott's Berry Farm, and Walter Elias Disney, and most Americans, there was simply no argument about its significance: to them, the frontier defined the American experience and synergistically shaped the American character and spirit. It made Americans a different (and better) people than even their (European) forebears. The East suggests Europe and European roots, and hence is tainted by the Old World, while the West suggests a *tabula rasa*, ready for new beginnings and opportunities.

Although Disney's Frontierland celebrated the triumph of Anglo American manifest destiny, his frontier actually reached *beyond* the West because it was synonymous with the American spirit. That spirit is ultimately political in that it is closely linked to the national expansion that continued long after the frontier ceased to be geographical and became ideological. This is to say that the frontier came to symbolize our national character even after the fact.

Disneyland and Frontierland are best viewed in the context of the Cold War. During that ideological dispute following World War II — a dispute that found the United States and other "free" countries pitted against the socialist and communist countries — Disney weighed in heavily on the patriotically conservative side. During those volatile times when the United States became obsessed with defending its ideology against communism, the word "frontier" also signified the boundary between two political systems. To pursue this thought further, Frontierland can perhaps be viewed, in an ideological sense, as a Cold War statement about the irrepressible spirit of America in overcoming the hostile frontier of that part of the world behind the Iron Curtain where individual aspirations were crushed. To a political conservative like Disney, who grew increasingly conservative as the Cold War heightened in the 1950s, the triumphs of the western frontier were applicable to meeting the international political challenges of both the present and future. This time, however, the battle would not be for land or resources *per se*, but for the minds and hearts of humanity. It is therefore no surprise that a man who would claim to do just that, Ronald Reagan, was present at the grand opening of Disneyland in July 1955. Reagan and Disney shared many conservative values regarding the evils of communism, the inviolability of individual rights, and the essential purity of the American spirit. Disney also shared these values with another political conservative, Walter Knott, whose Ghost Town in Knott's Berry Farm was created in 1953 with a political agenda in mind. In a booklet about his theme park, Knott candidly noted that:

> Ghost Town depicts an era in our nation's history when men were forging ahead and crossing new frontiers. Ghost Town also represents an era of free people who carved

out their salvation without let or hindrance. The people, the things, the buildings of
Ghost Town are long dead, but the same pioneer spirit still lives on [Knott 59].

Like Ghost Town, Frontierland is ultimately a statement about the role of the
individual in achieving success through faith, tenacity, and perseverance—
without the intervention or oppression of government. In the Disney version,
the victory could be couched using a play on words: The West was won, and
the West won.

Just as Disney never lived to see the victorious conclusion of the Cold
War, he likely never understood that the American West was not actually won
at all. As the New Western historians demonstrate, there remained much
unfinished business on the frontier, business that now forces the rethinking
of the concept of conquest: those indigenous peoples headed for oblivion in
Frontierland were not ever completely subdued or assimilated, but rather sur-
vived well enough to be participants in the multicultural West we know today.
However, because the Disney version of history is closely connected to American popular culture, which views progress and civilization marching to the
Pacific and settling everywhere along the way, it simplifies the western experience. It does so through allegory—defined as the expression by means of
symbolic fictional figures and actions of truths or generalizations about human
existence, and a symbolic representation. Frontierland is allegorical in both a
historical and a geographical/cartographic sense. Through its creation, Disney
shaped the West into a stylized iconic form, a place where heroes make history
and pave the way for civilization. To do so, he called upon historical western
figures such as Davy Crockett and Mike Fink to affirm the conservative tenet
that there is no civilization without individual freedom. The fact that two
famous and conservative actors, Fess Parker and Buddy Epsen, were present
at the opening of Frontierland confirmed a basic fact about the entire theme
park. It was an elaborate set where Disney's films could be further dramatized,
and where the park's visitors could actually take part in the drama they had
seen on movie and television screens.

Temporally, Frontierland depicted mythically heroic, herculean efforts
over a vague and rather long period of time, from about 1790 to 1890. And
yet, Disney presented this history as if it were currently in progress because
this would convey a deeper message: the spirit of the frontier was not dead.
He thus further refined Walter Knott's tenet about the frontier West, but with
a twist in the plot line. Although Disney and his designers were intrigued by
nearby Knott's Berry Farm's decadent western flavor, Disney elected not to
recreate a decrepit ghost town in Frontierland because this would imply failure.
Rather, Disney went one step farther than Knott and re-created a vigorous
West in its period of booming growth.[7]

A closer look at the spatial configuration of Frontierland reveals much about Disney's worldviews. To Disney, the penetration and settlement of the West was an ongoing drama that, by its continued replaying, taught both history and geography lessons about manifest destiny. This Disney version of the relationship between people and place forms the basis of Frontierland's historical geography, both real and imagined. It underscores Frontierland's function as both an environment and as a map. Through cartography, people conceive of, and then represent, places even as vague as "the frontier." Frontierland is a rich subject for cartographic interpretation, for it too has identifiable geographic antecedents and resulted from individual vision and group collaboration about where and when the frontier existed. If a map is, as dictionaries claim, "a representation ... of the whole or part of an area," then Frontierland indeed serves as a stylized, three-dimensional relief map.

Although Disneyland developed through a complex process of sketch mapping — most of which would up in the trash bin — Disney himself had a strong hand in designing Frontierland. What did Disney and his designers include in this map of the frontier? What, likewise, did they omit? Less concerned with the formalities of scientific mapmaking, Disney nevertheless used direction, scale, and proportions. Through miniaturization and stylization on one level, and constant refinement on another, Frontierland served several cartographic purposes. It was used for navigation (that is, to get people from one discrete place to another), but it was also didactically used to instruct individuals how to view places and the peoples who occupy (or should occupy) them. Disney used Frontierland as a stage on which to tell the story of how the western part of the country functioned in American history. Although Frontierland is idiosyncratic (i.e., Disney's), it is also populist in that it incorporated popular views. Embraced by large numbers of people, it tells or endorses "our" story, not Disney's story alone. Disney had a phenomenal ability to capture public sentiment in his products, stories, and theme parks; thus, Frontierland works so well because it fits popularly conceived images of the frontier (King, "Disneyland" 116–40). It served as a simplified depiction of how the West became part of America through the construction of towns and forts, and the development of transportation systems, that reached into the heart of the region. "Cartography is often intimate with imperial necessity..." and Disney's cartographic design of Frontierland is a less than subtle recollection of American empire building (Sleeve 45).

Disney's design of Frontierland also exhibits intriguing similarities to other stylized maps, some utopian, some ancient. When compared, Frontierland's design and that of an ancient Babylonian map are strikingly similar. Although the former is a stylized and miniaturized map of the frontier, while the latter depicts the known world and even the heavens surrounding it, both, significantly, are closely tied to narratives of origin and evolution. Both also feature centers that are, in effect, insular and surrounded by waters. Toward the outer edge of the Babylonian map, features become increasingly abstract and peripheral to local narrative because less is known about them so, too, in Disney's design there is a distinct core and a periphery. Both designs are, in effect, cosmological statements given recognizable form through the process of imaginative map making. Frontierland's cartographic design is also similar to Chinese world maps (ca. 1500 CE) and to the earlier narratives of Homer, which feature water as a central part of the narrative (Whitfield 1–11).

Like his cartographic counterparts in ancient and historic times, Disney used water to create boundaries and delineate arteries of travel. If Frontierland's essentially circular of kidney shape encloses a body of water and island at its center, these features are at once geographical and metaphorical: in the American West, especially in the West of popular imagination of the nineteenth century, water both beckoned settlers and entrepreneurs into the frontier and defined the perimeter of the known world. Water fascinated Disney as it has our culture for centuries. To Disney and generations of Americans preceding him, the western waters were alluring, even seductive. They both defined the physical world and hinted at the rejuvenation or regeneration of the American character that would be attained by following them to their sources, and then beyond. The goal of this search was either *youth* (as Ponce de León's search for the fountain or springs implies), or restored *health*—both mental and physical. It is thus not surprising that American culture, ever in search of renewal in the (westward) move into the interior, would cast the rivers as entryways and passageways to both opportunity and adventure. As hydrographer, Disney touched a deep chord that may even resonate across cultural boundaries. Water is often associated with creation, and especially spiritual birth/rebirth in recurrent creation myths of cultures worldwide.[8] Water serves as a powerful symbol in Frontierland, where Disney used it to convey visitors back into the American past.

Although Disney's love of the rivers in the trans–Mississippi West is beautifully revealed in the Rivers of America, it is not simply a personal infatuation. Rather, Disney's view is deeply embedded in popular culture and history, where the rivers were widely portrayed and promoted as beckoning explorers into the interior of the region — and even through it to the Orient. One can speculate that these waters were in a sense symbolically uterine, drawing the traveler deeper into mystery and, ultimately, to the forces of creation. In building upon this metaphor of exploration and discovery in the Rivers of America, Disney thus perpetuated a folk narrative reaching back at least five hundred years. As early as 1498, on his third voyage, the beguiled Christopher Columbus reportedly used sexually charged and metaphorically loaded wording to describe the interior he had not yet seen (Zamora 152–79). In the centuries that followed, the quest continued as the river or water passages promised a rebirth of empires. Both the Spanish explorers' search for the Straits of Anian and the British, French, and Anglo American quest for the Northwest Passage are manifestations. Aware of these quests and visions, both historians and common folk came to believe that "the river is a defining agent in the metamorphosis of colonies to republic, serving as entrance or border but always a symbol of what might be obtained beyond" (Sleeve 7).

It is worth restating that Disney played a crucial role as both storyteller and cartographer in Frontierland. He *personally* designed the river system and its centerpiece, the intriguing Tom Sawyer Island. Because his designers seemed stymied by the challenge, Disney "laid out the island to scale, with all the little inlets on the island" admonishing his designers to "quit fooling around and draw it as it should be" (Gordon and Mumford 99). The Rivers of America have their mythical headwaters in the springs that issue from the mountain close to the geographic center of Frontierland. Cascading from their source, they soon take on the status of full-fledged rivers in a creative example of selective compression. Due to their relatively small size and height, the mountains in Frontierland appear distant (hence increasing their mysteriousness): they represent the higher peaks of the West that rise above the timberline. Like the Rockies and Sierra Nevada, these peaks are devoid of trees and perpetually snow clad. Despite the prominence of these mountain peaks, however, it is the rivers that they feed that are obviously the most important topographic — or rather hydrographic — feature in Frontierland. Waterfalls and rapids are seen near their headwaters in the mountains, but throughout most of their course, the rivers are broad, and fairly placid. The depiction of rivers considerably downstream from their source (that is, where the gradient has flattened at the Great Plains) is significant, for that is where Disney experienced them in his youth.

As cartographer, Disney manipulated American geography to conform to his perceptions of the frontier. He insisted that a part of the Rivers of America depict a distinctly southern locale, as evidenced by a plantation house located on one bank. Like the early nineteenth-century frontier, Disney's West evidently began in the South in the vicinity of New Orleans, a reminder, perhaps, that this part of the country was popularly called the "Southwest" in the early nineteenth century. Disney's West also began on the great Ohio River, that "shining gateway" to the Old Northwest in the late eighteenth and early nineteenth century. Frontierland's Rivers of America thus represents the generic "Western Rivers" that rise west of the Appalachians and extend into the fabled lands of the Louisiana Purchase. But Pacific slope rivers are also represented, at least subliminally, by Disney — as suggested by the name of the *Columbia* sailing ship that plies the Rivers of America. The actual *Columbia* became the gem of the ocean, on one occasion sailing into the aptly named Columbia River, the artery by which the Pacific Northwest would be explored and settled.

Water is a dominant element in Frontierland, occupying approximately 30 percent of the area of this part of the park. This is significant for, in reality, water bodies occupied only about 2 percent of the Trans-Appalachian and Trans-Mississippi West. Some might argue that Disney and his designers *had* to devote that much space to water for simple logistical reasons. River boat rides, for example, take space. However, Frontierland's design reaffirms both the actual importance of the western rivers to transportation and their symbolic importance to Disney's (and America's) imagination. Also significant is the manner in which Disney configured Frontierland's Rivers of America to form a circular, rather than liner or dendritic, system. The rivers surround the land at the center of the river system, which is configured as a large, irregularly shaped island. This design reflects a deep literary heritage that is evident in Disney's appreciation of the writings of Mark Twain (and the islands of the Missouri/Mississippi system that Twain depicted). It also reflects the thrilling discovery-and-exploration-based eighteenth century and early nineteenth century novels, such as *Treasure Island*. By placing literary events and characters in an island setting, Disney geographically isolated them — an action that further emphasized their importance and sacredness in American popular culture. Frontierland's design suggests that the frontier was, for Disney and America, both geographical/historical and imaginary/literary. Although Disney himself intimated that he designed the Frontierland experience to provide a history lesson to the public, one suspects that Disney's history was — both metaphorically and literally — never far from fantasy[land].

As cartographer, Disney configured the frontier to depict many ecotones. Closely related to hydrography and topography, Frontierland's diversity of vegetation varies from boreal forest to sub-tropical desert. Stylized saguaro cacti and Joshua trees evoke the desert areas of the Southwest (Sonoran and Mojave deserts, respectively). The nearly barren, colorful, stratified, and heavily eroded sedimentary rocks in parts of Frontierland personify the badlands seen in parts of the semi-arid West. Disney undertook an ambitious geographic depiction: he created in Frontierland a microcosm of the American West, capturing a glimpse of the environmental variation that exists there. Disney's role as storyteller of both natural *and* cultural history is underscored by his juxtaposition of man-made features, notably towns, with natural/wilderness features, including deserts and spectacular rock formations. In the portion of Frontierland called Nature's Wonderland, he abstracted many of the distinctive features of western topography and vegetation found throughout the entire region. By way of analogy, Disney's Frontierland depicts the scenic highlights seen in the national parks of the West, which, like their counterparts in Frontierland, were reached by an elaborate transportation system that included railroads. To people of Disney's parents' generation, the national parks and railroads were closely tied in an elaborate pattern; Glacier, Yellowstone, Grand Canyon, and Bryce were reached by — and promoted by — the railroads (Runte). These parks became meccas for the patriotic. To see their natural wonders was to reaffirm one's sense of nationalism and to confirm that American civilization respected the sublime. Spectacular topography continued to be equated with political strength throughout Disney's life, as evidenced by 1966 California billboards that featured then gubernatorial candidate Ronald Reagan posing in front of a mountain range backed by the slogan "A Man to Match our Mountains."

Despite its suggestion of unconquerable wilderness in Frontierland, the human presence is also palpable there. To the cultural or social historian, Frontierland exhibits considerable cultural and ethnic diversity. It also depicts the frontier as the proving ground of both agrarian pioneers and industrial capitalists. Disney wanted the public to experience the colorful history of the frontier period of the West in this special part of the park, the economic agenda of private enterprise being an important subtext. Thus, most of Disney's "frontiersmen" are Anglo Americans performing varying roles, such as miner, riverboat crew member, saloon keepers, and dance hall girls (all, or course, sanitized) — occupations popularly depicted as "opening the West" for settlement. But if Anglo Americans dominate Frontierland's cultural landscape (in keeping with the prevailing popular interpretation of western history as the progressive, westward move of "civilization"), they are not the only people represented here. A closer look at the social geography of Frontierland reveals that Disney did indeed populate this land with other peoples — notably Hispanics and Native Americans. Reminiscent of the way in which cartographers depict "Apaches" here and "Comanches" there, Disney provided a place for ethnicity. That these ethnic peoples lived in separate communities is telling, for it mirrors the racial segregation that only became illegal at about the same time (1954) that Disney's theme park opened.

And yet, despite segregation, Anglo America has long had a fascination with ethnicity vis-à-vis mainstream culture. No popular depiction of the West, such as restaurateur and hotel owner Fred Harvey's string of attractions across the region, left out Indians. Working closely with the Santa Fe Railroad, Harvey helped both popularize and preserve aspects of the Native American cultures in the West and Southwest. The Indians' communities and "primitive" or "ancient" cultures were contrasted with the "civilization" of the Anglo-American travelers who gazed at them from railroad car windows. Given Disney's ability to perpetuate commonly held sentiments and his admiration for Fred Harvey and the Santa Fe Railroad, Native Americans were destined to be part of Disney's characteristically American drama. Present in the frontier of Disney's youthful imagination, Indians were portrayed at river's edge as part of the Frontierland experience. Disney would concur with the observation that "as the river opening inland provides the epic route for the New World hero, so the Indian becomes his chief ally and his most treacherous and ubiquitous threat" (Sleeve 12). When Frontierland opened in 1955, Disney located Native Americans peripherally, that is, at the far [western] edge near the railroad that circles the perimeter of the park. These Indians (many of whom were Native American actors) were depicted as a variable part of the "drama" of the West. The script recited on the Santa Fe and Disneyland Railroad ride around the park in 1962 is noteworthy. It commented on the "authentic Indian Villages ... where Indians of thirteen tribes perform ancient ritual dances." After noting that the Frontierland stations was "also the embarkation point for the Indian War Canoes which encircled Tom Sawyer Island," the message then admonished passengers to "watch for Indians and wild animals along the riverbanks." It further noted that "some Indians are hostile, and across the river is proof ... a settler's cabin afire. The pioneer lies in his yard ... victim of an Indian arrow."

That not all the Indians were menacing was apparent in the script's next words: "Ahead is a friendly Indian village with the inhabitants active in their daily tribal chores."[9] These were industrious, "good" Indians that existed on Disney's frontier. Although some of the Frontierland Indians were non-threatening, Disney cast others as savages. The burning settler's cabin thus made a statement at several levels. It obviously signified danger and loss, but at yet another level it may be interpreted as a mythic "need fire," which is to say it had a role in "reenacting the fundamental drama by which humanity distinguished itself from the rest of creation, playing on myths in which fire destroyed and renewed, appeasing the gods through burnt sacrifice" (Pyne 69). If so, this would be the ultimate "trial by fire" wherein a culture's mettle is tested. The individual settler would thus be vanquished to confirm that the ultimate sacrifice had been made. This trope would in turn validate the colonization of the wilderness by a chosen people. One suspects that visitors to the park intuitively know that regeneration will occur from the ashes; that for every such cabin burned a dozen will sprout, endorsed, as it were, by a higher power. It is worth noting that in more recent times, all references to Native Americans as threatening or war-like were expunged. The burning cabin is now described as the result of a lightning strike, not human conflict!

Just what Indians did Disney depict on his allegorical map of the American West? As designed by Disney, the Indian village glimpsed from the *Mark Twain* riverboat suggests a Plains Indian encampment, perhaps along the Upper Missouri. Their dress suggests Cheyenne and Arapaho, but others are also represented. Disney felt obliged to include these Native Americans, for they were not only part of the real West, they also figured heavily in the Wild West shows and dime novels read by Disney and the preceding generation. Although Disney depicted ethnicity selectively, he built on widely held racial stereotypes. Disney's generation continued to believe that Native Americans could become good citizens by assimilating (a central tenet of the Dawes Act of the late nineteenth century — that Indians could even become pioneer yeoman farmers). Yet, Americans also recognized, even endorsed, Indian tribal identity by the 1930s, as manifested in the passage of the Native American Reorganization Act of 1934. This legislation helped set the scene for today's widely accepted tribal self-determination.

But what of the other ethnic peoples? How did they fit into Disney's map of the West? In contrast to the independent (war-like or defiant) Native Americans, Disney depicted Mexican/Hispanic Americans as somewhat innocuous, even passive. Disney romanticized the action-oriented Zorro (originally a 1919 Anglo American pulp novel about Spanish/Mexican California) and thus perpetuated mainstream myths about the golden days of Spanish California. As sets for this frontier action, the architecture of vestigial New Spain, or Mexico, was stereotyped and commercialized in Frontierland. The original Casa de Fritos, and the stylized adobe "Casa Mexicana," reaffirm the Hispanic presence. The design and cultural complexion of early Frontierland suggests that Disney himself was likely ambivalent about the multicultural makeup of the West. He evidently recognized that non–Anglo peoples were important in the history of the region. Yet, he stereotyped them and put them in their "place" (often peripheral) in the Anglo-centric cartographic order and design of Frontierland.

Frontierland reminds visitors that the American westward moving frontier was both irrepressible and tyrannical, for "the United States was ... an unusually severe imperial state, not just because of its enormous and ever expanding material power, but because it was intolerant of cultural diversity in territorial form" (Meinig 12). The Cold War era romanticized the power that Americans wielded over other non–Western peoples and over the environment. Disney captured the consequences of this unstoppable westward move on various indigenous ethnic peoples in Frontierland. Like the post-colonial West itself, Frontierland compartmentalized peoples of Indian and Mexican origin, so that they lived in enclaves, when in fact they were once nearly omnipresent. Disney certainly did not initiate the cruel process of expansion, but he justified it by inclusion in his map of Frontierland. Although it is easy to criticize such treatment of peoples from today's more culturally sensitive perspective, Disney simply reflected and espoused the mainstream values of his time. In the final assessment, Disneyland is largely about assimilation and conformity to American (i.e., Anglo American) values in the 1950s (Francaviglia, *Main Street* 175–6).

There was, however, a glimpse of non-conformity in Frontierland. Disney cast some characters on the frontier as rough or shady. These included pirates, outlaws, and other miscreants. Their presence squares with Disney's vision of the frontier as a place of adventure and risk taking. In perpetuating this image of the frontier, many of Frontierland's rides emphasized "close calls" with both natural hazards (raging rivers, falling rocks) and cultural/social misfits (stage coach robbers, marauding Indians). By overcoming these physical and cultural hazards, Frontierland allowed proper Anglo American civilization to penetrate to the very interior of the untamed West.

This was accomplished, in part, by an elaborate transportation infrastructure. Frontierland — which is connected to the rest of the theme park by the Santa Fe and Disneyland Railroad and a series of walking paths that convey the guests from either the plaza or (later) New Orleans Square — is internally served by transportation network that doubles as rides. This network is the only way to experience much of the landscape. Central to the circulation pattern of Frontierland, the Rivers of America showcases developments in transportation technology, notably keelboat, sail, and steam power. These various transport forms are in turn linked to varied frontier experiences; for example, swashbuckling sailing adventures or a more genteel and serene steamboat journey. (The pirate ship was said by Disney to depict Jean Lafitte, and thus has a Gulf of Mexico connection.) The *Columbia* sailing ship that traverses the rivers provides a direct reference to U.S. expansionism: because it replicates the real sailing vessel *Columbia* that circumnavigated the globe carrying the U.S. flag from 1787 to 1790, one suspects that Disney's "frontier" actually transcended the American West. It was, in a sense, the entire, not-yet-Americanized globe.

No late-nineteenth-century map of the West was complete without railroads, and Frontierland also reveals Disney's near obsession with them (Broggie). Frontierland had a station on the line that encircled the entire park, and featured another railroad line that ran into the heart of Nature's Wonderland. Beginning in 1956, the narrow gauge mine train through Rainbow Caverns conveyed visitors through a simulated underground cave. In 1960, the expanded mine train began operating through Nature's Wonderland in yet another intrusion of the machine in the garden. Frontierland also hints at other industrial developments that transformed the map of the American West. One of the region's stereotypes — a booming mining town — forms the backdrop for the narrow gauge trainride. To further link the western experience with industry, Disney's early railroad equipment in Frontierland bore the evocative name "Rainbow Mining and Exploration Company." That reference to "exploration" suggests Disney's never-ending fascination with geographically based adventure and its corollary, exploitation. Although mining is still represented in the runaway mine train (which is in reality a small roller coaster added in 1979), a wrecked narrow gauge mine train is now preserved as a reminder of the earlier railroad. Seen from the *Mark Twain* riverboat, this wrecked train confirmed that even a theme park has its own history.

If railroads girdled much of the West (and much of the colonized world) by the late nineteenth century, they also girdled the theme park, where they serve several purposes. They symbolically open (and hint at the taming of) Disney's frontier, while serving yet another more immediate purpose. Disney actually developed the park's encircling Santa Fe and Disneyland Railroad as a huge model railroad that he could operate, in part as therapy, on the days that the park was closed to the public.[10] This railroad replaced the large-scale live-steam railroad — the Carolwood Pacific — that encircled Disney's home in the hills above Los Angeles. Significantly, the e scale, steam powered railroad around Disneyland had only one other major stop — Main Street. The locations of the two stations appear to reflect Disney's never-ending fascination with both the small town and the West.[11]

Disney's cartographic interpretation of the West was built on the changing role of technology. The transportation technology depicted in Frontierland spans a broad time period, celebrating *transitions* in the industry, notably the nineteenth-century shift from manual, animal, and sail power to steam technology. For Disney, the Frontier without both the riverboats, *and* the railroads that ultimately replaced them, would be unthinkable. This transition to steam captivated Disney, for it symbolized the Anglo American domination of the West by technology. The touted superiority of steam-driven technology may have helped Disney and others of his generation define the West racially/culturally in much the same way that Euro-centric, technologically advanced peoples thought of themselves as racially superior to indigenous people who did not possess such technology (Adas 112–13). However, as early as the nineteenth century, Euro-American culture itself often looked back with a mix of nostalgia and derision at early technology and the peoples — sometimes their own forebears — who possessed it. Paradoxically, Anglo Americans revered the industrial/technological process that transformed the West (and helped exclude the peoples who did not possess it), yet they also longed for the lost or vanished era of the pioneer as the frontier receded. As Washington Irving lamented as early as 1852, gone were the "good old times before steamboats and railroads had driven all poetry and romance out of travel" (Irving 73). That magic word — travel — suggests the mobility that Disney built into his evolving map of the West. Unlike Washington Irving a century earlier, Walt Disney had it *both* ways in Frontierland. Like Irving, he romanticized the earliest (i.e. most "primitive") aspects of Native American and Anglo American technology to the region (canoe, keel boat, and the sailing vessel *Columbia*) and, without a hint of anxiety about anachronism, he also joined the barons and magnates in celebrating the most "modern" developments of the mid–nineteenth century, such as the ornate steam train and the elaborate steamboat *Mark Twain*.

The steam power that so enthralled Disney was itself a complex and arresting metaphor for geographic expansion. In wedding two of the basic classical elements, water and fire, steam suggested both urgency and power. Through the machines it propelled, steam proved a perfect metaphor for the march of civilization into the wilderness. Simply stated, "steam replaced flame as the symbol of human power" by the late nineteenth century (Pyne 225). Through both the commanding note of the steam whistle and the persistent chugging of cylinders, the steamboat and steam locomotive may be interpreted as bringing the Victorian's sense of regimentation and control to the frontier lands they penetrated. The use of steam power connoted, above all, the ingenuity of Western technology in shaping the map of the West. As the diesel-powered streamlined train came to symbolize the 1940s and 1950s, Disney enshrined its steam predecessor in Disneyland. But by the time he depicted it, steam power was doomed, and Disney knew it.

Walt Disney beautifully exemplified "technostalgia" — the nostalgic appreciation of earlier forms of technology for what they conveyed about our lost connections with time and place (Francaviglia, *Hard Places*). Although he and his designers partly copied the pioneer western-themed Knott's Berry Farm, which featured operating restored Denver and Rio Grande narrow gauge equipment, Disney also built upon the traditions of nineteenth and early twentieth century fairs and expositions. In the company of railroad buff and designer Ward Kimball, Disney attended the 1948 Chicago Railroad Fair, a major exposition at which the more modern forms of railroad machinery/technology were exhibited side by side with the old for comparison. As in all such expositions, that comparison was never value-free, for one would secretly admire and fear the new, while simultaneously berating and romanticizing the old. This dichotomy had both technological and cultural implications; in Frontierland, the presence of Native Americans, that most romanticized group of pre-technological peoples, suggested what the West, and perhaps all human culture, had been like before industry transformed it. In this regard, the Disney message again mirrored that conveyed by the Fred Harvey Company, which worked in close harmony with the Santa Fe Railroad to depict Native Americans as a people both lost/doomed and yet pure/noble (Weigle and Babcock).

The three elements of Frontierland discussed in some detail above — scenery, culture, and technology — reveal that everything had both a meaning and a place in this carefully engineered, but ever-evolving, part of the park. These elements were enunciated as historical metaphors positioned in time. Through their placement in a carefully arranged spatial pattern, Disney created more than a contrived *place*. In Frontierland, he presented a simplified image of the region that reaffirmed widespread popular beliefs about the historical geography of the West. It may be tempting to dismiss such popular conceptions, but we do so at our own peril: like the dime novels and Wild West shows originating in the nineteenth century, they sustain the region's past as a significant mythological element in American culture.

Viewed symbolically, Frontierland's design reveals deeply embedded binary distinctions — such as nature *vs.* man, them *vs.* us, past *vs.* present, technology *vs.* pre-technology — that continue to characterize not only American, but also Western civilization. It is ironic that Disney depicted the western frontier as a place of individual initiative when, in fact, its settlement resulted from large scale federal presence in the form of troops, infrastructural improvements (roads), and economic incentives such as land grants. This irony is doubled when one realizes that Disney romanticized the West of the individual frontier at just the time that federal dollars poured into the region's Cold War defense industry.

It is telling, too, that in designing the Rivers of America, Disney elected to omit the story of the active construction of canals and dams, much of it subsidized, that transformed America's western waters in the nineteenth century (although his entire project was, in fact, just such a hydrologic engineering coup). Those untamed rivers were essential to Disney, who employed them to contrast transportation technology with the force of nature. This juxtaposition reveals Disney's nostalgia and romanticism. To Disney, the primordial Western American landscape was an instructional stage setting. It demonstrated both the purity of that supposedly pristine landscape and the inevitability of the frontiersman transforming it into civilization. That inherently irresolvable dilemma is essentially tragic. And yet, it is a common theme that reaches back to the Enlightenment and the Renaissance — if not into earlier classical times.

Frontierland is a cartographic icon with a deep narrative story line; it is ultimately a story about, and a longing for, what would be lost in the transition from nature to civilization. Disney, that master of visual imagery and design, plumbed American culture for inspiration. Cartographically speaking, Frontierland's essentially concentric design — with its *core* embedded in narratives of creation, its circular waterway, surrounding the core and serving as a middle ground, and its periphery of wild lands and communities that portend the encroachment of civilization and the order that would soon follow — is significant. Frontierland's design imitates a *mandala*, the abstract representation of the cosmos within a circle. However, in keeping with Disney's pragmatism, the design would change, as would everything in a progressive America. To continue the cartographic analogy, Frontierland as a map of the West is not static. It is constantly evolving to accommodate new values and philosophies in edu-tainment, and so must be revised from time to time. Viewed in this way, Frontierland is a constantly revised sequential map, much like the Sanborn fire insurance maps that are updated periodically through the addition of new overlays to answer present needs. As in Six Flags Over Texas, the history lessons in Frontierland have yielded somewhat to the demand for faster and more thrilling rides; yet, Disney's fundamental vision of history and geography is still visible in Frontierland (Francaviglia, "Texas History" 34–42).

In its spatial organization, Frontierland represents the cartography of expansion: it is a locale in which the process of imperial colonization is *constantly* depicted and celebrated. As an allegorical map, Frontierland is perpetually animated, much like the sequential weather maps on the evening news or on the Weather Station. In much the same manner that the sequential replaying of these maps depicts changes in weather patterns that we grasp only by replaying, the drama of western expansion is reenacted in Frontierland until the sequence is learned by heart. The looping of railroad, sailing vessels, steamboat and mine train, all reaffirm the circularity of a model that runs like clockwork, conveying the observer through the once-exotic, now-familiar, territory of the stylized West.

Like all maps, Frontierland is also a representation of place in time(s) that contains deeply embedded messages about power and ownership. As a microcosm of one section of the world — the Trans-Appalachian and Trans-Mississippi West — Frontierland reveals that the supposed conquest of the West was an event so significant, and so instructive, that it needed to be repeated endlessly as part of both the education and entertainment of first

American, and then world, culture. Walt Disney himself concluded that "in Frontierland we meet the America of the past, out of whose strength and inspiration came the good things of life we enjoy today " (Gordon and Mumford 53). What better way to reaffirm that unabashedly patriotic message than through miniaturization and stylization — processes that, like all map-making, transform places like the real West into both icons and symbols.

Notes

1. In reality, the western cartographic tradition builds on African, Arabic, and even Chinese traditions as described in Harley and Woodward's *History of Cartography*.

2. See Harley's introduction to David Buisseret's *From Sea Charts to Satellite Images: Interpreting North American History through Maps*.

3. For a discussion of such maps of Texas, see Francaviglia's *The Shape of Texas: Maps as Metaphors*.

4. This term was inspired by the title of Richard Schickel's *The Disney Version: The Life, Times, Art and Commerce of Walt Disney*, which provided an interpretation of Disney in context. For other interpretations see Christopher Finch's *The Art of Walt Disney: From Mickey Mouse to Magic Kingdoms*; Bob Thomas's *Walt Disney An American Original*; and Alan Bryman's *Disney and His Worlds*; Randy Bright's *Disneyland: Inside Story*. For more recent revisionist interpretations of Disney's impact, see Joe Flower's *Prince of the Magic Kingdom: Michael Eisner and the Re-making of Disney* and Stephen M. Fjellman's *Vinyl Leaves: Walt Disney World and America*.

5. That scholars are taking Disney and other shapers of popular culture seriously is evident in a spate of recent book chapters and journal articles. See, for example, Dorst's "Miniaturizing Monumentality: Theme Park Images of the American West and Confusions of Cultural Influences" and Mike Wallace's *Mickey Mouse History and Other Essays on American History*.

6. This change is revealed by comparing the many illustrations in Bruce Gordon and David Mumford's *Disneyland: The Nickel Tour — A Post Card Journey through 40 Years of the Happiest Place on Earth*.

7. Wally Boag, Disney employee, phone interview with author, 28 May 1997, Santa Monica, CA.

8. Water figures heavily in myths of emergence: see, for example, Northrop Frye's *The Great Code: The Bible and Literature*, 144–7; Joseph Campbell's *The Myth Image*; Carl G. Jung's *Man and His Symbols*; and Mircea Eliade's *Images and Symbols: Studies in Religious Symbolism*.

9. This quote and those in the preceding paragraph that refer to the railroad script come from Michael Broggie's *Walt Disney's Railroad Story*, 256–8.

10. Karal Ann Marling, interview by author, 27 January 1995, Anaheim, CA; see also Marling's essay "Disneyland, 1955: Just Take the Santa Ana Freeway to the American Dream," 168–207.

11. Disney's romanticism came face to face with reality when he depicted transportation in the West. Statistics show that nineteenth-century travel by rail and river boat was hazardous and horse and wagon travel was especially so. In transporting the theme park visitors, Disney compromised (as did other parks, including Six Flags Over Texas): Whereas park guests originally rode horse-drawn stage coaches and traversed Frontierland's waters in real canoes, these yielded to more vicarious, and safer, rides after a number of minor

accidents and close calls raised Disney's concerns about liability and adverse publicity. To Disney's disappointment, the more or less "authentic" forms of transportation were replaced by safer rides that were more controllable. As originally designed, the Frontierland transportation experience was, in retrospect, too realistic.

Works Cited

Adas, Michael. *Machines as the Measure of Men: Science, Technology, and Ideologies of Western Dominance.* Ithaca, NY: Cornell University Press, 1989.

Allen, John L. *North American Exploration.* 3 vols. Lincoln: University of Nebraska Press, 1997.

An American Tail. Dir. Don Bluth. MCA/Universal Studios, 1986.

An American Tail: Fievel Goes West. Dirs. Phil Nibbelink and Simon Wells. Universal Pictures, 1991.

Basso, Keith H. *Wisdom Sits in Places: Landscape and Language Among the Western Apache.* Albuquerque: University of New Mexico Press, 1996.

Bright, Randy. *Disneyland: Inside Story.* New York: Abrams, 1987.

Broggie, Michael. *Walt Disney's Railroad Story.* Pasadena, CA: Pentrex, 1997.

Bryman, Alan. *Disney and His Worlds.* New York: Routledge, 1995.

Campbell, Joseph. *The Myth Image.* Princeton, NJ: Princeton University Press, 1974.

Disney, Walt. "Frontierland." *True West* 5 (May-June 1958): 10–1.

Dorst, John. "Miniaturizing Monumentality: Theme Park Images of the American West and Confusions of Cultural Influences." In *Cultural Transmissions and Receptions: American Mass Culture in Europe,* edited by R. Kroes, et al., 253–70. Amsterdam: Vu University Press, 1993.

Downs, Roger M. "Maps and Metaphors." *Professional Geographer* 33 (August 1981): 287–93.

Duchemin, Michael. "Walt Disney's Wild West." Annual Meeting of the Western History Association. St. Paul, MN. 18 October 1997.

Eliade, Mircea. *Images and Symbols: Studies in Religious Symbolism.* London: Harvill, 1961.

Fjellman, Stephen M. *Vinyl Leaves: Walt Disney World and America.* Boulder, CO: Westview, 1992.

Finch, Christopher. *The Art of Walt Disney: From Mickey Mouse to the Magic Kingdoms.* New York: Abrams, 1975.

Findlay, John. *Magic Lands: Western Cityscapes and American Culture After 1940.* Berkeley: University of California Press, 1992.

Flower, Joe. *Prince of the Magic Kingdom: Michael Eisner and the Re-making of Disney.* New York: Wiley, 1991.

Francaviglia, Richard. *Hard Places: Reading the Landscape of America's Historic Mining Districts.* Iowa City: University of Iowa Press, 1991.

_____. *Main Street Revisited: Time, Space and Image Building in Small Town America.* Iowa City: University of Iowa Press, 1996.

_____. *The Shape of Texas: Maps as Metaphors.* College Station: Texas A&M University Press, 1996.

_____. "Texas History in Texas Theme Parks." *Legacies: A History Journal for Dallas and North Central Texas* 7 (Fall 1995): 34–42.

Frye, Northrop. *The Great Code: The Bible and Literature.* New York: Harcourt Brace Jovanovich, 1982.

Gordon, Bruce, and David Mumford. *Disneyland: The Nickel Tour—A Post Card Journey through 40 Years of the Happiest Place on Earth.* Santa Clarita, CA: Camphor Tree, 1995.

Harley, J.B., and David Woodward, eds. *The History of Cartography*. 6 vols. Chicago: University of Chicago Press, 1987–2009.

_____. Introduction. *From Sea Charts to Satellite Images: Interpreting North American History through Maps*. Ed. David Buisseret. Chicago: University of Chicago Press, 1990.

Humphrey, William. *The Ordways*. New York: Knopf, 1965.

Hyde, Anne F. "Cultural Filters: The Significance of Perceptions in the History of the American West." *Western Historical Quarterly* 24 (August 1993): 351.

Irving, Washington. *The Home Book of the Picturesque or American Scenery, Art, and Literature*. New York: G. P. Putnam, 1852.

Jung, Carl G. *Man and His Symbols*. Garden City, NY: Doubleday, 1964.

King, Margaret J. "The Audience in the Wilderness: The Disney Nature Film." *Journal of Popular Film & Television* 24 (Summer 1996): 60–8.

_____. "Disneyland and Walt Disney World: Traditional Values in Futuristic Form." *Journal of Popular Culture* 15 (Summer 1981): 116–40.

Knott, Walter. *Ghost Town & Calico Railway*. Buena Park, CA: Knott's Berry Farm, 1953.

Lewis, Sinclair. *Main Street*. New York, Harcourt Brace, 1920.

The Living Desert. Dir. James Algar. Walt Disney Pictures, 1953.

Marling, Karal Ann. "Disneyland, 1955: Just Take the Santa Ana Freeway to the American Dream." *American Art* 5 (Winter-Spring 1991): 168–207.

Meinig, D. W. "Strategies of Empire." *Culturefront* (Summer 1993): 12–19.

Norris, Frank. *The Octopus*. New York: Doubleday, Page, 1901.

Pagden, Anthony. *European Encounters with the New World: From Renaissance to Romanticism*. New Haven, CT: Yale University Press, 1993.

Pyne, Stephen J. *Vestal Fire: An Environmental History, Told through Fire, of Europe and Europe's Encounter with the World*. Seattle: University of Washington Press, 1997.

Robinson, Arthur, et al. *Elements of Cartography*. 5th ed. New York: Wiley, 1984.

Runte, Alfred. *Trains of Discovery: Western Railroads and the National Parks*. Niwot, CO: Roberts Rinehart, 1990.

Schickel, Richard. *The Disney Version: The Life, Times, Art and Commerce of Walt Disney*. New York: Simon and Schuster, 1968.

Seelye, John. *Beautiful Machine: Rivers and the Republican Plan, 1755–1825*. New York: Oxford University Press, 1991.

_____. *Prophetic Waters: The River in Early American Life and Literature*. New York: Oxford University Press, 1977.

Steiner, Michael. "Frontierland as Tomorrowland: Walt Disney and the Architectural Packaging of the Mythic West." *Montana: The Magazine of Western History* 48 (Spring 1998): 2–17.

Stevenson, Robert Louis. *Treasure Island*. London: Cassell, 1883.

Ten Who Dared. Dir. William Beaudine. Walt Disney Pictures, 1960.

Thomas, Bob. *Walt Disney: An American Original*. New York: Simon and Schuster, 1976.

Thrower, Norman. *Maps and Man: An Examination of Cartography in Relationship to Culture and Civilization*. Englewood Cliffs, NJ: Prentice Hall, 1972.

Tuan, Yi Fu. "Language and the Making of Place: A Narrative-Descriptive Approach." *Annals of the Association of American Geographers* 81.4 (December 1991): 684–96.

The Vanishing Prairie. Dir. James Algar. Walt Disney Pictures, 1954.

Wallace, Mike. *Mickey Mouse History and Other Essays on American History*. Philadelphia: Temple University Press, 1996.

Watts, Steven. *The Magic Kingdom: Walt Disney and the American Way of Life*. New York: Houghton Mifflin, 1997.

Weigle, Marta, and Barbara Babcock. *The Great Southwest of the Fred Harvey Company and the Santa Fe Railroad*. Tucson, AZ: Heard Museum, 1996.

Westworld. Dir. Michael Crichton. MGM Studios, 1973.

Whitfield, Peter. *New Found Lands: Maps in the History of Exploration.* New York: Routledge, 1998.

Wood, Denis. *The Power of Maps.* New York: Guilford, 1992.

Zamora, Margarita. *Reading Columbus.* Berkeley: University of California Press, 1993.

The Dark Ride of Snow White
Narrative Strategies at Disneyland

Suzanne Rahn

Of all the traditional fairy tales, the most closely associated with Walt Disney is *Snow White and the Seven Dwarfs*. The 1937 movie, his first feature film, was also the first feature-length cartoon; it brought him immense profits, international fame, and a special Motion Picture Academy Award. Today, it is the Disney version of *Snow White* that most children know — whether they have seen the film, read a Disney picture book, or taken the ride called Snow White's Scary Adventures at a Disney theme park.

Disney's films and their effect on children are frequently scrutinized, as are the theme parks themselves, but little detailed attention has been given to individual theme park attractions. Thus, it is important to consider the Snow White ride at Disneyland as a work of children's literature — specifically, a dramatic adaptation of a folktale — examine it in terms of theme and narrative structure, and compare the "literary" quality of its original and revised versions.

Such an analysis would make sense to the actual designers of Disney's imaginary worlds — the Imagineers, as they call themselves — for storytelling is embedded in everything they do. The original team who created Disneyland was recruited almost entirely from Disney's and other motion picture studios, when Walt Disney realized that conventional architects and engineers could not fathom his concept of an amusement park (Bright 45). The studio designers consciously applied the same narrative techniques to their new assignment that they had perfected in film. "We just started dreaming a lot of storyboards with notes on them, the way they do in typical Disney fashion," art director Richard Irvine recalls (qtd. in Bright 48). Storyboards are large wooden panels on which sequences of sketches are pinned to create a visual narrative. In addition to individual rides, the park as a whole was organized as a narrative experience for the visitors. To keep people moving from the entrance and Main Street to the center of Disneyland, for example, the designers placed the spectacular Sleeping Beauty Castle on a direct line of sight, as a sort of visual magnet; such a device, called a "marquee," is a common element in film design (Bright 61). "Long shots" and "close-ups" were used to encourage movement from one attraction to another; simple but interesting masses of shape and color seen in the distance revealed fascinating details as visitors approached (Rafferty 158). A smooth and gradual transition from one "land" to another was achieved by the three-dimensional, multi-sensory equivalent of the "cross-dissolve" in film.[1]

Traditional amusement park attractions — roller coasters, Ferris wheels, carrousels, bumper cars — offer novel physical sensations, but no narrative context. Even the traditional "dark ride" — in which the customer rides in darkness through a labyrinth, encountering various surprises — is not usually conceived as a narrative, but as a random sequence of shocks and scares.

In a Disney theme park, on the other hand, every attraction is planned out using storyboards "that reflect the beginning, middle, and end of our guests' park experience" (Rafferty 40). In addition, the attraction has its own "back story," which may or may not be made known to "our guests" — a "myth or legend" in the form of "a basic outline, oral or written story, or even a poem" (42) which "explains" how the attraction came to be. Today's Imagineers create elaborate back stories even for restaurants and swimming pools.[2]

Thus a Disney dark ride is conceived much like a cinematic or theatrical production. In fact, the analogy is closer to theater than to film. The scenes one sees are not simply projected on a screen, as in a film, but have a three-dimensional reality. In a conventional play, the audience sits motionless in the theater while the sequence of scenes is performed. In a dark ride like Snow White's Scary Adventures, the sequence of scenes is fixed in place — it is the audience which moves physically, in small vehicles, from one scene to the next, literally *drawn into* the story. The aim is to make the audience feel like participants, as Walt Disney emphasized when he described the three original dark rides of Fantasyland:

> What youngster hasn't dreamed of flying with Peter Pan over moonlit London? Here in the "happiest kingdom of them all," you can journey with Snow White through the dark forest to the diamond mine of the Seven Dwarfs; flee the clutches of Mr. Smee and Captain Hook with Peter Pan; and race with Mr. Toad in his wild auto ride through the streets of old London Town [qtd. in Bright 81].

One might assume that these rides simply retell the stories told in the films, reducing them to a few key scenes which the audience views as it rides past. In fact, the designers developed two distinct approaches to pre-existing films. The first, recapitulating the film, was used for Peter Pan's Flight. For Mr. Toad's Wild Ride and Snow White's Adventures, however, the designers used material from the films to create what were essentially new stories. Mr. Toad was (and still is) a fairly simple story about reckless driving, in which the visitor, playing the role of Toad, dodges and smashes his way through a variety of settings before running headlong into an oncoming railway train and finding himself in Hell. Snow White's story was much more complex.

To see clearly the differences between three versions of Snow White — the film of 1937, the original dark ride of 1955, and the dark ride as revised in 1983 and 1994 — it helps to focus on the locations where the main scenes take place.

The film of *Snow White and the Seven Dwarfs* begins at the castle of the Wicked Queen, where Snow White briefly meets a passing Prince. When the Queen orders her huntsman to murder the girl, he takes her to the forest; warned by him, she flees deeper into the woods, where friendly animals lead her to the cottage of the Dwarfs. A brief scene shows the Dwarfs digging for jewels in their mine before they return to their cottage and discover Snow White there. Back at the castle, the Queen learns that Snow White is still alive; she takes on the form of an old woman (or Witch) and concocts a poisoned apple. Finding her way to the cottage, she succeeds in getting Snow White to take a bite. Meanwhile, the animals have run to the mine to warn the Dwarfs what is happening; the Dwarfs arrive too late to save Snow White, but pursue the Witch up the mountainside until, in an attempt to crush her enemies with a giant boulder, she falls to her death. The film concludes in a forest glade, where Snow White lies in a glass coffin, the Prince arrives to waken her with a kiss, and the two ride off together, bidding farewell to the Dwarfs.

The sequence of locations in the film, then, may be expressed as Castle — Forest — Cottage — Mine — Cottage — Castle — Cottage — Mountainside — Forest.

The film omits the tender opening scene of Snow White's true mother, adds her first meeting with the Prince, adds the friendly animals and the scene at the mines, reduces the Queen's visits to the cottage from three to one, and changes the occasion and manner of the Queen's death in a way that leaves no one to blame for it but herself.[3] But on the whole, the film follows the basic storyline of the folktale — more closely than Disney's subsequent *Cinderella* (1950) and *Sleeping Beauty* (1959) follow Perrault.

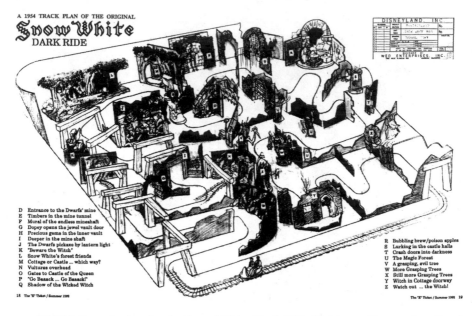

A 1954 TRACK PLAN OF THE ORIGINAL

Snow White
DARK RIDE

D   Entrance to the Dwarfs' mine
E   Timbers in the mine tunnel
F   Mural of the endless mineshaft
G   Dopey opens the jewel vault door
H   Precious gems in the inner vault
I   Deeper in the mine shaft
J   The Dwarfs pickaxe by lantern light
K   "Beware the Witch"
L   Snow White's forest friends
M   Cottage or Castle ... which way?
N   Vultures overhead
O   Gates to Castle of the Queen
P   "Go Baaack ... Go Baaack!"
Q   Shadow of the Wicked Witch

R   Bubbling brew/poison apples
S   Lurking in the castle halls
T   Crash doors into darkness
U   The Magic Forest
V   A grasping, evil tree
W   More Grasping Trees
X   Still more Grasping Trees
Y   Witch in Cottage doorway
Z   Watch out ... the Witch!

The 1954 track plan for the Snow White Dark Ride (© Disney Enterprises, Inc.).

Completed barely in time for the opening of the park, the 1955 dark ride was called simply Snow White's Adventures. Even before the ride began, it signaled its divergence from film and folktale. Imagine yourself a visitor nearing the loading area. Like Fantasyland's other two dark rides, it looks from the outside like a colorful tournament pavilion. On the back wall of the loading area, a cheerful mural depicts characters and scenes from the film, with Snow White herself at the center. Climbing into a "wooden" mining cart, you are swiftly propelled through the entrance doors into the blackness of a mine shaft. Rapid twists and turns take you deeper into the dark tunnels, past a scene of the Dwarfs working by lantern light. Dopey, perched on a rock, points to a sign reading "Beware of the Witch." Then the cart shoots out of the mine into daylight and the forest, where you are surrounded by friendly animals. Ahead, through the trees, you can see the sunlit cottage of the Dwarfs. A signpost points, in opposite directions, to "Dwarfs' Cottage" and "Witch's Castle." The track appears to be heading for the cottage, but at the last moment, your cart swings toward the castle instead. Suddenly, the forest is more menacing; two vultures peer nastily down from a bare branch, as the gray stone wall of the castle looms before you. Passing under a heavy spiked portcullis, you catch through another gate a glimpse of sunlit trees and a sign reading "To Dwarfs' House" — and again the cart swerves away, carrying you into the castle dungeons.

A skeleton chained upright to the wall croaks "Go baaack ... go baaack!" But you can't.

Through an archway, veiled by a huge spiderweb, is the silhouetted shadow of the Witch. Rounding a corner, the cart heads straight into the Witch's laboratory, just as she lifts the apple from her cauldron; a book propped on the table behind her is opened to a recipe for "Poison Apples." The cart dodges away from her, but she springs out from behind a stone column, dangling the apple in your face. Dodging again, the cart crashes through the stone wall of the castle and out into the forest — an evil forest of dead, twisted trees with gaping mouths and branches that reach out as you hurtle past. Ahead, the Dwarfs' cottage appears, the front door swings open — and the Witch is there, offering the apple! The cart swerves in the nick of time, heading into the rocks of the mountainside. Suddenly, on a cliff-top overhead, you see the Witch once more. She is prying loose a giant boulder! The boulder falls toward you, lightning flashes, and you are catapulted straight into the rock wall — through a pair of crash doors, and out into the sunshine.

All this has happened in about two minutes.

Clearly, the ride does not "tell the story of Snow White," even in curtailed fashion. Although some incidents and all the principal locations from the movie reappear, their sequence is now Mine — Forest — Castle — Forest — Cottage — Mountainside. The role of the mine has been expanded, and at no point do you find yourself inside the cottage, where a large part of the film takes place. In the film, the forest seems evil at the beginning only because Snow White is afraid of it; the trees do not clutch at her except in her imagination, and when her panic subsides, she is ashamed of having misjudged the friendly, harmless creatures who live there. In the dark ride, the forest is transformed from good to evil rather than the reverse, and the evil is real; the change seems to take place when the cart turns toward the castle. Strikingly, the story no longer has a happy ending. As the boulder falls, the Witch is triumphant; in your imagination, at least, you do not escape destruction.[4]

A major shift in the cast of characters reinforces the darkness of the narrative. Show White and her Prince are nowhere to be seen once you begin the ride, while the Dwarfs and the friendly animals are shown only once, at the beginning. The Witch, on the other hand, confronts you repeatedly, completely dominating the latter half of the ride. The cottage, a refuge you cannot seem to reach, turns out to be only another of her strongholds.

Ken Anderson, the ride's chief designer, had been an art director for the film of *Snow White*. In 1955 he had few resources and very little time; construction crews were racing to finish the park by an all but impossible deadline. Technologies that Imagineers would later come to rely on, including audio-animatronics, fiber optics, and holography, had not yet been invented. Anderson had to make do with the rudimentary technology of the traditional dark ride — vehicles run on a swerving track through a labyrinth constructed mainly of flat plywood cutouts. The clutching tree that just misses the visitors, the falling boulder that stops just above their heads, and the final crash doors were all adapted from features of the time-honored spook house. Only a few of the figures, including the Dwarfs and the Witch, were sculpted in the round and given some degree of movement. According to Anderson, "You didn't need a lot of animation because you were moving. You were going so darn fast that what you did was supply the movement for the characters" (qtd. in Janzen 22). And the illusion worked. In 1955, Snow White's Adventures was the scariest attraction at Disneyland — too scary for some children.

In *The Unofficial Guide to Walt Disney World*, Bob Sehlinger warns parents about its Snow White ride:

> We get more mail from our readers about this ride than any other Disney attraction. In short, it terrifies a lot of kids six and under. The witch is both relentless and ubiquitous, while Snow White is conspicuously absent. Many readers inform us that their small children will not ride any attraction that operates in the dark after experiencing Snow White's Adventures [347].[5]

He quotes a mother from Tennessee: "The outside looks cute and fluffy, but inside, the evil Witch just keeps coming at you." A mother from Long Island complains, "My daughter screamed the whole time and was shot for the day. Grampa kept asking, 'Where the hell is Snow White?'" (348).

In 1983, as part of an overall remodeling of Fantasyland, both the exterior building and the ride itself were completely redone, and the ride became essentially what it is today. A few lesser touches were added in 1994. (In late 1994, the ride at Walt Disney World Resort was revised along the same lines.)

In 1983, to warn parents, the name was changed to Snow White's *Scary* Adventures. In place of the "cute and fluffy" pavilion now looms the gray stone castle of the wicked Queen. High above the castle door is a Gothic window with red curtains; every half minute the curtains part, to reveal the Queen peering through. Below the window runs a row of stone supports in the shape of ravens perched on human skulls. The loading area represents the castle dungeons, and if your small child is already crying, you can drop out before it is too late.

The revised version seems to begin where the film and folktale begin — at the castle of the Queen. However, the visitors still climb into mining carts, and the first scene of the ride takes place neither at the castle nor in the forest nor even in the mining tunnels; instead, visitors find themselves instantly in the cottage, where the Dwarfs are singing "The Silly Song," as Snow White climbs the stairs to the upper floor. Any representation of the frightening journey to the cottage has disappeared; rather, the cottage now seems to be located on the castle doorstep.

Leaving the cottage, one sees the Queen lurking outside, saying, "Soon I'll be fairest in the land." From the forest, the carts follow a sign pointing to "Dwarfs' Mine" and briefly tour the tunnels, inexplicably exiting into the castle again. Here visitors see the Queen changing into the green-eyed hag before her Magic Mirror — before heading into the dungeons, where the Witch is creating the Poison Apple. Outside once more, the carts pass through the evil forest and turn toward the cottage of the Dwarfs — whose door opens to reveal the Witch offering visitors the apple. The cart swerves toward the mountain, where the Witch attempts to roll the boulder onto the pursuing Dwarfs, is struck by lightning, and falls with a scream (as in the film). At this point, the cart bursts out into brightness, where a large mural shows Snow White riding away with her Prince. In this version, which takes about three minutes to complete, the sequence of locations is Castle — Cottage — Forest — Mine — Castle — Forest — Cottage — Mountainside.

The revised version, though clearly meant to respond to the concerns of visitors, still fails to redress them. Snow White appears, but in a minor role; the Witch remains the dominant character; small children are still too scared to enjoy themselves. Indeed, it is difficult to imagine any version which would capture the atmosphere of the Disney film and *not* be too frightening for very young children. The evil Queen before her Mirror, Snow White fleeing in terror through the forest, the descent into the dungeons, past the skeletons of long-dead prisoners, the Queen transforming herself into the Witch — these scenes from the film are detailed and prolonged far beyond any frightening moments in the folktale.

At the same time, the revised dark ride has lost much of its dramatic impact. Jack E. Janzen, while acknowledging the technological superiority of today's version, sees the original as psychologically better crafted:

> Today's audience demands a more sophisticated entertainment ... but the old ride was more truly a "dark ride." In the dimly lit mine tunnels we lost our direction, and were all the more susceptible to the frights that were to come at us out of the dark [25].

When older children reviewed the revised ride at Walt Disney World Resort, they agreed that "this attraction doesn't fit well into any age category. It's very scary for young children and a little boring for older kids" (Birnbaum 43). They gave the ride their lowest, one-star rating (Birnbaum 56). Is this simply because more thrilling and technologically sophisticated dark rides are now available — rides such as Star Tours, The Haunted Mansion, Pirates of the Caribbean, Splash Mountain, and Space Mountain? Perhaps.

Or perhaps not. Despite its problems, the original "Snow White" ride was effective theater, a well-constructed narrative with a serious, interesting subtext. The revised version has abandoned both narrative logic and thematic interest. Neither version "tells the story of Snow White," but the revised version tells no story at all.

In the original ride, Snow White was never depicted — just as Toad was never depicted in Mr. Toad's Wild Ride — because the designers intended visitors to imagine *themselves* as Snow White. "As you rode the attraction," Ken Anderson explains, "you were taking Snow White's place ... you were the girl that was being threatened. And nobody got it. Nobody actually figured out that they were Snow White. They just wondered where the hell Snow White was" (qtd. in Janzen 24–25).

In the Mr. Toad ride, visitors found it easy to imagine themselves being Toad. From the outset, they were doing what Toad did — driving a primitive motorcar badly and recklessly — first through Toad Hall, then through the surrounding countryside, and finally in city streets. The surprise came at the end, when instead of escaping by locomotive (as in book and film), they crashed into it and went to Hell — a denouement found in neither source, but eminently logical. Snow White, on the other hand, never rolls through the mine in a cart. Nor does she return home to the castle (instead of reaching the cottage), tour the dungeons, see the Witch concocting the Poison Apple, or flee back through the forest to the cottage with the Witch in pursuit, only to be crushed by a boulder in the end. Her role, in folktale and film, is static and almost passive once she becomes the guest of the Dwarfs. Since movement and action are essential to the dark ride, the designers were forced to create an *alternative* story about Snow White, filled with thrilling adventures she had never had.

In this story, Snow White somehow finds her way into the tunnels of the Dwarfs and (apparently) becomes so confused and terrified that she ends up fleeing back to the castle — just in time to see the wicked Queen, now transformed into the Witch, concocting the Poison Apple for her. Not only is this an unlikely scenario, but one bearing so little resemblance to the original that visitors were hardly to blame for not grasping that it was about Snow White. The main thing both stories had in common was the heroine's panic-stricken flight.

The protagonist of the drama, as actually experienced, became not Snow White but "you," entering Snow White's world. At the beginning, disoriented by the dark tunnels, you received a warning to "Beware of the Witch." As you emerged from the mine into the forest, signs forced you to choose between "Dwarf's Cottage" and "Witch's Castle"; despite the warning, you "chose" the path to the castle, ignoring the ominously changing forest, the vultures, and even the chained skeleton's "Go baaack!" Forfeiting your last chance to escape from the castle, you suddenly found yourself face to face with the Witch. At this point your doom was sealed. Again and again, the pursuing Witch headed you off, confronting you even at the cottage door, and finally succeeded in destroying you.

Judged by its intentions, the alternative story was a failure, but as a drama about "you," it had a logic and effectiveness of its own.

The plot showed a nice sense of symmetry. The first half of the ride generated suspense by foreshadowing the encounter with the Witch — in fact, you *saw* her shadow just before meeting her in the castle — and giving you three chances to retreat. In the second half, much as in the original folktale, the Witch attacked you three times and was successful on the third try.

The series of "choices" gave visitors a strong sense of participation.[6] This almost interactive effect was heightened by the posted signs and by the way in which the vehicle seemed to become an extension of yourself as it ventured into the unknown and desperately dodged the Witch.

In addition, the drama had a theme — choices and their consequences. Despite the inviting appearance of the cottage, you might hesitate at the forking of the ways. Perhaps those Dwarfs were enemies, luring you into a trap. Perhaps an element of perverse curiosity — an itch to taste the forbidden fruit — played its part. Or perhaps free will was only an illusion, and you were predestined to choose the way of death. The forest withered as you swerved toward the castle, vultures circled overhead; the skeleton of a dead man croaked a warning. Instead of turning back, you penetrated to the very heart of evil — encapsulated in the glowing apple — and unleashed that evil upon yourself. Now there was no refuge anywhere — the entire forest, even the cottage, had been corrupted. With a liberal use of traditional symbolism, Snow White's Adventures spelled out the damning consequences of choosing *the wrong path*.[7]

For a younger audience, the theme may have been less about moral choice than about trust. Knowing when one can place one's trust in a strange adult or venture safely into a strange environment does not, unfortunately, come by instinct. Indeed, the ability to judge such situations correctly is one of the most crucial and difficult survival skills children have to learn. Some traditional folktales seem consciously designed to teach children the dire consequences of misjudgment. In "Little Red Riding Hood," the silly girl confides in the wolf and then fails to recognize him in disguise. In "The Seven Little Goats," the goats let the disguised wolf into the house, despite their mother's warning. In "Hansel and Gretel," the two children trespass onto dangerous territory.

In "Snow White and the Seven Dwarfs," Snow White makes the right choice when she trusts herself to the Dwarfs, but (like the seven little goats) opens her door to a deadly enemy. Adults who analyze this folktale may focus on the subtext of sexual jealousy and the complex character of the wicked Queen; for children, Snow White and her decisions are at the center of the story.

The Disney film, far from ignoring this interpretation of the folktale, amplifies it. A single sentence in the folktale, describing Snow White's fear of the forest, is expanded into one of the film's most memorable sequences, as Snow White flees in panic from imaginary dangers till she collapses from exhaustion. The episode becomes a lesson about the unreasonable fear of unfamiliar places, and how such fear can cause one to misinterpret one's surroundings — as Snow White sees the sinister glowing eyes resolve themselves into the eyes of rabbits and squirrels. At least, she knows enough to trust her new animal friends — in folktales, you can always trust an animal — and the shelter they lead her to. Later, there is a lengthy — perhaps unduly lengthy — scene in which the Dwarfs decide whether or not to trust *her*, and Snow White devotes considerable effort to winning Grumpy over. These variations on the theme all precede the pivotal scene in which Snow White, foolishly ignoring the warnings of the birds, invites a stranger into the cottage — and dies.

In 1955, the original Snow White's Adventures, though it failed to reproduce the plot of the film, created a kind of objective correlative for the themes of trust and choice in the geography of the dark ride. The bewildering but harmless forest was replaced by a similar environment — the mining tunnels. The evil forest of Snow White's imagination acquired objective reality in the territory of the Witch. Snow White's choices about whom to trust found an equivalent in the rider's "choice" of paths. Even the skeleton in the Witch's dungeon took on new meaning. In the film, it is only glimpsed in passing, a silent witness to the cruelty of evil. In the dark ride, it actively attempts to save the visitor from its own fate. This is the only moment in the dark ride in which good, somehow surviving death, fights back against the ruthless evil of the Witch.

If the original ride presented a brief but memorable drama, the revised version has abandoned both narrative logic and thematic content. Visitors, no longer faced with "choices," are now merely observers of a few, mostly disconnected scenes; the only coherent sequence is that closest to the original — the repeated encounters with the Witch. The Imagineers of 1983 chose to jettison plot and theme for a series of sensations — from anxiety at the loading platform, to cheeriness at the cottage, to increasing fear, and then back to cheeriness again. The differences between the two versions raise interesting questions about "story" itself. How much narrative and thematic coherence is necessary to create something that feels like a story? And how does this perception alter the audience's response? At Disneyland, it seems, boredom or fear were all that remained once narrative and theme were gone.

The Imagineers' abandonment of the original narrative can be explained in part by changes in Disneyland as a whole, which in turn reflected changes in American culture. As cultural historian Karel Ann Marling expresses it, the Disneyland of the 1950s represented "a world view grounded in Main Street's values. Frontierland sets forth the story of how the West was made safe for homesteaders — and suburbanites. Adventureland appropriates the Third World and untamed nature to serve as the frontiers (and boutiques) of today, while a corporate Tomorrowland, intent on the conquest of space, is the profitable frontier of the future" (10). Only in Fantasyland did one find "flirtations with the dark and irrational" (200–201), with its "flat, unnuanced contrasts between good and evil, light and dark, so evident in the cold war politics of the 1950s" (197). (And only, I would add, in tales of European, not American, origin.)

Past, present, and future were all presented as benign in this world-vision. In the late 1960s, however, morally ambiguous dark rides began spreading like an infection. Pirates of the Caribbean (1967) invited visitors to enjoy the spectacle of pirates looting a helpless town, humorously depicting scenes of rape and torture. The Haunted Mansion (1969) surrounded the visitor with ghosts and skeletons which were sometimes funny, sometimes frightening, but neither "good" nor "bad." Both rides were located in New Orleans Square, a new area squeezed between Adventureland and Frontierland (and representing, perhaps, the decadence of the Deep South). "Out of control" rides combining the dark ride with the roller coaster entered the park, first the Matterhorn Bobsleds on the border between Fantasyland and Tomorrowland (1959), then Space Mountain in Tomorrowland (1977) and Big Thunder Mountain Railroad in Frontierland (1979).[8] Lawlessness, recklessness, and terror, no longer confined to "Once upon a time," now permeated the past, present, and future of the world.

Real-world childhood was changing, too, as children were exposed to increasingly violent films, television, and video games at home, and decreasing freedom to venture outdoors on their own. Walt Disney envisioned his theme park primarily as a place where parents and children could enjoy the same entertainment. He did not foresee either the protectiveness of today's parents, who attempt to shield children from any remotely dangerous experience, or a growing audience of teenagers and childfree adults looking for more "mature" thrills.

In 1961, Disney began offering the park as a safe, liquor-free, but festive

venue for high school "Grad Night" celebrations. The students naturally gravitated toward Snow White's Adventures, still the scariest dark ride there. Just
as naturally, they viewed the scariness as an amusing challenge. It became a
tradition not to shy away from the Witch's apple as she offered it — but to
snatch it from her hand, symbolically defying death and embracing evil, as
teenagers often feel compelled to do. The custom spread beyond Grad Night
and downward in terms of age. As older children became more exposed to
scenes of violence and danger, in their entertainment media and even in real
life, so they grew less afraid of the Witch and increasingly likely to steal the
apple. This in turn became a problem for the "cast members" of Disneyland.
By the 1990s, they found themselves having to race through the dark ride
between carts to replace the apple, sometimes twice a day, from a bag of fake
apples kept behind the scenes.[9] This problem, at least, found a satisfying
solution. In 1983, using the technology now available, the apple was replaced
by a holographic image; today, anyone who tries to steal the apple finds his
hand "magically" passing right through it. At the same time, a way was found
to allow daring visitors the chance to flirt with death. The approach to the
ride now features a bronze apple sitting near a bronze book of magic spells
inscribed with the legend, "One taste of the poisoned apple and the victim's
eyes will close forever in the Sleeping Death." Those who touch this apple
hear a peal of thunder and the cackling laugh of the Witch.

Today, ironically, Fantasyland — with the adjacent Toontown — is no
longer the scariest but the "safest" area of the park. Once "the happiest kingdom of them all," it is now merely "the kingdom most suitable for children
under six." Snow White's Scary Adventures is stuck here in limbo, boring
older children, frightening younger ones, and upsetting protective parents
who believe that children should not be frightened at all. Were the film of
Snow White less central in the Disney canon, the ride might have been jetti-
soned years ago.

If the ride is to survive, it should, I think, abandon the failed attempt
at compromise and create a dramatic experience suitable either for one age-
group or the other. The Imagineers could create a pleasant entertainment for
younger children by selecting from the fanciful and comic elements of the
film — more Dwarfs! more Snow White! more friendly animals!— and drasti-
cally reducing the role of the Witch; in this version, she would never confront
the visitor as she does now. Or they could create a gripping drama for older
children and adults by restoring a strong and meaningful storyline and realizing it with all the technological resources now at their command. Then the
Snow White ride might become again what it once was — the darkest dark
ride of them all.

The author thanks Ian McFeat, Patsy Rahn, Hamida Bosmajian, and her husband, John, for their valuable contributions to this essay.

Notes

1. Rafferty describes one such cross-dissolve:
   A stroll from Main Street to Adventureland is a relatively short distance, but one experiences an enormous change in theme and story. For the transition to be a smooth one, there is a gradual blending of themed foliage, color, sound, music and architecture. Even the soles of your feet feel a change in the paving that explicitly tells you something new is on the horizon. Smell may also factor into a dimensional cross-dissolve. In a warm summer breeze, you may catch a whiff of sweet tropical flora and exotic spices as you enter Adventureland [90].

2. For "Blizzard Beach" at Walt Disney World Resort, for example, the Imagineers wanted to combine the usual pools and slides of a water park with the architecture of a ski resort.
   So the team created a legend that a freak winter storm blew through central Florida, stopping just long enough to dump a mountain of snow on the area's highest hill, thus prompting the construction of the state's first-ever ski resort. As the legend goes, the hot tropical sun returned and quickly melted all the snow. The ski runs turned to water, and the run-off created some of the tallest, fastest, and wildest water slides found anywhere in the world [Rafferty 26].

3. In the Grimms' version of the folktale, the Queen's death is notoriously nasty; she is forced to dance at Snow White's wedding in a pair of red-hot iron shoes until she falls down dead. Presumably, the Prince orders her punishment, and Snow White does not object.

4. John Hench, one of the original Imagineers, argues that
   Actually, what we're selling throughout the Park is reassurance. We offer adventures in which you survive a kind of personal challenge — a charging hippo, a runaway mine train, a wicked witch, an out-of-control bobsled. But in every case, we let you win. We let your survival instincts triumph over adversity [Bright 237].
   This seems to me dubious in the case of "Snow White's Adventures." Analogously, a novel would have a happy ending as long as the reader was still capable of closing the cover on it.

5. (New York: Macmillan, 1995), 347. When this edition of the *Unofficial Guide* was written, the Snow White ride at Walt Disney World Resort was still essentially the same, inside and out, as the original ride at Disneyland.

6. In "Mr. Toad's Wild Ride," the sense of active participation is heightened by having a steering wheel in the car. The wheel turns readily to left or right, but (naturally) has no effect whatsoever on the course taken by the car, causing a pleasant degree of panic in the visitor.

7. It is a well-known supernatural law that an evil being — such as a witch or vampire — cannot invade a house until it is *invited* to enter by someone who lives there; after that initial invitation, it can come and go freely. In the folktale of "Snow White," for example, the girl has to be tricked into inviting the old woman into her home; the Witch cannot simply break down the door by force. (Something of the same sort may have happened in *Beowulf*, to allow Grendel free access to Heorot.) On a spiritual level, evil cannot enter one's heart without one's own consent. In the original Snow White dark ride, consenting to evil seems to be symbolized by one's "decision" to turn toward the castle; once this has happened, evil can go anywhere, even into the cottage.

8. In "Big Thunder Mountain," for example, a mine is supposed to be haunted by dri-

verless trains running madly through the tunnels on their own. In September 2003, one of these trains actually did go out of control. The engine became detached from the passenger car and then rolled backward into it, with a crash that killed one passenger and injured ten more.

9. See *http://www.hiddenmickeys.org/Disneyland/Secrets/Fantasy/SnowWhite.*

Works Cited

Birnbaum, Stephen, ed. *Birnbaum's Walt Disney World for Kids, by Kids.* New York: Hearst Business, 1997.

Bright, Randy. *Disneyland: Inside Story.* New York: Harry N. Abrams, 1987.

Janzen, Jack E. "The Original Snow White Dark Ride." *The "E" Ticket* 13 (1992): 22–25.

Marling, Karel Ann. "Disneyland 1955." *American Art* 5 (1991): 168–207.

Rafferty, Kevin, and Bruce Gordon. *Walt Disney Imagineering: A Behind the Dreams Look at Making the Magic Real.* New York: Hyperion, 1996.

Tom Sawyer Island
Mark Twain, Walt Disney, and the Literary Playground

MARK I. WEST

Mark Twain and Walt Disney both achieved iconic status during their lifetimes, but that is certainly not all that they that they had in common. Both spent part of their boyhood years in small towns in Missouri. In 1839, when Twain was nearly four years old, he moved with his family to Hannibal, a town in eastern Missouri located on the banks of the Mississippi River. In 1906, when Disney was four years old, he moved with his family to Marceline, a town in north-central Missouri. For both Twain and Disney, the experience of growing up in a small Midwestern-town helped shape their identities and provided them with a wealth of memories that they later drew upon in their creative work. Both Twain and Disney had distant fathers and affectionate mothers. Both grew up in families that were barely in the middle class economically. Both were avid readers during their childhoods, but neither excelled in school. Both spent part of their early adult years in Kansas City, and both sought their fortunes in California. Both became successful in part by tapping into the popular tastes of the American public, and both helped shape the nature of American culture (Burnes 154–55). In addition to these biographical similarities, both Twain and Disney had a deep understanding of how children respond to stories.

Twain and Disney understood that children often treat their favorite stories as playgrounds for their imaginations. For children who are inclined to engage in pretend play, shared stories can provide a loose structure for this type of play. These children often pretend to be characters from their favorite stories, or act out plot elements, or imagine that their play is taking place in

101

the settings described in the stories. As reader-response theorist Robert Proth-erough points out, many child readers describe this "experience as being 'there' in the books with the characters" (22). In their pretend play, such children often deviate from the actual storyline found in the printed version, but they tend to honor the basic literary conventions associated with the story.

When responding to literature in this way, children often gravitate toward stories that are set in self-contained worlds. As both Twain and Disney under-stood, island settings are especially well suited for this type of pretend play. Jackson Island, the setting for several chapters in Mark Twain's *The Adventures Tom Sawyer*, and Tom Sawyer Island, an attraction in Disneyland, provide intriguing examples of how island environments can function as multi-leveled literary playgrounds for children who enjoy projecting themselves into story-based situations.

Mark Twain's 1876 classic novel, *The Adventures of Tom Sawyer*, contains several instances of children incorporating stories in their pretend play. How-ever, the most notable example is when Tom Sawyer, Huckleberry Finn, and Joe Harper take a raft to Jackson Island, a small, uninhabited island located in the middle of the Mississippi River, where they pretend to be pirates. It is clear from the text that Tom is very knowledgeable about pirate lore. When Huck asks what pirates do, Tom readily responds, "Oh they have a bully time — take ships, and burn them, and get the money and bury it in awful places in their island where there's ghosts and things to watch it, and kill everybody in the ships — make 'em walk a plank" (119).

Under Tom's direction, the boys assume pirate names. Huck is renamed Huck Finn the Red-Handed, Joe takes on the name of Joe Harper the Terror of the Seas, and Tom dubs himself the Black Avenger of the Spanish Main. While on the island, they play out scenes from pirate stories. Lucy Rollin, the editor of the Broadview Edition of *The Adventures of Tom Sawyer*, explains that these pirate stories are based on a series of tales by Ned Buntline that first appeared in a weekly paper called *Flag of Our Union* in 1847 and then came out as a book titled *The Black Avenger, Story of the Spanish Main*. During his boyhood years, Twain read Buntline's pirate stories, and he drew on this aspect of his childhood when he created the character of Tom Sawyer (Rollin 306).

As a boy growing up in Missouri, Disney gravitated toward the works of Mark Twain. Disney especially enjoyed *The Adventures of Tom Sawyer*, which he originally read during his childhood and remembered fondly for the rest of his life (Burnes 56; Thomas 36). Disney's love of Twain's classic surfaced when Disney set out to create Disneyland during the early 1950s.

Of all Disneyland's attractions, the one that Disney was most heavily

Artistic rendering of Tom Sawyer Island (© Disney Enterprises, Inc.).

involved in designing was Tom Sawyer Island. As Bob Thomas recounts in *Walt Disney: An American Original*, the task of designing Tom Sawyer Island was initially assigned to Marvin Davis, one of the main designers of Disneyland:

> Marv Davis had labored over the contours of Tom Sawyer Island, but his efforts failed to please Walt. Give me that thing, "Walt said. That night he worked for hours in his red-barn workshop. The next morning, he laid tracing paper on Davis's desk and said, "Now *that's* the way it should be." The island was built according to his design [264–65].

In creating this attraction, Disney drew heavily on his childhood memories of reading Twain's classic. He set out to create a special environment where children could feel as if they had magically entered the pages of *The Adventures of Tom Sawyer*. Disney especially liked the chapters in the book that take place on Jackson Island in part because these chapters convey the experience of being in a secondary world where the rules associated with the ordinary world do not apply. Disney wanted the visitors to Tom Sawyer Island to enjoy this same type of experience. Like the character of Tom Sawyer, they could ride a raft, explore a mysterious cave, and engage in pretend play. When talking to a reporter from *Reader's Digest* about his plans for Tom Sawyer Island, Disney said, "I put in all the things I wanted to do as a kid—and couldn't" (Wolfert 147). He deliberately avoided putting rides or other mechanical devices in this space because he wanted it to be open to multiple interpretations and to present children with opportunities to exercise their imaginations. Disney included many specific references to *The Adventures of*

Tom Sawyer on Tom Sawyer Island, such as Injun Joe's Cave and Harper's Mill.

Tom Sawyer Island opened to the public in June 1956, one year after the official opening of Disneyland. Walt Disney himself presided over the dedication of Tom Sawyer Island, and he used the opportunity to celebrate his Missouri roots. He arranged for a boy and a girl from Hannibal to participate in the dedication ceremony. These children brought with them bottles of water from the Mississippi River, and this water was used to "christen" the island (Janzen 18).

As Chris Strodder states in *The Disneyland Encyclopedia*, Tom Sawyer Island came to be known as "one of the most unique and most entertaining" attractions in Disneyland (425). One of the aspects of Tom Sawyer Island that soon distinguished it from most of the park's other attractions is its absence of rules and restrictions. Visitors reach the island via rafts, and as soon as they exit the rafts they are at liberty to play and explore. In an article published in *The E Ticket Magazine* in 2002, Jack and Leon Janzen discuss this aspect of Tom Sawyer Island:

> On the island there are no waiting lines, few rules or restrictions and kids freely explore one site or another for as long as they want. Even in this era of increased litigation, running, jumping and climbing are activities still welcomed on the island, and kids quickly outdistance their careful parents, Tom Sawyer Island is big enough to get a little bit lost, and unsupervised access to cave, bridges, escape tunnels and secret passages lets each kid script his or her own exciting story. Most other theme park rides control the route, the ride length, whether you stand or sit, the direction you turn and look, and what you see and hear. Because of this, each rider inline receives the same experience. In contrast, kids of all ages make their own discoveries on Tom Sawyer Island and adventure is experiences from each child's point of view. It is this difference that accounts for much of the attraction's timeless popularity [14–15].

The success of Tom Sawyer Island led to the creation of two similar attractions at other Disney theme parks. In 1973, a somewhat expanded version of Tom Sawyer Island was included in the Magic Kingdom within Disney World (Kurtti 55). A decade later, a third Tom Sawyer Island made its debut at Tokyo Disneyland in Japan. Mark Twain's *The Adventures of Tom Sawyer* served as the inspiration for all three of these attractions, but they are not identical.

In part because Walt Disney played such an important role in designing Tom Sawyer Island, the management of Disneyland made only minor changes to the island during its first fifty years. However, as *The Adventures of Tom Sawyer* gradually fell off the required reading lists for many school systems, fewer and fewer children who visited Tom Sawyer Island could fully appreciate the attraction's many connections to Twain's novel. Finally, in the fall of 2006,

Disneyland decided the time had come to revamp Tom Sawyer Island. The redesigned attraction, called Pirate's Lair on Tom Sawyer Island, opened to the public on May 25, 2007, the same day that the *Pirates of the Caribbean: At World's End* opened in theaters.

When the management of Disneyland decided to introduce a pirate theme to Tom Sawyer Island, they hoped to tap into the immense popularity of the *Pirates of the Caribbean* movies, but they still wanted to preserve the Mark Twain connections to this attraction. To accomplish this goal, Disneyland relied on the leadership of its experienced "imagineers," including Michael Sprout, senior concept writer, and Chris Runco, senior concept designer.

Sprout and Runco found their inspiration in the pages of *The Adventures of Tom Sawyer*, especially the chapters set on Jackson Island. Sprout and Runco read this part of Twain's classic with great care, and they used it as a blueprint for their redesign of Tom Sawyer Island. As Sprout explained during an interview conducted on March 22, 2007, "The idea is that everything that Tom and Huck imagined to be on the island is actually there. We're just trying to live out a little bit more of the fantasy. We're being very careful not to disturb the bones of the original design. It's still called Tom Sawyer Island, but we want it to seem as if it has just been taken over by pirates, and it is now a pirate's lair."

Visitors to the redesigned Tom Sawyer Island still take rafts to the island, but the rafts now fly the Jolly Roger flag and have pirate names. One is called Blackbeard and the other is named after Anne Bonny, the female pirate who became famous for her exploits in the Caribbean during the 1720s.

Most of the original buildings and structures on the island remain, but their names have changed. For example, the first building visitors encounter after exiting the raft had long been known as Harper's Mill, but it is now called Lafitte's Tavern, named after Jean Lafitte, a famous pirate from the early 19th century who often frequented New Orleans.

One of the long-time features of Tom Sawyer Island is a cave dubbed Injun Joe's Cave. This cave remains a main feature but with a new name. "We've given it a pirate name," Sprout said. "It's called Dead Man's Grotto. It's the same cave, but we've hidden more treasures in it. We've also added special effects that sort of guard these treasures."

Another feature that remains is Tom and Huck's Tree House, where children can still climb up high and spy on the other visitors down below. The tree house includes specific references to the characters of Tom Sawyer and Huck Finn. Sprout explained, "We added their pirate names to the wall of the tree house. We're using the names from the book, such as Huck the Red-Handed. I hope that these touches will lead children back to the book."

Sprout and Runco provided other Twain references that less observant visitors might not even notice. For example, near the dock where visitors board the rafts to reach the island, there is a glass-covered bulletin board with a sign that reads "River Notices." Posted on this bulletin board is what appears to be a newspaper article from *The St. Petersburg Journal*, dated November 30, 1835. The article is titled "Lost Boys Found," but it is really a retelling of the episode from *The Adventure of Tom Sawyer* in which Tom and his companions return from their adventures on Jackson Island in time to attend their own funeral service. The bulletin board also includes a replica Twain's original of the pilot's certificate that authorized him to operate river boats on the Mississippi River.

Although the revamped version of Tom Sawyer Island has fewer references to *The Adventures of Tom Sawyer* then was the case with the Disney's original design, the new version is still true to the original spirit of the book. Child visitors to the redesigned version of Tom Sawyer Island may not be inclined to pretend that they are Tom or Huck, but by pretending to be pirates, they are doing exactly what Tom and Huck do while visiting Jackson Island. The new version still provides children with opportunities to engage in pretend play and to draw on stories while doing so. In this regard, the new version of Tom Sawyer Island has much in common with the memorable depictions of imaginative play found in Twain's classic novel.

Works Cited

Burnes, Brian, Robert W. Butler, and Dan Viets. *Walt Disney's Missouri: The Roots of a Creative Genius.* Kansas City, MO: Kansas City Star Books, 2002.

Janzen, Jack E., and Leon J. Janzen. "Tom Sawyer Island." *The "E" Ticket Magazine* Spring 2002: 14–28.

Kurtti, Jeff. *Since the World Began: Walt Disney World, the First 25 Years.* New York: Hyperion, 1996.

Protherough, Robert. *Developing Response to Fiction.* Milton Keynes, UK: Open University Press, 1983.

Rollin, Lucy. Appendix D. *The Adventures of Tom Sawyer.* By Mark Twain. Ed. Lucy Rollin. Peterborough, ON: Broadview Editions, 2006. 287–310.

Sprout, Michael. Personal interview. 22 March 2007.

Strodder, Chris. *The Disneyland Encyclopedia.* Santa Monica, CA: Santa Monica Press, 2008.

Thomas, Bob. *Walt Disney: An American Original.* New York: Simon and Schuster, 1976.

Twain, Mark. *The Adventures of Tom Sawyer.* Hartford, CT: American Publishing Company, 1876.

Wolfert, Ira. "Walt Disney's Magic Kingdom." *Reader's Digest* April 1960: 144–152.

A Southern California Boyhood in the Simu-Southland Shadows of Walt Disney's Enchanted Tiki Room

CRAIG SVONKIN

Growing up in the late 1960s and early 1970s in Monterey Park, a sub-urban bedroom community just east of Los Angeles and twenty-five miles from Disneyland, I was bombarded by simulacrum of Polynesian and Hawaiian culture, by the faux–Tiki spaces that permeated Southern California at the time. Long before I became an English major and learned from Jean Baudrillard that reproductions or simulations of the "real" often feel more real or authentic to us than the "real"—his theory of hyperreality—I probably couldn't have told you what cultural practice felt more alive or authentic to me—that all-important annual family pilgrimage to Disneyland—and thus to my favorite Disneyland show, Walt Disney's Enchanted Tiki Room, a robotic bird show themed to Hawaii and Polynesia—or a Sabbath morning trip to my family's synagogue. If someone had explained to me when I was eight years old that, to quote Baudrillard, "Disneyland [was] presented as imaginary in order to make [me] believe that the rest was real, when in fact all of Los Angeles [...] surrounding it [was] no longer real, but of the order of the hyperreal and of simulation," I might have agreed (Baudrillard 428). One of the central appeals of Disneyland for me was not that it was a world of illusion and simulation in contrast to a "real" world of authenticity, but rather that it took the simulacrum that surrounded me to a logical conclusion. It was the height of beautiful fakery, and for the ten-year-old Craig, the fake often felt more vivid and real than the "real" itself, assuming I could discover the "real" in Southern California or knew what it was to begin with.

As a Jewish American kid growing up in a multicultural suburbia, I certainly had no idea of what constituted "authentic" Hawaiian culture. Likewise, as a Jewish American kid growing up away from the Jewish ghetto that my grandparents had lived in, I also lacked a clear idea of what constituted "authentic" Jewish culture. Given the common acceptance in the 1960s of cultural appropriation, any critique of the Tiki-obsessed fakery that surrounded me as inauthentic or insensitive to actual Hawaiians never reached my ears. My favorite things were pretty much all fake, many of them being Polynesian or Hawaiian simulacrum, with the king of them all being Walt Disney's singing robotic bird and Tiki show added to Disneyland's Adventureland area in 1963. It is likely that these simu–Southland Tiki spaces were all the more beloved due to their very inauthenticity. I, a Jewish, middle-class, suburban, somewhat assimilated American kid, experienced Jewishness itself, what with its ancient stories and rituals so foreign and distant from my everyday life, as a form of Exotica. If the mechanical Tikis at Walt Disney's Enchanted Tiki Room chanted in an inauthentic parody of Oceanic languages, I was too ignorant to notice, and even if I had known, I probably wouldn't have objected. After all, my friends at Hebrew school and I parodied the Hebrew prayers that we chanted but didn't understand by replacing the foreign, and to us, somewhat fake-sounding words with comical English substitutes. Jewish culture seemed akin to the exotic, magical spaces, stories, and rituals of Tiki-culture in other ways too. Disneyland's Enchanted Tiki Room appealed to me partly due to its moody, dim lighting, lighting that I associated with the dark, spiritual lighting found in my synagogue's sanctuary. The inauthentic but fantastic and appealing stories about Tiki Gods created for the Enchanted Tiki Room's pre-show waiting area seemed just as fantastic, appealing, and inauthentic to me as my rabbi's stories of Abraham binding his son to be sacrificed or tiny David killing the giant Goliath.

In my childhood obsession with Tiki culture, in my craving for "Tiki" artifacts and Hawaiian "experiences," I followed many other non–Hawaiian, mainland Americans in turning faux–Polynesian culture into a simultaneously commodified and spiritual if inauthentic practice, one that represented for us, perhaps, the impossible hope for escape from the perceived limitations of American, middle-class, suburban life. The fact that we consumers of pop Polynesia were, in the words of George Lewis, "appropriating the culture of indigenous island peoples and redrawing this culture to reflect" our own "dreams and desires" did not trouble us as much as it perhaps should have (Lewis 123). I was too focused on experiencing an aesthetics of wonder to notice how my pursuit of faux–Hawaiian culture might have been damaging or hurtful to indigenous people. Critics such as Mary Louise Pratt and Stephen Greenblatt point out that the European's initial sense of wonder in the face of an encounter with an exoticized other can easily turn into a desire to touch, catalogue, inventory, and possess that other (Greenblatt 22).

If wonder can act "as an agent of appropriation," as Greenblatt persuasively asserts (24), then the sense of wonder at the "others" of the Enchanted Tiki Room experienced by so many generations of children like me could have had all sorts of troubling imperialist results. But at eight or nine I simply didn't understand that I was a part of the long and troubling practice of First World cultures taking "the Third World's emotional and expressive practices and arts," or "emotional capital" to use the term coined by Marta Savigliano, and turning that emotional capital, through homogenization, "into commodities suitable for consumption" by Anglo Americans (Lewis 124; Savigliano 237). I was part of a wider practice of consuming Hawaiian culture as "exotic culture under the subcategories of 'mystery,' 'untamed wilderness,' 'the primitive,' and 'raw passion'" (Savigliano 237). This Orientalist practice accelerated in the United States after World War II, when returning American GIs spread stories of "exotic" locations from the South Pacific to Africa and demanded Americanized recreations of the foreign bars and other liminal spaces they had come to associate with pleasure, excess, and freedom.

One of my earliest memories is describing my Hawaiian trip on the first day of kindergarten, even though I had never been to Hawaii. I based my description largely on my careful study of the Dole-sponsored Hawaiian travelogue/commercial that played in the pre-show area of the Enchanted Tiki Room. The film educated me to what I, as a future tourist to Hawaii, would need to do in order to fully experience Hawaii — I would have to go to a luau, eat pineapple, listen to Hawaiian ukulele music, and learn to surf. So, when my kindergarten teacher, Mrs. George, asked me what I had done that summer, I told an elaborate tale of participating in a luau, eating roast pig, bathing on black-sand beaches, and sipping delicious, frothy, tropical fruit beverages served in hollowed-out pineapples (just like my grandmother would serve us delicious Fresca in plastic pineapple-shaped mugs). My story was quite convincing, and my lie worked just fine until Mrs. George asked my mother about our Hawaiian vacation. My lie was unsurprising, really, given our annual family pilgrimages to Disneyland, where the Enchanted Tiki Room robot-bird and talking–Tiki show was my very favorite attraction in my very favorite Disneyland "land" — Adventureland. On virtually every Disneyland trip, on both the drive to and the drive back home from the theme park, I would torture my parents and siblings by singing endless, tone-deaf refrains of the chorus to the Enchanted Tiki Room theme song. The song was composed by Disney songwriters Richard and Robert Sherman, the songwriters later made famous by their penning of "It's a Small World (After All)" and the songs for Disney's hit musical *Mary Poppins.*

Other facets of "Tiki" culture permeated my childhood. My family's suburban track-home was surrounded by banana trees, petrified wood, birds of paradise, and lava-rock planters, and an "Orientalist" Moderne design was placed prominently on the large front garage door of the house. There was even a rubber tree plant-dominated "jungle" right outside my bedroom window. Monterey Park was also the home to one of the shrines to fake Tiki culture — Danny Balsz's Tiki–themed luau grounds and theme-park — "The Tikis," created in the 1960s (Kirsten 106–113). Throughout my childhood, I begged my parents to take me to The Tikis, but, given the fact that The Tikis served alcoholic drinks and marketed itself to an adult audience, my parents refused. When the Tiki theme park that was walking distance from my home and that we would drive by so often closed, I had still never experienced the thrill of going. At some point, my father had brought home a souvenir matchbook from The Tikis, with the following description of the park on the inside cover:

The Tikis
- Three acres of lush atmosphere
- 200 ft. underground volcanic cave
- Erupting volcano — waterfalls
- Large lagoons — thunder — rain
- Bird calls — monkeys chattering
- 3 dance areas — individual huts
- 100 foot snake bar — barefoot bar
- Complete indoor & outdoor party and banquet facilities, up to 1500
- 5 acres of paved free parking
- Tiki's banana train ride

1001 N. Potrero Grande Dr. Monterey Park — Calif. [Kirsten 110].

Staring at that matchbook, which I had added to my growing Tiki souvenir collection, I dreamed of going to The Tikis; my dreams of this unattained and unattainable paradise continued for years after the park had shut down. The lack of ever visiting "The Tikis" long haunted me, and by extension, my entire family. When we went to Walt Disney World Resort in 1977, my parents made sure to take me to a luau at Disney's Polynesian Resort Hotel, perhaps in order to atone for the sin of having never taken me to The Tikis.

Tiki-themed spaces were typically designed with adults in mind. Tiki bars, Tiki restaurants, and The Tikis all gave off a faint whiff of sexuality and excess, making Walt Disney's decision to build a Tiki-themed restaurant at Disneyland a bit surprising. However, it is important to note that Walt Disney often integrated adult themes into his park, thus complicating the general myths of the theme park as an innocent child's paradise. My own childhood love of Disneyland may very well have been related to Disneyland's cleverly designed so as to be unnoticed adaptation of adult themes and tropes, and the mixing of these adult tropes with tropes and stories associated with childhood. This mixing of adult and child tropes at Disneyland turned the park into a liminal space desired by children and adults alike. While as a child I couldn't go to The Tikis or to a Tiki bar, as much as I might have wanted to, and while I had to go to bed before the more adult television shows came on, Disneyland was child-approved entertainment despite its common use of images of death and horror, and despite its embrace of risqué sexual moments such as those found in the Golden Horseshoe Review (where Slue Foot Slue, performed by Betty Taylor, flirted with male customers in a manner reminiscent of Mae West), the Pirates of the Caribbean ride (where the Disney Imagineers originally played for laughs images of women being auctioned off or chased by predatory male pirates), and even in the Enchanted Tiki Room show and it's a small world ride (where respectively "female" robotic birds and "female" robotic dolls dressed as Can Can dancers or as Cleopatra were presented as eroticized fetish objects of desire).

Walt Disney, a frequent visitor to the many Polynesian gourmet restaurants dotting the Southern California landscape (Kirsten 191), first planned for his Enchanted Tiki Room to be the ultimate Hawaiian-themed dinner show. Disney undoubtedly was a fan of the same sort of Polynesia-themed restaurants that I loved as a child, such as San Gabriel's Bahooka, Trader Vic's in Beverly Hills, and Laguna's The Royal Hawaiian. However, when tests of the show conducted by Disney's Imagineers, his attraction designers, proved that people wouldn't eat while the show was progressing and that there was therefore no way to keep up with reservations or make a profit, Disney dropped his plans for a dinner show, cancelled his sponsorship deal with Stouffer's, and took over sponsorship of the show himself, opening it as Walt Disney's Enchanted Tiki Room (Gordon and Mumford 188–189; Marling 83). He retained ownership of the show for a year through his private company, WED Enterprises, before enticing United Airlines to take over sponsorship (Gordon and Mumford 175, 90).

While the stories of Walt Disney's perfectionism do ring true, he was also a savvy businessman, willing to change his concept for a Disneyland attraction such as the Enchanted Tiki Room based on market or profit forces. However, while I agree to some extent with Steven Fjellman's assertion that the Disney "Company — especially at its theme parks — produces, packages, and sells experiences and memories as commodities" (11), it is important to qualify Fjellman's assertion somewhat. While the Disney company was always a corporation intent on profits and on selling, the current multi-national Walt Disney Company clearly differs from the Disney company of Walt Disney's time in terms of degree. Walt Disney was happy to provide a total themed environment that, by integrating themed stores, restaurants, and attractions, would encourage visitors to consume out of a desire to become participants in the thematic totality of the park. However, Walt Disney was not only focused on encouraging consumption and selling commodities for the sake of profit. He arguably was using profit to allow him to fulfill personal ideological and psychological desires, as part of a utopian plan to design a theme park that could somehow fill a lack that he, and by definition we, felt. Disneyland, and by extension the Enchanted Tiki Room, were personal projects meant to communicate a political ideology to his visitors while allowing him to deal with personal anxieties.

The layout of Disneyland, like the design of the Enchanted Tiki Room itself, brings together many of Walt Disney's ideological and psychological contradictions, given their simultaneous and seemingly contradictory nostalgic celebrations of the past and obsessive fixation on the future and technological progress. Disneyland is designed so as to create a strange blend of futurism and nostalgia or wishful primitivism. Disneyland's Fantasyland focuses its thematics on nostalgia for a lost youth, but it is also indicative of Walt Disney's intellectual colonization of European fairy tales. Disneyland's Frontierland celebrates a mythic American past while inculcating the American theme of Manifest Destiny and triumph over the American "frontier." Adventureland offers a strange example of trans-exoticism or cultural slippage by bringing together an architectural and cultural "sampler of forms from most of the exotic parts of the planet" — from Asia, Polynesia, Mexico, Arabia, Africa, the Caribbean, and British and French colonial regions (Charles Moore et al. 41). By confusing and mixing all of these "exotic" foreign locales into one thematic melting-pot, the Disney Imagineers created the ultimate simulacrum of American primitivist desires. As Susan Willis explains, writing about the later Walt Disney World Resort theme park Disney's Animal Kingdom, a park predicated, like the Tiki Room, on a Gauguin-like desire for primitivist escape, Disney's trans-exotica themed parks and shows are "a Third World Never-Never Land amenable to American sensibilities," or, in other words, simultaneously "exotic but comfortable" (59). Scott Hermanson puts it this way:

"Disney constructs a landscape that relies on nostalgic myths and mediated images" (207). Disney thus attempts to accomplish two seemingly opposed purposes through this trans-exotic cultural primitivism — both fulfill American tourists' nostalgic or escapist desires for an encounter with an exoticized otherness, and, by depicting the exoticized other, reinscribe the boundary between that other and white American normalcy.

Like the nineteenth-century white viewer of blackface minstrelsy, the American visitor to Disneyland's Jungle Cruise or Enchanted Tiki Room can vicariously enjoy an escape from his middle-class white Americanness when he views the objectified, fetishized African bodies visible from the Jungle Cruise or listens to the Mexican-accented parrot, Jose, who dominates the Tiki Room show. At the same time, the viewer is reminded of his own superiority over those African villagers, or over Jose, voiced by Disneyland's Golden Horseshoe Review comic Wally Boag. Boag's Mexican accent indicates a brown-face performance, for it is only through the most stereotyped of inflections and his use of "ch" rather than "sh" in lines like "Ole, ole, it's chow time" or "I think somebody has left the chower running," that Boag indicates that Jose is a Mexican parrot. Jose is, like earlier minstrel figures, both a comic Harlequin mocking the very show he is in and a figure that the show and by extension the audience mocks. For example, when a "Bird Mobile" of all-white female birds descends from the ceiling of the room, introduced by the French-accented parrot Pierre as "the lovely ladies of the ensemble, just like the Follies Bergere with all the feathers," Jose asks, "I wonder what happened to Rosita?" This joke, like many of Jose's, is an ethnic joke that no longer plays all that well for contemporary audiences. However, like other ethnic jokes in the show, it can be read in a double-manner, as Jose questioning the all-white, all French ethnic make-up of the female parrots (who have names like Fifi, Mimi, Colette, Suzette, and Josephine), and at the same time the show mocking Jose for his assumption that a Mexican bird somehow belongs in this all-white harem.

The ethnic make-up of the parrot hosts of the Tiki Room is so strange as to be worthy of analysis. Other than Jose, the other three primary bird characters all possess faux–European accents. Michael has an Irish accent, Pierre a French accent, and Fritz a German accent. What are three European-accented parrots doing in a Polynesian-themed show set in an "exotic" Colonialist "Adventureland"? The answer appears to come out of the restaurant-roots of the show and out of the simultaneously appealing and horrifying neuroses of 1950s American culture. The presence of these three European and one fake–Mexican accents in an Adventureland show demonstrates the cultural slippage at the heart of American imperialism, for the

history of American themed restaurants seems tied to shifts in American imperialism. It is as if one foreign bird is as good as any other. The American
movement from restaurants themed to Germany or France to restaurants
themed to Mexico to restaurants themed to Hawaii (paralleling my family's
dining practices — our favorite restaurants were the Bavarian Inn in San
Gabriel, La Parisienne in Monrovia, Ernie's Taco House in Pasadena, and the
Royal Hawaiian in Laguna — all beautifully themed, immersive dining experiences) parallels the return of American GIs, for when American GIs came
back from Germany and France, Americans wanted German or French restaurants, and when GIs came back from Hawaii or other parts of Oceana, Americans craved faux–Polynesian restaurants. Reyner Banham argues that faux
Polynesian restaurants are merely the most extreme Southern California variation of a long line of "plushly underlit" and "gourmet" restaurants from the
Brown Derby to the Velvet Turtle to any number of Spanish Colonial–themed
restaurants (121–122). According to Banham, visiting, living in, or eating in
a building "as strikingly and lovingly ridiculous" as many of the faux–
Polynesian restaurants is an indication that the "traditional cultural and social
restraints have been overthrown and replaced by the preferences of a mobile,
affluent, and consumer-oriented society, in which 'cultural values' and ancient
symbols are handled primarily as methods of claiming or establishing status"
(124). Banham's concept of the adoption of a themed-environment or themed-
architecture as a sign of a cultural shift toward viewing culture as a commodity
and identity as protean and as claimed rather than given is useful for an analysis of both the popularity of Polynesian theming in general and of Disneyland's
popularity specifically.

Walt Disney's decision to build an Enchanted Tiki Room at Disneyland,
as well as his decision the year before, in 1962, to open a Tahitian Terrace
restaurant next door to the future Tiki Room where visitors could view a
"real" luau show, was clearly a response to Hawaii becoming a U.S. state in
1959 and to the growing popularity of Hawaii and Polynesia in the American
consciousness. Following World War II, when GIs returned from the Pacific
theater, more and more books and films about Asia, Polynesia, or other
"exotic" foreign lands began to appear. In 1949 James Michener's collection
of stories about American soldiers serving on "exotic" islands was turned into
the hit Broadway musical *South Pacific* (Marling 82, 86). Norwegian adven-
turer Thor Heyerdahl published his best-selling book *Kon-Tiki* in 1950 (Curtis). The film version of *South Pacific* came out in 1958. Elvis Presley's hit film
Blue Hawaii came out in 1961. With all of these media images depicting Polynesia as a sun-drenched utopia, it was little wonder that Walt Disney added
the Swiss Family Treehouse, the Tahitian Terrace, and the Enchanted Tiki

Room to Disneyland — after all, the allure of escape, now associated with the South Seas, was important to the allure of Disneyland as well. This image of Polynesia as the perfect escape from a hectic life of work for Caucasian and non–Caucasian Americans continues to exist, as writer Sandra Tsing Loh mockingly makes clear in her essay "Tahiti!": "'I'm old, I'm fat, I'm going to Tahiti.' Gauguin thought it, Brando thought it, and last month it was my turn" (111).

The idea that Disneyland is about free play and not about work permeates popular and scholarly literature about the theme park. For example, Pauline Hunt and Ronald Frankenberg argue that "Disneyland is about play, not work" (121). Their contention that the "park fosters a sharp dichotomy between work and play" where even adults "are allowed to re-experience an ideological reconstruction of partially remembered childhood where idling time away in play is legitimated" bears deeper analysis (Hunt and Frankenberg 121, 122). The Enchanted Tiki Room provides us with the perfect artifact with which to test Hunt and Frankenberg's thesis, for the show offers a challenge to Hunt and Frankenberg's contention that Disneyland plays upon adult (and child) nostalgia for a "free" but lost childhood. Walt Disney's Enchanted Tiki Room, as the first of many subsequent Audio-Animatronics shows, illustrates that so much of Disneyland, while clearly pleasurable, is in no way about free-play. On the contrary, with the Tiki Room the Disney Imagineers began to hone their craft of people-moving and audience manipulation that continues with today's generation of Disney theme park rides and shows.

A close analysis of the Tiki Room show demonstrates that the audience is almost never freely playing, but is rather led through the story of the show in a not-so-subtle manner. For example, much of the robotic birds' dialogue is fundamentally about manipulating the audience to act in a certain desired manner. Throughout the show, there are clear cues to the audience indicating that they should act or respond in a certain way. Jose opens the show with "Ah, my siestas are getting' chorter and chorter. Oh, look at all the people. Welcome to Walt Disney's Enchanted Tiki Room." This opening dialogue adds little to Jose's character development and isn't all that humorous or entertaining. Rather, these lines are primarily meant to get the audience's attention focused in the correct direction. This focusing of attention continues with Jose's repeated refrain of "it's chow time." Often, the dialogue is simply what I would call "pointing" communication — in other words, it is designed to "point" the reader's attention in the proper direction, as with dialogue such as: "Look, here come the girls."

The theme song to the attraction that I was obsessed with as a child includes a heavy-handed indication to the audience that they should be happy to be part of the audience. This bragging does not begin to grate on the audience because those who are telling us how great they are are mechanical birds, and because the show offers rude, corn-ball repartee or self-mockery in response to the bird-bragging. For example, Michael, the Irish tenor parrot, states, "I sing so beautiful I should sing solo," to which Jose responds, "Si, so low we can't hear you." And after another song Jose states, "No one laid an egg but me."

This practice of priming the audience pump continues throughout the show, for after every musical number our four robot bird emcees call on the audience to applaud: "Aha! Applause, applause... Si amigos, applause." Not only is the audience constantly being asked to applaud by mechanical birds repeating back a pre-recorded show, but the audience is being encouraged to sing along, both by being told to "Sing along with us" and by the Imagineers' clever placing of people's pre-recorded voices singing throughout the theater in order to cue the actual audience to sing, reassuring them that they won't be alone. The Disney show designers were clearly aware of the realities of group behavior, and used the newest technology to manipulate the group. While we could label the experience of watching the Enchanted Tiki Room as "play," the level of control and manipulation inherent in the design of the show makes the term "play" questionable. This "play" seems much more like "work" in many ways, but work that is hidden as play. In this confusion of the work/play binary, Disney was clearly at the forefront of a shift in the American practice of leisure.

The Enchanted Tiki Room show concludes with more audience manipulation, including reminding the audience members of all the wonderful things they saw, evidently so that they will remember to help Disney to publicize the show to others:

> PIERRE: Messrs, and Mme., it's time to say adieu, but we hope you'll always remember the amazing things which happened in Walt Disney's Enchanted Tiki Room.
> MALE CHORUS: The birdies had their fling [birds sing] / You've heard the flowers sing [flowers sing] / Tikis played the drums [they do so] / Hear them do the chant [Tiki totems chant] / Farewell and Aloha to you.

Finally, the Imagineers, ever worried about moving the last theater full of people out quickly so as to move the new group in a timely fashion, designed a final "joke" and a final song set to the Snow White and the Seven Dwarfs tune "Heigh-Ho":

> JOSE: "Let's give the birds a standing ovation.... Everybody stand up, on your feet, Ole!"
> MICHAEL: "And now as long as you're standing..."
> JOSE: "We have a wonderful trick for you."
> FRITZ: "Ja, a wunderbar trick. Everybody face the door, and the trick is we're going to make you all disappear."

After this last piece of would-be comic business, the song parody of "Heigh-Ho" begins. The humor is used to make the seeming rudeness of the order to the "guests" to leave as quickly as possible more palatable, but the important element of this conclusion is that it once again demonstrates a clear attempt to control the audience and move them.

Just as Walt Disney was attracted to the new Audio-Animatronics robotic technology, used for the first time at the Enchanted Tiki Room, because it removed pretty much all possibility for the unpredictable or the unforeseen, so to did the Disney show designers attempt to eliminate all possibility for unforeseen or unwanted audience behavior from their shows. Thus, while the myths of Disneyland emphasize free play, the reality is that Disney was moving more and more toward a design culture that attempted to eliminate randomness and free play. The irony of the Enchanted Tiki Room thus lies in its juxtaposition of themes of freedom and escape inherent in its trans-exotic Orientalist tropes with its innovative use of cutting-edge Audio-Animatronics technology designed to eliminate the unpredictability of real animals, and new theatrical methods designed to turn the human audience into predictable automatons. Disney's desire to eliminate the random or the unexpected from his theme park shows and attractions demonstrates an anxiety concerning the unpredictability of human behavior too. Disney's use of human-shaped Audio-Animatronics in such attractions as Great Moments with Mr. Lincoln, Pirates of the Caribbean, the Haunted Mansion, and the Carrousel of Progress clearly demonstrates this anxiety.

While critics like Hunt, Frankenberg, and Yoshimoto agree that the Disney theme parks demonstrate an "absolute separation of leisure from work," this binary, as my discussion of the Enchanted Tiki Room demonstrates, appears overstated (Yoshimoto 189). Perhaps Mitsuhiro Yoshimoto is somewhat correct when he argues that "Disneyland succeeds in creating the impression of a utopian space of leisure, from which any trace of work is diligently erased" (189). Certainly, Walt Disney's increasing turn to Audio-Animatronics figures in his theme parks, and his long-time interest in automatons and mechanical simulations of animals and people, might indicate a discomfort with the messiness of actual animals and people or with the display of actual work. On the other hand, as already discussed, the regimentation and control at the heart of this Disney show certainly cannot be read as a sign of a promise of eternal play. Rather, the Disneyland of the Enchanted Tiki Room entices the adult visitor with a false promise of her or his own free play, but in fact gives the visitor an experience so regimented that it would take years for the United States to learn that level of social engineering. Disney's Imagineers were indeed ahead of their time.

Given the dramatic changes that people noted in Disney's personality after his studio was hit by a major animators' strike in 1941, the point at which Disney arguably began to move to the right politically, Disney's turn to Audio-Animatronics might have been a result of an increasing discomfort with real workers. Speaking of his experiments with Audio-Animatronics figures in a 1960 interview, Disney said of these robotic figures: "There is where I am *happy*" (Barrier 290). Despite this reading, I would argue that the allure of Audio-Animatronics figures, both for Disney and his audience, was not simply about the hiding of work, although that might have been one factor. For a perfectionist like Disney bent on total creative control, Audio-Animatronics held the promise of allowing him to "dictate and sequence great numbers of actions for one or more figures," thereby making it "possible to program specific movements of face and head, limbs and body, the character's words and music, and even [to] coordinate the actions of many performers within an entire attraction or show" (*"E" Ticket* 18).

For audiences, and possibly for Disney as well, the appeal of Audio-Animatronics might also have been about the threat of mortality, which could help to explain the seeming paradox of Disney's simultaneous interest in nostalgia and in futurism, as well as his tendency to bring the two together. Disney's earliest experiments with three-dimensional animation demonstrate a tendency to bring together technological futurism and nostalgia. His earliest robotic experiment involved designing a miniature Dancing Man who seemed to be performing on a Victorian-era vaudeville stage; before the Orientalist Tiki Room birds, Disney tried to create another Orientalist dinner show starring an Audio-Animatronics version of Confucius; and Disney was obsessed with creating an animatronic version of President Lincoln (Gordon and Mumford 233; Imagineers 118–119; Stafford 37). In interviews, Disney emphasized the futuristic technology of Audio-Animatronics by calling attention to their use of space-age technology, and Disney's press machine continually underscored the realism of the Audio-Animatronics figures. Despite this emphasis on "realism," it was the audience's awareness that the Audio-Animatronics figures were not real, and the juxtaposition between using futuristic American technological ingenuity to depict nostalgic figures from the past or from the symbolic "past" of Asia, Polynesia, or Africa, that created the ideological power of the Audio-Animatronics. By using the newest technological means to present the past, Disney was subtly underscoring the troubling mythic message of American Manifest Destiny — the United States was the future which would, by capturing the "past" of non–U.S. cultures, appropriate and thus preserve them. And in order to point out that utopian American power to control the world through technology, and thus to overcome national and perhaps even personal death, Disney was willing to highlight the very inauthenticity and deception inherent in Audio-Animatronics, if only fleetingly. Thus, while the Disney Imagineers could have programmed the mechanical birds of the Tiki Room to be "alive" and moving from the very moment the audience entered the theater, they chose not to. Disney and his Imagineers made that choice, perhaps, because they wanted the audience to fully experience that moment when the inanimate, "dead" birds came to life. It was in that moment that Disney made his greatest ideological claim to American technological imperialism. It was also in the moment when the birds transformed from immobile and lifeless to seemingly alive that Disney may have expressed his own, and his audience's, full-throated desire for a reprieve from death.

Nostalgia is a longing for a lost past that cannot be reclaimed and that possibly never existed in the first place. And utopianism is a longing for an ideal future that will never be seen and may never exist. Both nostalgia and utopianism therefore show evidence of a desire for transcendence, as well as an existential anxiety concerning mortality and the present. For the person, like Disney, fixated on the past and the future, it is the present and the ineluctable reality of mortality that is the problem. The automaton offers a strangely spiritual if uncanny promise of escape from mortality. As Victoria Nelson explains, the modern electrical puppet of the twentieth century, while "empirically speaking" a lifeless object, appears on the silver screen or in the theater to be alive, sometimes more so than a human actor (249–250). Longtime Disney artist and Imagineer John Hench explained that Disneyland was usually about reassurance; namely, the reassurance that we will somehow live despite the constant threat of death: "You know, since we're born, the first thing we fight for in life is that feeling of being alive — and it's the last thing, too. We never want to give up that experience of being alive. And that is the secret of Disneyland" (Littaye 157). Disneyland, Hench asserted, offered much-needed reassurance.

Walt Disney's Enchanted Tiki Room, opening as it did in 1963, arguably at the end of one era of American cultural and political history and the start of another, summed up much about post–World War II U.S. culture: a faith in technology and a firm belief that the United States was at the forefront of technological progress sure to bring about a better world, and a sense of nostalgia, wonder, and loss for those "exotic" cultures thought to be not easily assimilated by the increasingly dominant American culture. Walt Disney's first true Audio-Animatronics show, given its connection to aesthetic and ideological issues as diverse as nostalgia and technological utopianism, cultural slippage, wonder, American hegemony, and the creation of the American subject in opposition to the depiction of ethnic otherness, therefore stands as a fascinating and complex work of art worthy of thoughtful cultural analysis.

Works Cited

Banham, Reyner. *Los Angeles: The Architecture of Four Ecologies.* New York: Penguin, 1971.
Barrier, Michael. *The Animated Man: A Life of Walt Disney.* Berkeley: University of California Press, 2007.
Baudrillard, Jean. "Simulations." In *Continental Aesthetics: Romanticism to Postmodernism: An Anthology,* edited by Richard Kearney and David Rasmussen, 411–430. Malden, MA: Blackwell, 2001. Originally published as *Simulations.* New York: Semiotext, 1983.
Curtis, Wayne. "Tiki." AmericanHeritage.com. (Article first appeared in *American Heritage,* August/September 2006).
The 'E' Ticket. 25 (Winter 1996).
Fjellman, Stephen M. *Vinyl Leaves: Walt Disney World and America.* Boulder, CO: Westview, 1992.
Gordon, Bruce, and David Mumford. *Disneyland: The Nickel Tour.* Santa Clarita, CA: Camphor Tree, 1995.
Greenblatt, Stephen. *Marvelous Possessions: The Wonders of the New World.* Chicago: University of Chicago Press, 1991.
Hermanson, Scott. "Truer Than Life: Disney's Animal Kingdom." In *Rethinking Disney: Private Control, Public Dimensions,* edited by Mike Budd and Max H. Kirsch, 199–227. Middletown, CT: Wesleyan University Press, 2005.
Hunt, Pauline, and Ronald Frankenberg. "It's a Small World: Disneyland, the Family, and Multiple Re-representations of American Childhood." In *Constructing and Reconstructing Childhood: Contemporary Issues in the Sociological Study of Childhood,* edited by Allison James and Alan Prout, 107–125. London: Falmer, 1997.
The Imagineers. *Walt Disney Imagineering: A Behind the Dreams Look at Making the Magic Real.* New York: Disney, 1996.
Kirsten, Sven A. *The Book of Tiki: The Cult of Polynesian Pop in Fifties America.* Los Angeles: Taschen, 2000.
Lewis, George H. "Beyond the Reef: Cultural Constructions of Hawaii in Mainland America, Australia and Japan." *Journal of Popular Culture.* 30.2 (Fall 1996): 123–135.
Littaye, Alain. "Interview with John Hench, June 24, 1996." In *Walt's People—Volume 1: Talking Disney with the Artists Who Knew Him,* edited by Didier Ghez, 153–165. [United States]: Xlibris, 2005.
Loh, Sandra Tsing. *Depth Takes a Holiday: Essays from Lesser Los Angeles.* New York: Riverhead, 1996.
Marling, Karal Ann. *Behind the Magic: 50 Years of Disneyland.* Dearborn, MI: Henry Ford, 2005.
Moore, Charles, Peter Becker, and Regula Campbell. *The City Observed: Los Angeles: A Guide to Its Architecture and Landscapes.* New York: Vintage, 1984.
Nelson, Victoria. *The Secret Life of Puppets.* Cambridge: Harvard University Press, 2001.
Pratt, Mary Louise. *Imperial Eyes: Travel Writing and Transculturation.* New York: Routledge, 1992.
Savigliano, Marta E. "Tango in Japan and the World Economy of Passion." In *Re-Made in Japan: Everyday Life and Consumer Taste in a Changing Society,* edited by Joseph J. Tobin, 235–52. New Haven, CT: Yale University Press, 1992.

Schaffer, Scott. "Disney and the Imagineering of Histories." *Postmodern Culture* 6.3 (May 1996), *http://muse.jhu.edu/journals/postmodern_culture/v006/6.3schaffer.html*).

Stafford, Barbara Maria. "Revealing Technologies/Magical Domains." In *Devices of Wonder: From the World in a Box to Images on a Screen*. Barbara Maria Stafford and Frances Terpak, 1–142. Los Angeles: Getty, 2001.

Willis, Susan. "Disney's Bestiary." In *Rethinking Disney: Private Control, Public Dimensions*, edited by Mike Budd and Max H. Kirsch, 53–71. Middletown, CT: Wesleyan University Press, 2005.

Yoshimoto, Mitsuhiro. "Images of Empire: Tokyo Disneyland and Japanese Cultural Imperialism." In *Disney Discourse: Producing the Magic Kingdom*, edited by Eric Smoodin, 181–199. New York: Routledge, 1994.

Disneyland's Variations

Disneyland Paris
A Clash of Cultures

CHRISTIAN RENAUT

One day in the summer of 1987, Ollie Johnston,[1] one of the top veteran animators of the Disney Studios, asked me: "What do you think of that whole business over in France, the Disneyland Park, is it gonna work?" He thought I, as a Frenchman, could have a better understanding of what was to be expected. I answered him that I thought the Disney managers didn't realize how different the European visitors would be from the American ones. As a matter of fact, the first time I had been to Disneyland in Anaheim, I had been amazed at the quietness and discipline of an audience that was largely American. I couldn't imagine the same park near Paris with French people not trying to overtake others in the queues, or Italians not trying to crisscross Main Street even one minute before the beginning of the parade. My misgivings would prove partly right. In fact, from the beginning of the negotiations and all through the building of what would first be called Euro Disneyland, it is indeed the gap between two cultures which would make it hard to implement such an ambitious project. CEO Jay Rasulo, who managed Euro Disneyland in 1998, later admitted in *Time*, "We had not yet had an on-the-ground experience in a multicultural environment, it was really the first park that had the majority of its guests coming from very diverse cultural backgrounds" (qtd. in Chu 44). But that wouldn't be as visible as I anticipated in the lines of edgy visitors but more in what was intellectually at stake.

Before the Disney managers eventually decided that Marne-La-Vallée, a small village surrounded with huge flat fields of sugar beets, should be the spot, there were already amusement parks in France. A total of seventy parks could be visited, but most of them had difficulties. The most famous one is still open today, Parc Asterix, although many thought its days were numbered when Mickey would be around. Others like the Smurfs Park, the Zygofolies Park at Nice or the Mirapolis Park either closed down or were bought by other companies with huge layoffs and budget reductions, providing that French people weren't that interested in spending their money in such parks or that what they were offered didn't live up to their expectations. But, unabated, Robert Fitzpatrick, the first boss of Euro Disneyland, said in *La Vie Française*: "We have nothing to do with them! We are investing 15 billion francs in the first stage of our project while they are putting less than a billion" (qtd. in Silbert 16). In reality, most French people and many around France didn't really know what the Disney park was all about, except for the lucky few who had traveled to Florida or California. As explained in *The Kansas City Star* in 1991, "According to Euro Disneyland spokesman Nicolas de Schnonen, misunderstandings have arisen with the union because people in Europe don't understand what an American-style 'resort' is" (qtd. in Powell). Of course, many TV shows had boasted of the magnificence and the fun of the two American parks, but still, most thought it would be another amusement park with merry-go-rounds, some thrilling roller-coasters, French fry stands all over the place with a few Mickeys shaking hands here and there.

But for some people in France who knew better about the parks and all that one might carry in terms of ideologies, boosting of American supremacy over Europe, the project was clearer. Very soon, the idea of an American park as famous as Disneyland in France looked like a terrible threat on European culture, and many intellectuals, journalists, and politicians started to voice their disagreement and sometimes their disgust. Of course, it is true that the relationship between France and the USA may be used as a backdrop to all that turmoil. It has been a love/hate relationship ever since Lafayette set off for America. Now and then, there have been clashes, often enhanced by narrow-minded journalists or frustrated politicians. The instance of the disagreement over the involvement in Iraq war in 2003 is revealing, with some of the American press urging a boycott of French products. But when it comes to remembering the past and what the French population owes to Americans, nobody will ever endanger the strong link. However, surely, one of the reasons for this chaotic relationship is jealousy. The French are certainly jealous of a country whose economy is unchallenged with all its cortege of cultural invasion. The Americans are jealous of the cultural and artistic legacy of a very old nation that does nothing to hide its arrogance about it. As a consequence, when the Disney authorities decide to invade the country of Victor Hugo, Voltaire and Baudelaire with Mickey, Pluto and Sneezy, many take it very badly. It is even worse when it is quickly realized that in front of the dollars that will soon pour in, it will be quasi-impossible to say "no." Money versus culture. That's how many understood it in the late 1980s.

The Disney films, although very successful in France, were scorned by some newspapers, which harshly criticized their stories for children, saying they harmed the original fairy tales from Europe. Papers like *Libération* or *Télérama*, the teachers' favorite, had scarcely praised any of the animated features, especially the lackluster achievements of the 1980s. From *The Black Cauldron* in 1985 to *Oliver & Company* in 1988, that period was an all-time low in the history of animation at the Disney Studios. Journalists and reviewers displayed a marked preference for Eastern-European cartoons or Tex Avery parodies. Very soon, the whole operation was nicknamed "a cultural Chernobyl" by Ariane Mnouchkine, a celebrated movie and stage director. That phrase was used again and again by the French *intelligentsia*. What happened to Jean-Luc Choplin, the former director of French ballet at the Opera de Paris, is very revealing. After five years at the Opera, he decided to join Euro Disneyland and also became head of the millennium ceremonies for Disney in the United States. Here is what he answered in *Telerama*: "In France, people are locked up in categories. I belonged to the cultural world, so, I had betrayed them and sold my soul to the devil — at least, that's what most people told me at the time" (qtd. in Pascal-Mousselard 16).

One of the most anti–Euro Disneyland spokespeople was the famed and charismatic French Culture and Education Minister, Jack Lang. In his typical way, he tried to please everyone by saying in *Newsweek*: "I have never, never denounced the American 'cultural invasion.'" I'm horrified by the expression, which is not mine. I'm one of the principal propagators in Europe of modern American culture. The America of the daring, the inventive of ideas, is dear to my heart. It's another matter, I'd say, when you talk about culture of standardization, the culture of the lowest common denominator. That is not so much an American culture as it is a marketing one" (qtd. in Dickey 12). In fact, the difficulty for Jack Lang was to be believable, given that, as a left-wing politician belonging to a government who couldn't refuse the 12,000 jobs it meant in a context of high unemployment, he had no choice but to go along with it. The left-wing president of France himself, François Mitterrand, would years later acknowledge he would never visit the park, as it wasn't his cup of tea. An article in *Panorama* in 1992 confirms it: "After criticizing the American culture and denouncing its wild imperialism until 1981, the left-wing government had but to negotiate with Disney to fight against unemployment and carry on with the development of the Ile-de-France region" (Leboucher 66). A few people wouldn't go along with the general outcry, like the sociologist of free time, Joffre Dumazedier, who said in *Le Journal du*

Dimanche in 1991: "At the time of Louis XIV, Europe spoke French. Then England fascinated the 19th century. Today, it's up to the Americans, then it'll be the Japanese. It is a stupid scare. Who cares Disney is American as long as it's well made" (qtd. in Johanns 8).

Here lay the key to the project: with the priority in France being employment, who could turn down so many job offers and win the following elections? The government did lose the next elections, but they had approved of the project before. The following government, headed by then Prime Minister Jacques Chirac, was far more pro–Disneyland, in the tradition of right-wing people who admired any sense of enterprise, whatever the cost, as well as the American model. As Michael Eisner wrote in his biography, "Chirac would prove more sympathetic to our project, but his arrival meant dealing with an entirely new group of officials" (267). It would have been interesting to know what would have happened had the unemployment rate been far lower.

As aforesaid, this terrible reality wounded French people's pride, and especially the left-wingers. So, their representatives did their best to look like they defied Disney people and imposed a whole array of criteria. The idea was as follows: if we are to be invaded by American culture on our own soil, let's do our best to counter-attack it and impose our culture as much as we can. In *Le journal du dimanche* in 1985, Michel Giraud said: "All along the negotiations which are being started now, I intend to put the French cultural interests forward by introducing French or European themes in the park" (qtd. in Schlumberger 20). So, then started a very hypocritical series of statements and dead-born projects to gain the *intelligentsia*'s sympathies, a vain endeavor anyway. In many interviews, it was said over and over that after all, most Disney movies were born out of European stories and that it was a fair return to pay a tribute to those tales from Denmark, Germany or France. As reported by *La Croix*, the writer Ray Bradbury, a friend of Walt Disney's, stated at the opening of the French park: "France and Europe are witnessing a just return of what they had given to America. It's a real cultural exchange" (qtd. in Royer 25).

To be honest, it is true that the Disney Imagineers[2] back in Glendale, California, tried to devise new attractions which could glorify the old European legends and books. But, as we will see later the whole thing eventually boiled down to a few details here and there. I had the very rare privilege to see a model of the future French park when I was doing interviews for my first book,[3] and there were clear attempts to do so.

These few concessions and a whole seduction operation were nothing compared to what the French government would yield in the end, and many thought that the cunning Disney businessmen were slowly but steadily fooling them, which caused even more anger and bitterness. As a whole, in order to convince the Disney managers to choose the eastern side of Paris instead of the Barcelona area, the government did things they had never done for any other company, including, the French Parc Asterix. Among the concessions were "to cut the value-added tax on ticket sales to just 7 percent instead of the usual 18.5 percent" as reported in *Fortune*. In addition, the State and local governments agreed to extend the mass transit line to the site and pay $125 million for this. Additional highways were paid for by the same organizations, paying another $105 million, not to mention funds for the roadways, sewers and telephone lines. The price of the acre was $100,000, very far from its actual value then. It was in fact, the price of the early 1970s. Furthermore, incredibly good loans were granted. All those efforts were meant to make up for the numerous assets that Barcelona in Spain was said to have, in particular, the sunny weather. This was rather a flimsy argument when we remember that many attractions at Tokyo Disneyland were built to protect the visitors from the very rainy climate. In fact, from a vantage point, it seems that the Disney people were extremely smart in dealing with the two possible options between Paris and Barcelona. The truth is, as some Disney executives now say off the record, very early, the decision had been made to go for Paris but that sounding reluctant was an excellent way of blackmailing the French politicians who kept thinking of the offered jobs. In his book, Michael Eisner almost acknowledges this by saying, "My heart was with France from the start" (265) after making a long list of the assets of the French zone. To top it all, the preliminary studies quickly showed that the bad geographical position of the Spanish city would entail a low rate of visitors, i.e., six million a year, compared to about twelve million people in Paris.

But The Walt Disney Company quickly realized that with all these negotiations and the anti–Disney campaign in the press, they had to react and try to give a better image. That's what we called "Seduction Operation." First, some Disney executives and publicity men started to advocate a strong link between France and Disney. There was the never-proved theory, as suggested by Bob Thomas, Disney's official biographer, that Disney was from Norman descent and originally called D'Isigny. So how would the French be aggressive towards a friend of the family? Then, there were speeches — for example, "I wouldn't want to be arrogant, but we are bound to succeed for three reasons. The first one is that Walt Disney has been in Europe for generations. No grandma or dad or child has ever grown up without the animated features, or read Journal de Mickey from time to time. We have left here a sixty-year-old cultural legacy," as Robert Fitzpatrick told Frank Johannes. In *La Vie Française*, he was reported saying: "Europe has always been very important to Walt Disney" (qtd. in Silbert 15). By the way, it is true that the creator of the empire had a fascination for Europe, and had traveled there as often as he could. It is during one of his travels in the summer of 1949 that he went from France to Scandinavia and drew many ideas for his future Disneyland park in California and, especially, made it clear what he'd rather not see in his park. He was impressed by the Tivoli Gardens of Copenhagen in Denmark. In the book *Inside the Dream*, the TV celebrity Art Linkletter tells about that visit with Walt Disney: "He was making notes all the time — about the lights, the chairs, the seats, and the food. I asked him what he was doing, and he replied, "I'm just making notes about something that I've always dreamed of, a great, great playground for the children and families of America" (qtd. in Greene 106).

But all this wasn't enough; the local mayors and civil servants had to be persuaded that paradise was ahead. It is true that many mayors of the little towns near Marne-La-Vallée like Magny-Le-Hongre or Bailly-Romainvilliers hated the idea of the park on their grounds. Therefore, around thirty of them were invited to see for themselves what Walt Disney World was all about. Back home, they had difficulties concealing how impressed they had been. Needless to say, they had been welcomed in a way that could flatter the egos of then-anonymous mayors of unknown villages. Who can beat the Americans when it comes to public relations? Later, a store with Mickey's pointed hat as a logo was built up to invite would-be visitors to have an inkling of what they could expect. Robert Fitzpatrick boasted in *Entreprises:* "The public has already shown their interest for the park as, since last December, 160,000 people have visited the information center" (qtd. in Haas and Lafont 6). The choice of Robert Fitzpatrick himself was part of that whole operation. He was beyond doubt the most French of the Disney executives: fond of French literature, married to a French wife and speaking French.

So, there was just no stopping Disney's steamroller and the deal was signed on March 24, 1987. Some die-hard farmers or intellectuals tried to thwart Eisner whenever they could, but the deal was on.

Yet, the cultural clash was not visible yet. It took the first months of recruiting workers — craftsmen, plumbers, electricians, foremen, cooks — to start unveiling the reality of this gap between two worlds. Very soon, thousands and thousands of people rushed to the employment offices set up by the Disney employers. And very quickly, the smiles faded away. For months on TV and in the press, dozens of witnesses were interviewed, voicing their protest, along with trade-unions, about the endless list of restrictions in order to work for Disney: no beard, no moustache (unlike Walt Disney), hardly any make-up, short fingernails, no earrings at all for men and only 2 cm-long ones for women. France was discovering the Disney Style: a whole special mentality and hard work. When the lucky ones then learned they would have to go to a "Disney University," they thought they were dreaming. That university, which doesn't seem to cause any trouble in the United States, was taken as a brainwash training camp and, French people being who they are, many would rebel, not accepting to be as submissive as they were asked to be. Among many stories of disappointed or laid-off employees, there's one by a former executive who testified in *Capital*: "One month after I was recruited, I was sent to be trained in Florida. Once at the hotel, I eat hardly anything at the bar, that is beer and hamburger. On the next day, a top-man of the hotel section welcomes me, cold as ice, in his office. Not a single word. Not a handshake. With a closed face, he ends up saying: 'the next time you drink alcohol in public, you will be fired.' I had been spied" (40).

We can easily understand that, seen from an American standpoint, being so touchy about the rules in a country with between 10 percent and 12 percent unemployed people was a bit too much. Suddenly, the French were discovering how much they loved a certain quality of life whereas the Americans focused on the salary and climbing the ladder of success.

Year after year, more and more employees left, resigned, or complained about working in the park. In the meantime, the Disney bosses were busy repeating that smiling to the "guests" and not the "customers" was essential. For many young waiters, waitresses, hostesses or dancers, long hours of work for a low wage was reason enough not to smile. Later, the firm had to be less demanding in terms of level of English spoken or credentials in some fields.

When the park opened in 1992, there were only a few problems caused by bitter trade-unionists. Recounting the event, the *Los Angeles Times* reported, "Strolling down the circa–1900 American 'main street' with his French-born wife, Sylvie, and a handful of security guards, Fitzpatrick described the rail strike, which shut down a major line leading from Paris and the western Parisian suburbs to the site, as 'part of the simple fundamental reality of living in (strike prone) France.'" Anyhow, the public rushed as expected. It is interesting to note that for the VIP opening day, many people came without any hesitation. Bernard Kouchner, a well-known left-wing politician, Bernard-Henri Levy, a famous member of the Parisian intelligentsia, and even Bob Geldof were there. But, some months later, many complained about the expensive restaurants and the impossibility of drinking alcohol in the land of wines. In fact, Disney people acknowledge now that they made a few mistakes in handling the French public and the media. Blunders included the refusal to offer special discounts to an English charity taking care of ill children, a comment by an executive in the press saying Disney is better than anyone else, and saying that Disneyland was as immortal as the Egyptian pyramids. The use of the character Scrooge during the launching of the buying of stock was also a terrible mistake. Michael Eisner had the honesty to mention some of these errors in his book. But, as time went by and the profits were not so high, things changed. Disney got more humble, recruited a French manager to replace Fitzpatrick and made more and more concessions. It is true that the situation, in spite of the masses of visitors, got alarming, with 7.1 billion francs lost in two years (in 1995). As a consequence, most of the projects were shelved or delayed like the second park, Walt Disney Studios Park.

We might think that what is now called Disneyland Paris is a failure. It surely is for stock holders: in 1992 the share was worth 23 euros, but it collapsed to a mere 1 euro. Anyway, it is far from being a flop in terms of architecture. We could even assert that it is probably the best as compared to the other parks, because it is obvious that the designers felt a real challenge to achieve something exceptional in the very land where real chateaus and medieval castles were just a few kilometers away. In addition to feeling they had to surpass themselves, they also benefited from years of experience and new technologies. All they had learned from building three parks from Anaheim to Tokyo could be used to avoid any snafus. I haven't been to the Tokyo park but I have been on several occasions to the Florida and California ones, and I can say that, even though we miss some American favorites such as Splash Mountain, New Orleans Square or the Country Bear Jamboree, the French park is probably the most beautiful. Many who have been to the others agree. The landscaping is particularly well done, be it in Fantasyland, Adventureland or Discoveryland. The Imagineers did their best to work everything to the minute detail. But what about the promises to make it a tribute to the European tales, which was one of the pledges of the Disney administration?

If we compare the Paris park to the others, the European touch is not that easy to see at first sight. Main Street is still a reminder of Victorian America that was so dear to Walt Disney. It had even been thought at one time to make a reminder of the violent 1920s Chicago, but it was quickly dropped. The Sleeping Beauty Castle is another rendition of the castles in the other parks, but what is most pleasing is the preservation of the famous square trees designed by Eyvind Earle[4] in the feature. It is true that the castle is magnificent, but there's nothing more European in it. Of course, Adventureland is not the place where Disney could pay homage to Europe as it is dedicated to exotism and the Caribbean. Next to it, Frontierland is the same glorification of the Wild West in America. Too bad Disney didn't put a replica of the New Orleans district, which is such a great achievement. After all, who built up Louisiana? The best area to make the park more European is undoubtedly Fantasyland. There is a wonderful carrousel named "Lancelot Carrousel" but there's no allusion to the Knights of the Round Table except beautiful horses. All the rest, from "Peter Pan's Flight" to the "Mad Hatter's Tea Cups" is the same. We can mention Alice's Garden, which is a labyrinth, but it is all a reference to the Disney version, not Lewis Carroll's, which sounds sensible. Indeed, nothing has been added. It is in Discoveryland that we can see the European "plus." It is rather funny when we think that the original old Tomorrowland in Disneyland was based on American technology and the space adventure. This time the designers had chosen to go for a nineteenth-century look with many references to Jules Verne: the Nautilus (but it was already there in the other parks), a movie featuring Jules Verne and H.G. Wells, the entrance to Videopolis with a Jules Verne type of balloon, and "Space Mountain," which is vaguely a tribute to the writer. As for the rest, "Star Tours" and "Captain EO" had nothing to do with Europe. As far as the hotels are concerned, the names speak for themselves: Sequoia Lodge, Davy Crockett Ranch, New York Hotel, Santa Fe Hotel, Cheyenne Hotel and Newport Bay Club.

There was no keeping that promise. Disney has consistently reworked the original tales and legends from Europe but the park was neither going to include characters Disney hadn't featured nor, for example, return to Tenniel's drawings of Lewis Carroll's characters so as to pay a tribute to British literature.

By the way, did the visitors expect to see that? Sure, they wanted to drink espressos and wine, sure they wanted more comfortable and cheaper restaurants, the possibility to picnic, but what the children, and even their parents wanted was Mickey, Disney's Peter Pan and Disney's Cinderella. That's the whole issue about it. Scholars believe that Disney has harmed and spoiled the original tales while others think they have more appeal and more chances to survive in the Disney version. This raises the question: why had the Europeans never built a park with attractions that would have been more faithful to ... to what? To illustrate the stories, you must first find a design, which may be rejected by many. The Disney machine is so powerful that only its versions of the stories remain, not the originals. But those who lament this seem to forget that most fairy tales were altered when the Grimm brothers or Charles Perrault decided to make one definitive version out of many oral ones. The problem is more economic. Disney imposes a version because Disney is a strong multinational.

In that case, why doesn't the park work so well? It has been in deep water for years although visitors come in masses. It seems that here again, the clash of cultures is prevalent. The European visitor is not the same as the American one. He won't spend his money the same way, or won't spend it at all. As said in *Le Monde*: "The Europeans spend about $12 a visit, that is half what the Americans spend" (Robert 40). And this study was based on the habits of the Europeans in the American parks, where the tickets are cheaper, leaving more options to buy dolls or food within the boundaries of the parks. Let's try to analyze the reasons.

First, the economy in Europe has not been so good, with its populations fearing a possible lay-off almost any time and a growing unemployment rate, especially in France, and more recently even in Germany. The visitors are thrifty, and won't buy so many items in the shops. For the same reason, they won't go to the expensive hotels around. This is the main cause of the trouble: the Disney managers thought visitors would rush to the luxurious hotels and they don't, while Japanese, Australians, or Americans do. They are never fully occupied, usually about 75 percent. Meanwhile many hotel chains understood they could make a profit by building some hotels in the neighboring towns. Last of all, the growing success of trailers adds to the Disney people's dismay.

Another reason is the lack of Disney culture. American families have been raised with the *Mickey Mouse Club*, the TV shows and the Disney songs. Such is not the case in France. We have many more celebrities with Asterix, Tintin or more recently Titeuf, who have really had an impact on our ways of thinking and enjoying ourselves. Many jokes from Asterix's albums have been in the French language. Although the market of comic strip merchandise and collectors is well known here, Disneyana is hardly ever sought, except by some fans. The showcases of the few Disney stores in France, including the shops within the Disney Village or the park, had to be thought over when it was realized that teddy bears, dolls and clothes were what kids would rather get. In *La Vie Française*, Gary Wilson, vice-president of The Walt Disney Company at the time said, "Surrounded with his whole family, Minnie, Donald, Dingo [Goofy], Pluto and other characters, that incredible little mouse is the leader of a much cleaner culture than the American one, the Disney culture" (12). Most Europeans just don't know what that culture is about.

Moreover, French people, or more largely, European people, especially from Northern Europe and Germany (the bulk of visitors) are not the kind to wear Goofy caps whereas it's not unusual to see fathers wearing them in the USA without a second thought. American people have a way of behaving like children, an old cliché in Europe that has always astonished French people. Here, people will always think twice. What will the others think? Can I really do that? Surely, our cultural heritage is heavy and in the country of cathedrals, Renaissance chateaus and Louis XIV, there's always something in the back of our minds that makes us refrain from doing what others would, regardless of any consideration. That's why you won't see the European visitors applauding like crazy at the shows or parades. They will keep some distance, or even look cold. It is less true of people from the countries neighboring the Mediterranean Sea, with their hot tempers and taste for feasting, but they are fewer. What must be difficult for Americans to understand is that Europeans feel more free in terms of relationships, drinks or language. Jacques Chirac, himself, kidded Michael Eisner about the well-known American Puritanism that prevents Americans from drinking alcohol or beer in the open or buying them in super-markets or kissing in public. But Mickey's world is not that world; it is definitely an American world.

So, what about the other French parks? Have they, as many foresaw, closed down? Have they multiplied? Have they been influenced by Disneyland? Most people believed the Parc Asterix wouldn't survive the opening of Euro Disneyland in 1992. After a time of doubts, the park has fared better and better. Of course, the number of visitors is far lower than at Disneyland: an average of 1.7 million. But what was decided in 1999 was to redesign the vil-lage, an idea that certainly came after seeing the superb landscaping of the Disney park. What happened is that many who wanted to express their disdain for the American park wanted to support the French one which had never benefitted from any of the government's gifts. Besides, the ticket is far cheaper, which is important as many come from the North of France, a region which has suffered a lot, economically speaking, in recent years with a high unem-ployment rate. Unlike Disneyland, the park appeals to French people first, and only 15 percent visitors come from abroad, as compared to about 60 per-cent in Disneyland. That's why the park has played the French card more and more regarding the attractions. All the other parks, and especially those estab-lished long before Disneyland, decided to improve their look. With Disney-land now in France, the standards were much higher, and many managers knew it. Without necessarily trying to copy, they all gained in efficiency, design and professionalism. The best examples are probably the Futuroscope in Poitiers and Le Puy-du-Fou in Vendée, where the technologies and story-telling shows are unchallenged by Disney now. But it's interesting to notice that these two parks have a clear pedagogical aim in mind. Strangely enough, the Disney people also decided to develop this strategy. For instance, 2004–2005 was Jules Verne's year in the park, and Disney executives promoted edu-cational visits for all teachers in France and their classes. Maybe they understand that somewhere, Europeans have always felt a need to justify their visits with a more serious reason. As if having fun couldn't be reason enough. As *Panorama* proclaims: "Hence, the three usual critiques about Disney cul-ture. It flatters the tourists' passivity, who come as entertainment consumers, without really creating or learning anything" (69). Still, the attendance at

Disneyland is greater than at any other park in France. At its lowest, it was still 8 million people, with the peak years so far having been 2002 (13.4 million) and 2006 (13.1 million).

When Disney managers started working on the project, they knew that dealing with the French, or more largely the European audiences would be a challenge. They might not have anticipated how hard it would be. All the estimations were very positive before the opening. Stockholders beamed with satisfaction and many were eager to see the park. Even more ambitious projects, like hotels and new parks were on the drawing boards. But things have been difficult. Perhaps the Japanese experience blinded The Walt Disney Company. On the contrary, there everything seems to have gone smoothly. But the Japanese people are not the French. Even though the French people are very influenced by the American model, from hamburgers to jeans, they seem less passionate about the United States than the Japanese are. And by the way, there are more and more manga buffs in France, who are crazy about Japanese cartoons and look down on Disney's. Moreover, although shaky for a while, the Japanese economy and especially the very strong yen must have contributed to making things easier.

Once in a while, and especially every time there's a new accounting balance published in the press, some foresee the worst, even a future closing down of the park, which is unlikely. But it is true that the second park, the "Walt Disney Studios" is far less successful than expected. As recalled by Corinne Scamama, in *L'Express*, "It was expected to reach 17 million visitors a year, and in the end, it almost deters some visitors from coming" (2). The Disney management counts a lot on the newly opened attraction "The Tower of Terror" to attract more visitors to that forsaken park. However, the Disneyland Park is beautiful, and that's what matters. Undoubtedly, both French managers and Disney's top people have learned from that experience. They have learned about the others, and probably about themselves too.

Notes

1. Ollie Johnston is known as one of the famous "Nine Old Men" of animation at the Disney Studios. He worked there from 1935 to 1978. He often worked with his long-time friend, the late Frank Thomas. Among his many characters are Bambi, Alice, Mr. Smee, Lady, Sleeping Beauty fairies, Baloo, Bernard and Bianca, and so many more.
2. The Imagineers are the designers, engineers, architects and technicians who work on designing the parks. It is a combination of the word *imagination* and *engineers*.
3. I was then working on *De Blanche-Neige à Hercule*. Dreamland, 1997. It was an analysis of 27 Disney animated features based on numerous interviews and illustrations.
4. Eyvind Earle worked at the Disney Studios between 1951 and 1960. He was a back-

ground artist who then became the art director on *Sleeping Beauty* (1959). He had a very particular style based on square shapes and angular lines.

Works Cited

Chu, Jeff. "Happily Ever After?" *Time* 25 March 2002: 44.

Dickey, Christopher. "The America of Ideas Is Dear to My Heart." *Newsweek* 13 April 1992: 12.

Eisner, Michael, and Tony Schwartz. *Work in Progress*. New York: Random House, 1998.

Greene, Katherine, and Richard Greene. *Inside the Dream: The Personal Story of Walt Disney*. New York: Disney, 2001.

Haas, Patrick, and Juliette Lafont. "Robert Fitzpatrick: Nous avons pris le meilleur de nos autres parcs." *Entreprises* 29 April 1991: 6.

"Introducing Walt d'Isigny." *The Economist,* 11 April 1992.

Johanns, Franck. "Premier Voyage á Mickey-en-France." *Journal du dimanche,* 15 September 1991: 8.

Leboucher, Marc. "EuroDisney la culture du Dollar." *Panorama* March 1992: 66+.

"Mickey arrives in France." *Los Angeles Times,* 13 April 1992.

Pascal-Mousselard, Olivier. "L'homme qui a 'trahi' l'Opéra pour Disney." *Télérama* 29 October 1997: 16.

Powell, Nicholas. "Mickey Mouse Clashes with French Unions." *Kansas City Star* 6 March 1991.

Robert, Marie-Christine. "Astérix, Gargantua, les Schtroumpfs et les autres." *Le Monde* 24 March 1987: 40.

Royer, Philippe. "Walt Disney a semé tous vents." *La Croix* 4 December 2002: 25.

Schlumberger, Judith. "Voici Disneyland comme vous y serez." *Journal du dimanche* 22 December 1985: 20.

Scamama, Corinne. "Contes et Mécomptes. " *L'Express,* 28 March 2007.

Silbert, Nathalie. "Mickey roi de la bourse." *La Vie Française* 7 October 1989: 12+.

Thomas, Bob. *Walt Disney: An American Original.* New York: Simon and Schuster, 1976.

Tully, Shawn. "The Real Estate Coup at Euro Disneyland." *Fortune* 28 April 1986: 172.

Hong Kong Disneyland
Feng-Shui Inside the Magic Kingdom

Derham Groves

In 1993 executives of The Walt Disney Company began searching Australia, East Asia and South East Asia for a suitable site for a new theme park — the company's eleventh worldwide. The selection criteria included a large flat expanse of land near a major city with significant tourism, an established hospitality industry, reliable communications and mild weather for year-round operations. In 1996 Disney appeared to be on the verge of announcing plans to build a park in Shanghai when the Chinese government suddenly ceased negotiations because the company had backed the film *Kundun* directed by Martin Scorsese, which dramatized the life of the fourteenth Dalai Lama and China's invasion of Tibet. Perhaps to make amends Disney soon afterwards released *Mulan*, the company's thirty-sixth animated feature film, which told the sixth-century Chinese folktale of a noble Chinese girl who fought in the emperor's army in place of her crippled father. While this film may have successfully placated the Chinese government, it failed to impress many Chinese filmgoers who thought that the story was too Westernised. The avid anti-communist Walt Disney (1901–1966) and the fervent anti-capitalist Mao Zedong (1893–1976) were probably spinning in their graves!

In 1999 Disney announced plans to build a new Disneyland style theme park on a 130-hectare site on Lantau Island, the largest of the 236 islands that comprise Hong Kong, about a 30-minute train ride from downtown. "We looked at potential sites all over the city, but most of them were surrounded by high-rise buildings that would have compromised the Disney experience," explained Wing Chao, The Walt Disney Company's executive vice president of master planning, architecture and design worldwide (qtd. in Krivda 10).

138

Walt Disney believed that nothing should violate the visual integrity of his theme parks; otherwise, their ability to distance visitors from the outside world would be seriously undermined. Discussing the original Disneyland at Anaheim California he explained: "I don't want the public to see the real world they live in while they're in the park. I want them to feel they are in another world" (qtd. in Sklar). So a berm twenty feet high and over a mile long was constructed to screen Disneyland from its mundane surroundings.

Named Hong Kong Disneyland the new theme park was a joint venture between The Walt Disney Company, which invested $316 million for a 43 percent stake in the park, and the government of the Hong Kong Special Administration Region (HKSAR), which invested $419 million for the remaining 57 percent. In addition the HKSAR loaned Disney $718 million over 25 years; it spent $1.81 billion to build the new theme park; and it spent another $1.75 billion on associated infrastructure works. The latter included a new rail link between Sunny Bay station on the suburban line and Hong Kong Disneyland capable of carrying over 7,000 passengers per hour. It has special carriages featuring bronze statues of some of Disney's most beloved characters in glass cases and even Mickey Mouse shaped windows and grab-handles. Walt Disney — who was a dedicated railroad enthusiast — would have loved it!

Talking about the Disney-HKSAR partnership at the topping-off ceremony for Sleeping Beauty Castle, the managing director of the Hong Kong Disneyland Group Don Robinson confidently predicted, "Together we will help drive job creation, tourism and economic growth, while creating a magical journey for Hong Kong" (Lyne). However a significant number of Hong Kongers believed that the HKSAR had been shortchanged by Disney. Hong Kong Disneyland is currently much smaller than the other Disneyland-style theme parks at Anaheim; Orlando, Florida; Paris, France; and Tokyo, Japan, which the Hong Kong media eagerly pointed out at every opportunity. But an even greater blow to the collective pride of the locals was Disney's desire to build another theme park near Shanghai in the not too distant future. Being big and new and located close to China's showpiece city, it will probably diminish the patronage and the prestige of Hong Kong Disneyland.

Disney estimated that a third of visitors to Hong Kong Disneyland would come from Hong Kong, a third from Mainland China and a third from the rest of Southeast Asia. A lack of cultural awareness had already cost The Walt Disney Company time and money in China, and it had no desire to make the same mistake that it had made at Euro Disney, the company's park near Paris. The French public roundly criticized Disney for ignoring French culture at Euro Disney, which was a major reason for the park's initial struggle to

Passengers on the Hong Kong MTR Disneyland Resort Train Line.

attract large crowds. It opened in April 1992 and lost 1.3 billion dollars in the first year of operation. However after making numerous changes including renaming the park Paris Disneyland, things turned around. By 1998 Paris Disneyland had overtaken Notre Dame as France's number one tourist attraction.

Conversely at the hugely popular Tokyo Disneyland, "The Japanese told us from the beginning, 'Don't Japanese us,'" said Martin A. Sklar, The Walt Disney Company's international ambassador for Walt Disney Imagineering. "What they meant was that, 'We came here for Disney. We came for America. Don't give us Japan because we know Japan'" (qtd. in Schneider). Therefore it was very important for Disney to strike the right cultural balance at Hong Kong Disneyland — not too American and not too Chinese.

Disney's initial foray into China came in the late 1930s when the company's first animated feature film *Snow White and the Seven Dwarfs* was released there. (Disney was recently planning a Chinese re-make of this film to be called *Snow White and the Seven Kung Fu Monks*). However, later Disney films were banned in Mao's China. Therefore, as the vast majority of Hong Kong Disneyland's potential customers had not grown up with Disney animation and Disney merchandise, the company launched a massive marketing campaign throughout China. *The Magical World of Hong Kong Disneyland* began screening on Hong Kong television in 2003 — the same year that construction of the theme park commenced. This family-oriented TV series produced by Disney and hosted by the popular Chinese actor and pop singer Jacky Cheung featured Disney animated films that had inspired many of the park's rides. Cheung also presented behind-the-scenes reports about Hong Kong Disneyland; interviews with the park's designers or imagineers; and film footage from the classic 1950s American TV series *Disneyland* of Walt Disney speaking about his first theme park at Anaheim (with Chinese subtitles). In fact, *The Magical World of Hong Kong Disneyland* was a contemporary Chinese version of *Disneyland* the TV show, which in its day had vigorously promoted Disneyland the theme park especially during the run up to the park's opening in July 1955.

And to lift the profile of its enduring superstar Mickey Mouse in China, The Walt Disney Company enlisted the help of the seventy million strong Communist Youth League of China to organize special events for its members who ranged in age from 14 to 28, such as Mickey Mouse drawing competitions, Disney product promotions and Disney story readings. Once again Disney relied on a tried-and-true technique to generate publicity, since Mickey Mouse was originally promoted in a very similar way in the West, although on a far smaller scale. Between 1929 and 1933 the Mickey Mouse Club was established in cinemas across the United States (and even as far away as Australia) to promote the character's animated films. The club also organized live stage shows and published a newsletter. In the 1950s Disney revived this concept with the hugely popular children's TV series the *Mickey Mouse Club*, hosted by the American singer and songwriter Jimmie Dodd and featuring about a dozen multi-talented children called Mouseketeers.

According to Hong Kong Disneyland's vice president of sales and marketing Roy Tan Hardy, "The biggest challenge of bringing a Disney park to this part of the world is that not all audiences grew up with Disney stories and characters, so there are varying levels of familiarity and understanding. Our priority has been to introduce audiences all over the region to the classic Disney experience" (qtd. in Ewing). But Disney need not have been so anxious because the Chinese public was already very familiar with "the classic Disney experience" even if nobody realized it. This is because many Chinese religious buildings in particular are literal analogies, such as the Ba Gua Shan Temple overlooking Changhua in Taiwan, which takes the form of a gigantic Buddha. What is more, it is possible to go inside the Buddha's head and peer through his eyes, ears and nostrils. In the West playful building forms like this are usually found only in places such as Disneyland.

\

Never had a Disneyland-style theme park been built so quickly as Hong Kong Disneyland, which opened in September 2005. The park was modeled very closely on the original Disneyland; however, many things were tweaked to appeal to local tastes. For example the park's food shops and restaurants sold Asian food, such as barbeque pork puffs, curry laksa, moon cakes, pineapple buns, roast duck, sushi and mango puddings served in containers shaped like Mickey Mouse's head. Shark's fin soup was removed from hotel menus following pressure from environmentalists.

The Jungle Cruise ride is available in Cantonese (the Chinese dialect most widely spoken in Hong Kong), English and Mandarin (but the corny jokes of the ride's boat operators probably fall flat in all three languages). Some of the boats have regional names such as Mekong Maiden — a reference to the Mekong, one of the world's longest rivers which flows through several Asian countries including China — and Lijiang Lady — named after Lijiang City in China, which is famous for its scenic rivers. The boats also sail past the ruins of an Asian style temple dedicated to an elephant king and guarded by a pair of dancing cobras.

To satisfy the Chinese public's passion for taking photographs Disney established Fantasy Gardens, a Tivoli Gardens–inspired attraction unique to Hong Kong Disneyland where visitors could have their pictures taken with Disney characters often dressed in Chinese style clothes. Indeed a lot of attention was given to greening the park so that high-rise-bound Hong Kong visitors might get some relief from the usual bitumen and concrete. Disney imported eighteen thousand trees and one million shrubs for Hong Kong Disneyland including a number of surreal looking baobab trees from Australia for Tomorrowland and an impressive fourteen-metre tall yellow flame-of-the-forest tree from rural Mainland China for Adventureland. Taking a trip around the perimeter of the park on the Hong Kong Disneyland Railroad, one has difficulty seeing anything but trees.

But perhaps the biggest difference between Hong Kong Disneyland and the other Disneyland-style theme parks is the absence of Frontierland, which Disney thought would be of little interest to most Chinese visitors. As a result the park has only four of the usual five main zones — Adventureland, Fantasyland, Main Street, U.S.A., and Tomorrowland. While Hong Kong Disneyland provided visitors with "a classic Disney experience," nevertheless this seemed somewhat watered down compared to the other Disneyland-style theme parks. However, this may change over time as Disney gradually adds more attractions to the park, which eventually will be double its original size.

Undoubtedly the most interesting concession to local Chinese culture was Disney's decision to consult with feng-shui (wind-water) experts con-

The Asian-style ruins on the Jungle Cruise ride.

cerning the design and the construction of Hong Kong Disneyland. Feng-shui is the ancient Chinese system of siting buildings in the landscape in order to obtain good fortune for their occupants. It is based on the belief that powerful forces inhabit the landscape: qi (the breath of nature) is a positive life-giving force that flows invisibly through the earth, while sha-qi (noxious vapour) is a negative destructive force that is produced by anything straight, such as roads and walls. In a nutshell the aim of feng-shui is to attract qi, which brings good luck, and to repel sha-qi, which brings bad luck. While the Chinese Communist Party banned feng-shui on Mainland China, it thrived under British rule in Hong Kong.

A place with good feng-shui ideally has a mountain to the north (symbolized by a black tortoise); lower mountains to the east (a green dragon); hills to the west (a white tiger); and an open plane and flowing water to the south (a red finch). By good design or good luck or both, Hong Kong Disneyland has all of these things. "It's a very prosperous and fortunate site," commented Disney's Wing Chao (qtd. in Krivda 10). Even so, it is at odds with Disney's golden rule that nothing from the outside world should be seen from within its theme parks, because the mountains that surround Hong Kong Disney on three sides dominate the skyline from inside the park. This has the unfortunate effect of making Hong Kong Disneyland appear to be even smaller than it already is. But Disney's Imagineers could do nothing about this except to make the best of it. "Everyone from Southern California walks in and it strikes them right away — the train station, Main Street, the castle, even the music are the same as in Anaheim... Then there's this beautiful mountain range right behind the castle. That's when you quickly realize you're in the South China Sea," said Tom Morris, one of Hong Kong Disneyland's chief Imagineers (qtd. in Himmelberg). However, this was the only case where it could be argued that Disney design principles did not tie in with good feng-shui practice at the park.

While the Imagineers could do nothing about the mountains surrounding Hong Kong Disneyland, they still constructed an even higher berm than the one at Disneyland in Anaheim to block out the park's offensive neighboring man-made environment, which included an ugly coal-fired power station with three enormous chimney stacks on nearby Lamma Island. In this case the Imagineers were not only following Disney design principles but also good feng-shui practice, because an eye sore is a potential source of sha qi and should be at the very least hidden from view. While they were probably completely unaware of it, the Imagineers were also following in the footsteps of the rulers of ancient China, who had built huge embankments to protect their palaces from sha qi emanating from the north (a comparison that Walt Disney would have probably enjoyed!). In his book *The Travels* the explorer Marco Polo (1254–1324) wrote: "On the northern side of the palace, at the distance of a bow-shot but still within the walls, the Great Khan has had made an earthwork, that is to say a mound fully 100 paces in height and over a mile in circumference" (Polo 27). Likewise the third Ming emperor Zhu Di (1360–1424) constructed a 46-metre high hill directly north of the Forbidden City in Beijing, which is named Jingshan (Coal Hill) but is popularly known as Feng-Shui Hill. The Imagineers also employed other more subtle Chinese landscaping techniques, such as view framing, view hiding and water reflection, which they had instinctively used before at Disney's other theme parks but only now appreciated their Chinese origins.

Disney's feng-shui experts suggested reorienting Hong Kong Disneyland's front entrance by 12 degrees from where it was originally planned to go and placing a fountain outside the front gates to block the straight road leading to the park, which is a source of the negative force sha qi. The fountain designed by Disney's Imagineers for this spot has Mickey Mouse surfing a jet of water spouting from Monstro, the whale in Disney's second animated fea-

Mountains surround Hong Kong Disneyland on three sides.

ture film *Pinocchio*. Water is the principal source of the positive counter force qi, which is why "the thing that is most visible is the heavy usage of water in the park," explained Disney's Tom Morris (qtd. in Ashman). The feng-shui experts also recommended strategic locations for lakes, streams and waterfalls inside Hong Kong Disneyland. And to stop good luck from escaping they also suggested putting ornamental rocks at certain places around the park. The thing about these landscape features is that visitors can enjoy them regardless of whether they know anything about feng-shui or not, which illustrates how seamlessly the feng-shui experts' recommendations were incorporated into the park.

The feng-shui experts also made some significant recommendations based on Chinese numerology. Four is an extremely unlucky number because in Cantonese it also sounds like the English word "die," thus Hong Kong Disneyland's two tourist hotels — the supposedly Victorian style Hong Kong Disneyland Hotel (which looks more like a grotesque version of Mr. Roarke's house on the 1980s TV series *Fantasy Island*) and the glitzy art deco style Hollywood Hotel — both lack fourth floors for fear that like will produce like.

The fountain outside Hong Kong Disneyland's front gates.

On the other hand, eight is a very lucky number because it physically resembles the Chinese character for happiness; consequently the ballroom at the Hollywood Hotel is exactly 888 square metres in area because in this case the hope — not the fear — is that like will produce like. For this reason, the ballroom is a very popular venue for wedding receptions in Hong Kong. Even before Hong Kong Disneyland had opened, over three hundred couples had already registered for in-park nuptials. Apparently one young woman was so desperate to be among the first to be married there that she signed up in spite of not having a boyfriend!

Another very lucky number is 2,238 because in Cantonese it also sounds like "easily generate wealth." This explains why the up-market Crystal Lotus restaurant at the Hong Kong Disneyland Hotel was decorated with 2,238 crystal lotus flowers — from a feng-shui point of view eating there is not an expense but an investment. The feng-shui experts also consulted the ancient Chinese almanac *Tung Shu* for the most auspicious dates on which to hold Hong Kong Disneyland's groundbreaking ceremony (January 12, 2003), Sleeping Beauty Castle's topping-off ceremony (September 23, 2004) and the park's opening ceremony (September 12, 2005).

In order to have good feng-shui the five elements of Chinese cosmology — earth, fire, metal, water and wood — must be balanced in the environment. Disney's feng-shui experts paid particular attention to this at the Crystal Lotus restaurant. As mentioned, it is decorated with crystal lotus flowers. These symbolize the first element earth. Images of the second element fire are projected behind a wall of bottles in the restaurant's bar. (The Hong Kong fire code precluded the use of real fire.) In addition the stoves in the restaurant's kitchen were put in favorable places, while other areas were designated no fire zones. The restaurant's furniture is made from two more elements — metal and wood. And last but not least, there is a virtual reality pond that symbolizes the fifth element, water. Furthermore, computer animated Japanese carp are swimming in the pond, which is lucky because in Cantonese "fish" also sounds like "surplus."

Auspicious symbols were often incorporated in the design of everyday objects in China to bring whoever came in contact with them good luck. Take, for example, the front door of an old house near Suzhou, China. The doorhandle was a replica of an ancient Chinese coin to represent wealth, the head of the door-bolt took the form of two peaches to symbolize longevity and the escutcheon around the bolthole was shaped like a bat to represent happiness. This also significantly improved the feng-shui of the house. A similar thing occurs at Hong Kong Disneyland's Hollywood Hotel as well. It is known locally as the "Hidden Mickey" because Mickey Mouse's stylized head, which is a talisman as far as The Walt Disney Company is concerned, can be found in almost everything at the hotel including carpets, curtains, doormats, furniture, grilles, light fittings, mirrors, planter boxes and windows.

The feng-shui experts fine-tuned the layouts of the stores along Main Street, U.S.A., as well, "right down to where the cash registers are placed in every shop" said Disney's Roy Tan Hardy (qtd. in Gluckman). They made sure that nothing sharp pointed at the doors and also recommended against selling clocks in the stores because in Cantonese "giving a clock" also sounds like "going to a funeral." Once again the fear was that like produced like. (However, clocks are sold elsewhere in the park and also at the two Disney hotels.) Green hats were not to be sold in Main Street, U.S.A., either because according to Chinese lore a man wearing a green hat is a cuckold (poor Goofy!). Finally the feng-shui experts suggested using red wherever possible throughout the park because it symbolizes joy and is therefore a very lucky color, which was why "particularly on Main Street, U.S.A., we see a lot of accents done in red" explained Tom Morris (qtd. in Ashman).

The Walt Disney Company took to feng-shui like Donald Duck to water. Perhaps this was a result of the company's growing cultural awareness and

The virtual fishpond at the Crystal Lotus Restaurant.

sensitivity as Disney spokesperson Marilyn Waters implied: "We spend a lot of time trying to understand the culture and areas where we're creating parks. You do the best you can to be cognizant and respectful of that and the additional lessons you learn as you go along" (qtd. in Showley). However, there is more to it than simply that. As mentioned, Disney design principles coincided extremely well with good feng-shui practice. This is largely due to the fact that feng-shui involves reading symbols—hills represent animals, fish symbolize money, numbers represent death or happiness and so on—which is a manner of storytelling that also happens to be Disney's bread and butter. The rides, the landscape, even the food at Hong Kong Disneyland are all meant to tell stories. "First, everything is fundamentally story-based—we are storytellers" said Jay Rasulo, Disney's president of theme parks and resorts. "We use a broad variety of tools, technology and devices to deliver stories; fundamentally every ride and attraction really is a story" (qtd. in Cellini). Similarly, "The landscaping is driven by the stories told at Hong Kong Disneyland," said Paul Comstock, Disney's director of landscape design. "It serves to support and exemplify the story lines inside the theme park including a jungle, a castle, fantasy themes, and a journey through space" (qtd. in "HK Disneyland"). And again: "We brought the importance of the story to them," said Karlos Siquueiros who travelled from Disneyland at Anaheim to train Hong Kong Disneyland's restaurant staff. "In Anaheim, we say keep the story alive right down to the last bite" (qtd. in Himmelberg).

The synthesis of Disney design principles and good feng-shui practice at Hong Kong Disneyland seems to have been very well received by the Chinese public. This can be evidenced by the fact that in February 2006 the crowds were so overwhelming that the park had to be temporarily closed — a Disney first. Despite some initial skepticism by many people, perhaps the feng-shui experts were worth their weight in gold.

Works Cited

Ashman, Mark. "Disney Uses Feng-Shui to Build Mickey's New Kingdom in Hong Kong." *USA Today* 7 September 2005. www.usatoday.com/travel/destinations/2005-09-07-feng-shui-disney_x.htm.

Cellini, Adelia. "New Generation." *Variety,* 28 April 2005. *www.variety.com/article/VR 1117921882.html?categoryid'1928&cs'1.*

Ewing, Kent. "Hong Kong a Roller Coaster for Disney." *China Business,* 6 January 2006. www.atimes.com/atimes/China_Business/HA06Cb01.html.

Gluckman, Ron. "Mickey Mouse Meets Mao." *Silk Road,* September 2005. www.gluckman.com/HKDisney.htm.

"HK Disneyland Unveils Landscape Design." *People's Daily,* 19 September 2003. www.chinadaily.com.cn/en/doc/2003-09/19/content_265594.htm.

Himmelberg, Michele. "Pacific Exchange." *Orange County Register,* 10 September 2005. www.ocregister.com/ocr/sections/business/oc_region/article_669877.php.

Krivda, Cheryl D. "Behind the Magic: Hong Kong Disneyland." *Primavera Magazine* vol. 4, no. 1 (2005): 10.

Lyne, Jack. "Hong Kong Disneyland Tops Out Centerpiece Structure." *The Site Selection,* 10 October. www.siteselection.com/ssinsider/snapshot/sf041014.htm

Polo, Marco. *The Travels.* Harmondsworth: Penguin, 1978.

Schneider, Mike. "Feng Shui to Guide Construction of Hong Kong Disneyland." *Asian Week* 11–17 January 2002. www.asianweek.com/2002_01_11/news_disneyland.html.

Showley, Roger. "Hong Kong Disneyland Blends the New, Borrowed." *The San Diego Union-Tribune,* 26 February 2006. www.signonsandiego.com/uniontrib/20060226/news_1t26hkdland.html.

Sklar, Martin A. (1964) *Walt Disney's Disneyland: The Behind-the-Scenes Story of How It Was Done ... of the Man Who Made It Possible ... and of the Millions of Visitors Who Have Helped Make It the Happiest Place on Earth.* Anaheim, CA: Walt Disney, 1969.

Hyperurbanity

*Idealism, New Urbanism, and the
Politics of Hyperreality in the
Town of Celebration, Florida*

ERIC DETWEILER

Once upon a time, in an essay entitled "Travels in Hyperreality," Umberto
Eco wrote of Disneyland's Main Street:

> Main Street — like the whole city for that matter — is presented as at once absolutely
> realistic and absolutely fantastic, and this is the advantage ... of Disneyland over
> other toy cities. The houses of Disneyland are full-size on the ground floor, and on a
> two-thirds scale on the floor above, so they give the impression of being inhabitable
> (and they are) but also of belonging to a fantastic past we can grasp with our imagi-
> nation. The Main Street façades are presented to us as toy houses and invite us to
> enter them, but their interior is always a disguised supermarket, where you buy
> obsessively, believing that you are still playing [43].

Eco was writing in 1975, and his observations regarding Disney focus almost
exclusively on the "toy city" of Disneyland. His discussion of Florida's Walt
Disney World Resort, which "is a hundred fifty times larger than Disneyland,
and proudly presents itself not as a toy city but as the model of an urban
agglomerate," is limited to a single paragraph. These were, after all, the days
of such Disney movies as *Robin Hood* (featuring a cartoon fox in the titular
role) and *The Apple Dumpling Gang* (featuring Don Knotts as an outlaw).
Disney's image and commercial interests seemed exclusively tied to toys and
childhood fun — not urban agglomerates. In 1975, Eco still had to travel
through the real world to reach his hyperreal Disneyfied destinations.

Twelve years later, Disney opened the first branch of the Disney Store in
a Glendale, California, mall, less than an hour's drive from Disneyland (The

Walt Disney Internet Group). Disney thus became connected with another realm in which the realistic and fantastic are merged in a slightly less well-disguised supermarket: the mall, where real stores and commodities come together in what Neil Harris calls an "architectural fantasy" (qtd. in Gibian 33). Given Disney's involvement in the hyperreal businesses of fantasy and cinema, the company's presence in the mall seems only natural. As Peter Gibian claims, "malls have now absorbed the movie-theater concept, offering their own multiscreen cinamettes ... at least one mall even has enclosed amusement park rides" (33). By inserting a small piece of Disneyland's Main Street into the "carefree inner circle" of the shopping mall (34), Disney went from being a tourist destination to part of the suburban consumer's everyday milieu.

It was twelve years after that—1999, on the cusp of the new millennium—when Andrew Ross published *The Celebration Chronicles: Life, Liberty, and the Pursuit of Property Value in Disney's New Town*. In the book, Ross records his experiences as a resident of Celebration, Florida: a town built, planned, and managed by the Disney Corporation—"a showcase town for 20,000 residents ... in Osceola County to the south of the theme parks" (Ross 5). The town, which broke ground in 1994, "was a bid to maximize the value of 10,000 acres of company land" (5). The "model of an urban agglomerate" presented by Epcot had given way to a (hyper)real planned community, populated by permanent residents ready to "bank upon a star" (Ross 2).

In this essay, I will demonstrate how Celebration represents a new realization of the hyperreal—what Jean Baudrillard describes as "the generation of models of a real without origin or reality" (1). By moving from theme parks to malls to residential communities, Disney has slowly made it possible for people to not just vacation in a hyperreal manifestation of Main Street, but to live their lives in a purportedly hyperreal world. Celebration is more than just a new twist on Eco's travels in hyperreality; it is the promise of the hyperreal life. In Celebration, as on Main Street, "[the houses] give the impression of being inhabitable," and indeed they are. Inhabitability is no longer just an impression, however, nor are the second stories built on a two-thirds scale. My exploration of Celebration as hyperreal community reveals how the town is a sort of crossroads between various exemplars of American hyperreality: New Urbanism, the shopping mall, suburbia, and the Disney Corporation itself. Celebration evokes the shopping mall via its ties to New Urbanism and Disney, and this evocation in turn challenges the notion that Celebration and New Urbanism stand in direct contrast to suburbia—indeed, there seem to be far more overlaps between New Urbanism and the suburbs than New Urbanist rhetoric would like to suggest.

Moreover, the hyperreal quality of Celebration eludes and is elided in

The Celebration Chronicles. Although Ross' book is rich in insights, his strict focus on Celebration's materiality necessarily works around and against the hyperreality overlaying the town. Early in his stay in Celebration, a fellow resident confides that "the pixie dust here wears off quickly" (qtd. in Ross 11). Ross opts to "nod knowingly and change the subject," writing off his neighbor's comment as "too much like the beginning of a southern gothic screenplay." Ross' desire is to avoid "Disney-bashing" (6), giving full credit to the "nonutopian residue [of Celebration residents'] former lives" and resisting the tendency to present a picture of Celebration too reminiscent of such dystopias as *The Stepford Wives* (9). Materialism, however, doesn't give full shrift to the rich web of signifiers that enmesh Celebration — a town where homes are bought and sold based on the reputation of a corporation largely known for screenplays and pixie dust.

From California to Florida

As mentioned, Disneyland overshadows Walt Disney World Resort in "Travels in Hyperreality." Disneyland opened in 1955. The Walt Disney Company itself attributes the park's genesis to Walt Disney's desire for "a place where parents and children could have a good time together" ("The Walt Disney Company"), while Ross claims it grew out of Walt's "disgust for the postwar urban sprawl of Los Angeles" (4). Either way, Walt Disney World — which opened in 1971— was still relatively new in 1975, and without the established cultural import of its twenty-year-old California cousin. It did at least dwarf Disneyland geographically, built on 28,000 acres versus Disneyland's 400 and featuring a "Disneyland-style theme park" supplemented with "hotels, campgrounds, golf courses, shopping villages and a monorail connecting them all" ("The Walt Disney Company").

If Walt Disney World was Disneyland's colossal country cousin in 1975, however, it is now the site of many of Disney's most well-known attractions and symbols: the Magic Kingdom, Epcot, a castle "far more Gothic" than Disneyland's (Eco 47), and the "hyperreal habitat" of Disney's Animal Kingdom (Scott 125). Although Eco argues that Disneyland is "much shrewder" at stirring the imagination and maintaining a hyperreal atmosphere, in subordinating Walt Disney World he also highlights an important shift in ethos between the two parks. At Walt Disney World, "Tomorrow, with its violence, has made the colors fade from the stories of Yesterday" (47–48). Disneyland's nostalgic look back at a magical past is countered in Walt Disney World's optimistic futurism. The California park may have been Walt's alternative to

L.A.–style sprawl, but it was a definitively whimsical alternative. Walt imagined Disney World's Epcot, on the other hand, as a serious alternative model for urban development, the sort of city on a hill that would "influence the future of city living for generations to come" (qtd. in Ross 54). Epcot, that is, was not planned to be in the same league as *The Apple Dumpling Gang*. As Shelly Scott puts it, while the "Magic Kingdom entertains, Epcot entertains and teaches" (111).

Ultimately, however, the Epcot Walt envisioned was not to be. According to Ross,

> Walt's ur–Epcot was the last gasp of the paternalist company town.... Only the "unacceptably optimistic" Walt Disney Company would take up such a challenge in the midst of urban renewal, with the ghetto uprisings in Watts, Newark, and Detroit just around the corner [55].

Instead of a new urban model, the realized Epcot (which opened seven years after Eco's "Travels in Hyperreality") was built as a nonresidential and "perfectly schizophrenic affair," a park featuring attractions "already outdated" on its opening day. In the end, Disney traded in "the space-age version of the future" for retro "[g]eewhiz futurism" à la Jules Verne. Disney gave up on producing the future, turning instead to romanticizing the future as imagined by the past (Ross 55).

Walt's dream for Epcot, then, was dashed. Although families and individuals were more than willing to visit Disneyland as a hyperreal escape from everyday life, the idea that The Walt Disney Company, with its fantastic once-upon-a-time ethos, could create a working city didn't hold sufficient water for Walt's coworkers and successors. The urban centers of the mid-century were fraught with crises, uprisings, and cold, hard realities too complex for Disney Imagineering. Disney, seen as a hyperreal company pushing hyperreal commodities, was too distant from the real struggles of everyday urban life to effect practical change.

From Main Street to Mall Stores

Five years after the disappointment of Epcot's initial futurism, the Disney Store introduced Walt's company to a venue far more compatible with Disney's practices and ideals: the mall (The Walt Disney Internet Group). In "An Ontology of Everyday Distraction: The Freeway, the Mall, and Television," Margaret Morse argues that the mall "is a spatial condensation ... it is 'a city, indeed a world in miniature.' Shops that are four-fifths of normal size are linked together within a vast ... atrium or hall, devoted solely to the pedestrian consumer (albeit served by autos and trucks)" (105). Morse's observation is strikingly evocative of Eco's description of Disneyland as a miniaturized and disguised supermarket. The mall — like the freeway, television, and (as Morse also claims) postwar suburbia — is a *"nonspace* of both experience and representation, an *elsewhere* that inhabits the everyday" (Morse 102). The mall is thus a significant shift from Disneyland, which, by virtue of being a tourist destination and vacation spot, did not inhabit the everyday — at least for most Americans. Malls extend the simultaneous miniaturization and commercialism of Disney, the sense of "dreamlike *displacement* or separation" from one's surroundings, to the realm of the mundane (103). In the mall, "miniaturization is an attempt to master and control the world," with the miniature stores (like the "miniature shops and concessions" of theme parks) "designed to evoke the nostalgic feelings the adult has when visiting the world of childhood" (120).

The implicit and explicit similarities Morse draws between Disneyesque theme parks and malls are certainly not lacking. In both cases, a commercial agenda is shrouded in nostalgia, making the act of purchasing feel like playing, as Eco suggests. A key difference is the sheer availability and prevalence of malls. Disneyland, as a vacation destination, is enchanted and glamorized by its absence from the visitor's everyday realities. The houses in Disneyland may be miniaturized, but they loom larger than life in the cultural imaginary of those who desire to consume the park's magic.

The individual mall, on the other hand (with the possible exception of such hyperbolic aberrations as Minnesota's Mall of America), is not hyperreal by virtue of its particular character. Malls are easily replicable, ready to be dropped into any suburban community with sufficient commercial interest and buying power. As Gibian points out, "reproduced clones of an entirely standardized mall design, in fact, often reappear throughout the continent" (39). While Walt Disney World may disguise its commercialism via miniaturization and nostalgia, the price tag and time required by the vacationer are substantial enough to deter most consumers from paying the park a weekly visit. Walt Disney World, that is, has little to no direct role in the everyday public life of most communities. The mall, however, powered by "the boom of highway construction in the Eisenhower era and the huge migrations of people to the suburbs" (33), became an important part of everyday life for postwar Levittowners and their kindred.

Morse claims that the rise of the freeway (Gibian's "boom of highway construction") makes possible the division of the everyday into two realms:

> what David Brodsy calls "local" and "metropolitan" (24) orientations. These also denote two realities: the one, heterogeneous and static; the other, homogeneous and

mobile.... Freeways and the suburbs they serve are thus examples of the "garden in the machine," which provides mass society with a pastoral aesthetic and rhetoric [104].

In this way, the freeway and the subsequent possibility of suburban life sever private and public life, and thus the public and private realms. Suburbs were (and are) homogeneous spaces that largely glossed over the realities of many political, racial, and class tensions in broader society. The suburbs were where people lived; the urban center was where they worked.

Not that suburbia was free from politics or conflict. In contrast with Morse's ideal pastoral aesthetic, Dana Cuff notes that early suburbs "democratized the Panopticon's principle of surveillance: at Levittown, everyone could openly police everyone else" (para. 20). These suburbs, like the suburbs of today, were the site of such public spaces as "schools, community stores, and parks, and residents started innumerable local clubs and branches of national voluntary organizations" (para. 21). The homogeneity of the suburbs allowed for — even encouraged — a certain elision of public realities and social ills, but a certain "authoritarian control [and] pressure to conform" arose as a result, creating a new sort of political atmosphere (para. 19).

Two things the "garden in the machine" tenor of Levittown and similar suburban communities often lacked, then, were (1) the anonymity of city life and (2) the "downtown activity and bustle" of the urban center — an urban center newly fetishized by the Foucaldian oppression of life in Levittown (Gibian 38). The separation from the city allowed by suburban life caused the city to become an idealized space (in contrast with the "nonspace" of the suburbs). The city — a thing of the past for suburban residents — became "a lost referential, that is to say [a] myth," a fate Baudrillard argues has also befallen history itself (43). Even if suburban residents didn't want to return to a city where "at least there was violence" (44), distance from the city allowed for a fetishization of the urban qualities found lacking in the hyperreal nonspace of the suburbs. The mall, by "successfully repackaging an idealized urban form into the suburban milieu" (qtd. in Gibian 38), allowed the suburbanite to take part in a hyperreal variety of urban anonymity, activity, and bustle, while still "offering ... 'a continued shelter from engagement with ghetto areas'" and the other messy facts of real city life (Morse 103).

Ross mentions the way in which "malls have threatened to displace parks, school libraries, post offices, town halls, and community centers as civic meeting places" by imitating "the traditional marketplace, plaza, or village green, and many have walkways that simulate the public bustle of urban streets" (50). Suburban malls are safe, privately-owned alternatives to the relatively unconstrained public free-for-all of actual urban centers. The mall's *raison d'être*, however, is not civic engagement but consumerism: "the basic point is ... to keep shoppers [not citizens] dazzled by each display as it rises before their eyes" (Gibian 39). Ross sees malls as threatening because they are "often run by corporate boards with no trace of accountability" (51).

Two important points are not present in Ross' critique of malls. The first is the impact malls have had on the suburban cultural imaginary and the way this impact relates to Disney's urban-planning aspirations. As mentioned above, Ross aligns Walt's original plans for Epcot with the "paternalist company town," a method of residential organization with which most Americans were thoroughly disillusioned by the postwar era. By the 1950s, however, the shopping mall was already a well-established feature of the American landscape (Gibian 35). Shopping malls normalized a hyperreal, simulated urban form: a form that became centrally important to many suburban residents' social, public, and commercial lives. Its relation to such popularized, idealized urban surrogates, a thin veil of publicity covering the reality of private ownership, grants Celebration a cultural context different than that surrounding Walt's original "ur–Epcot." The potential residents of that obsolete version of Epcot may have been haunted by the memory of oppressively patriarchal company-owned mining towns and the violence of real cities. Celebration, however, is much more indebted to the shopping mall than the company town, and the New Urbanist supporters who planned and populated it had the shopping mall and Walt Disney World's hyperreal urban spaces (or nonspaces) as ideals to gird their notions of what Celebration could and should be.

New (Sub)urbanism?

In addition to its ties to Disney and the shopping mall, the town of Celebration's design is indebted to the New Urbanist planning movement. New Urbanism came on the city-planning scene with the publication of the Ahwanee Principles in 1991 (Cuff para. 33), and the founding of the Congress for the New Urbanism in 1993 ("CNU History"). According to the charter of the Congress for the New Urbanism (CNU), the movement

> views disinvestment in central cities, the spread of placeless sprawl, increasing separation by race and income, environmental deterioration, loss of agricultural lands and wilderness, and the erosion of society's built heritage as one interrelated community-building challenge ["Charter of the New Urbanism"].

Peter Schuermer, in his review of *The Celebration Chronicles*, further glosses New Urbanism as "an attempt to transform the out-of-control development of the American suburban landscape" founded on "the belief that architecture and the organization of space have the power to influence social behavior; that, in short, the 'built environment' can create democratic utopias" (para. 7). New Urbanism attempts to elide suburban sprawl, segregation, and disinvestment in central cities by advocating "neighborhoods diverse in use and population," with communities "designed for the pedestrian ... as well as the car," with "universally accessible public spaces and community institutions," and "architecture and landscape that celebrate local history, climate, ecology, and building practice." Strong ideals, and ones that mesh well with "Walt Disney's disgust for ... postwar urban sprawl" (Ross 4).

Many of these standards are certainly present in the layout and ideology of Celebration, and Ross interviews and quotes Andres Duany, one of New Urbanism's founders, several times throughout the course of his book. Although Cuff claims "new urbanism has [already] been soundly criticized from nearly every academic perspective" (para. 33), what is worth noting here are the ways in which the movement's ideals are (or are not) manifested in Celebration. In terms of mixed income, Celebration offers everything from relatively low-rent apartments through townhouses to the "expensive estate houses" of the "millionaires on Golfpark Drive" (Ross 33). And despite income disparities, "the Celebration ethos of communitarianism demands that everyone is understood to be in the same boat" (32). Celebration is also a "place designed for walkability" (35), making it possible for Ross to adopt "the profile of a resolute pedestrian." As for "architecture and landscape that celebrate local history," Celebration is preternatural in its approach to local history: "the town is supposed to have grown up organically over time" (10), and "in the earliest planning stages, there had been some talk about dating [Celebration] ... with a themed backstory," one possibility being that "the town was built by survivors of a shipwrecked Spanish galleon" (22). Instead of celebrating local history, Celebration fabricates its past via "posterior dating," mythologizing both the town and history itself (10).

How these ideals play out in the everyday reality of Celebration, however, is a different matter. Despite Celebration's attempt to overcome "separation by ... income," the production homes sold in the first phase of the town's development cost "almost twice the median for a single family home in the Orlando region," of which Celebration is a part (Ross 32). The general property value inflation brought about by the town's connections to Disney wouldn't seem to leave many options for residents not making at least a solid middle-class wage. Celebration's lack of racial heterogeneity, meanwhile, was a disappointment for developers and residents alike. As Ross notes, "After two years, the town had attracted only one African American homeowning family, while three single women were living in rented apartments" (264).

On the issue of pedestrian-centeredness, Ross observes, "In a place designed for walkability, it is also surprising how often residents still use their cars to drive downtown and elsewhere" (35). In addition to in-town driving, many residents "[drive] substantial distances to work outside of Celebration, and a serious shopping trip entails driving well outside the orbit of what the town's own stores can offer" (30). The persistent necessity of driving is largely due to the priorities set by Disney when it came to choosing what retail options to feature in Celebration's commercial sector. Instead of "a hardware store, fast-food outlet, and other convenience shops" (83), Celebration "catered primarily to tourist custom, rather than resident needs," featuring a "children's specialty store offering unrealistically priced toddlers clothing" and "M Fashion, owned by a Tampa socialite who had privately acquired a dozen of Princess Diana's cocktail dresses" (82). If they needed everyday commodities not available at the grocery store, Celebrationites had to head for the commercial complexes closer to Orlando.

Celebration's physical reality thus prevents it from achieving some of New Urbanism's ideals. In many ways, the town seems to have more in common with the suburbs. As Paul Mason Fotsch writes in his review of Ross's book, "[Celebration residents'] primary concern over property value ultimately bonds them to problems created by suburbia" (784). Ross himself remarks, "the interiors [of homes] followed conventional suburban floor-plan standards" (29).

Celebration's initial instincts toward "posterior dating," hearkening back to Celebration's fabricated past, underscore the town's drive to maintain self-imposed hyperreal ideals. Consider this passage from Celebration's promotional literature:

> There once was a place where neighbors greeted neighbors in the quiet of summer twilight. Where children chased fireflies. And porch swings provided easy refuge from the care of the day.... Remember that place? Perhaps from your childhood... The special magic of an American home town. Now, the people at Disney—itself an American family tradition—are creating a place that celebrates this legacy. A place that recalls the timeless traditions and boundless spirit of who we are [qtd. in Ross 18].

Baudrillard claims, "History is our lost referential, that is to say our myth" (43). He specifically connects this notion with cinema in general and nostalgia pictures like *The Last Picture Show* in particular, claiming that such films are the fetishization of a historical moment "immediately preceding our 'irreferential' era" (44). Celebration works toward the same end as these films. Duany associates Celebration with "Neotraditionalism," a combination of "the security and responsibility of the 50s with the individual freedoms and personal choice of the "Me Generation" (qtd. in Ross 27). If "[n]eofiguration is an *invocation* of resemblance," then neotraditionalism is an invocation of traditional American community values, but both movements are "at the same time the flagrant proof of the disappearance of objects in their very represen- tation: *hyperreal*" (45). Disney claims Celebration is "[a] new American town of block parties and Fourth of July parades" (Ross 18), but block parties and Fourth of July parades are simply "the reinstitution of 1950s" neighborhood events (Baudrillard 45). Celebration is a town where "imports are passed over in favor of 'authentic reproductions'" (Ross 31).

The sort of careful (re)construction present in Celebration's civic ethos is another way in which the town is reminiscent of the mall, and these further similarities expose deep points of sympathy between malls and New Urbanism. As Gibian points out, "Both malls and Disney's Main Street derive from the townscape" (34). Malls have imitated endless iterations of public realms, from "the 'market town' styles which deliberately underplayed [malls'] large size" (35) to "the changing, irregular views of an 'English village' mall" (37). Espe- cially noteworthy here is Victor Gruen's Southdale Shopping Center, which "recreate[s] the effects of urban variety and energy ... a suburbanite's dream of an early 1800s *unplanned* city, offering substitutes for streets and an arena of concentration to those feeling the uniformity and isolation of suburban sprawl" (38, emphasis added). The mall, of course, along with Celebration, is carefully planned — all the more so in order to seem unplanned and ram- bling. In both malls and Celebration, the model of an idealized urban history precedes and predominates actual history. Both play on suburban assumptions of what the city should be — although Celebration has the extra assurance of Disney's caring, magical persona: Walt's shadow, or perhaps the unenduring "pixie dust" referenced above (Ross 11).

Another tie between the design philosophies of the mall, New Urbanism in general, and Celebration in particular is their relationship to cars. Malls, like Walt Disney World, work to separate "customers from cars and from any service activities — creating a carefree inner circle distant from outside concerns (forget your car, forget the street, forget services, forget yourself)" (Gibian 34). These "closed, cleaned stage-set 'streets' move in similar ways to keep practical services (deliveries, employee access, building supports, circuitry, etc.) behind or below the 'scene.'" The mall and Disneyland separate cus- tomers from cars and services with what William Severini Kowinski calls "the neutral zone of the parking lot ... the asphalt moat around the magic castle" (qtd. in Morse 104). In Celebration, this separation is more tenuous. As Ross observes, residents are reluctant to abandon their cars, even when it comes to driving around town. Cars are not left behind, but they are hidden. Celebra- tion garages are located at the backs of houses, accessible by "narrow (usually

10 feet) alleyways that ... were [also] used as service roads for trash haulage" (Ross 83). Indeed, the first issue of the resident-published *Celebration Independent* featured a "front-page story excoriating BFI garbage disposal company for ... its use of large trucks that ravaged the grass on back alley lawns" (339). Another civilian's protests would eventually result in mail deliveries being made to the rear of houses as well (40). Especially in the former case, residents' desire for services to remain out of sight is clear, and the intrusion of public vehicles onto private property serves as a clear reason for distress. Services may be more present than at Walt Disney World, but the push to elide their existence persists.

In addition to the relative invisibility of cars and services, and simulated connections to historical forms and events, Ross' book eventually unveils sympathies between the privatized political structure of many malls and Duany, the "figurehead" of New Urbanism (27). In a conversation with Ross, Duany states, "[Celebration] is clearly governed by a corporation, rather than government, and so what happens is that an American corporation is treating you as a customer. A customer is possibly treated better than a citizen in this country" (307). He goes on to say, "If it takes a corporation, I'll take a corporation. Because the free market will not sustain this.... It takes a closed market, a managed market, to keep a normal place going" (308). Despite Disney's attempts to background its name in presentations of the town (104), then, private financial backing is at least pragmatically, even if not ideologically, central to the future Duany imagines for New Urbanism. What is at stake here is the successful maintenance of the advantages of both suburbs and cities — without the alienation and negative enviro-social impacts of the former, or the often violent and tumultuous realities of the latter. This is precisely what the shopping mall aimed for: civic order in a social center, crowds and a veneer of pedestrianism without the ghettos and conflict that come with public urbanism. New Urbanism might reasonably be relabeled something along the lines of "Residential Mallism."

New Urbanism, at least as realized in the case of Celebration, is largely dependent on the denial of broader realities. Just as Walt Disney World and malls use the parking lot as a moat around the magical castle, Celebration is surrounded by rural Osceola County. The parking lot serves as a transition zone between the real and the hyperreal, a border between the protected, automobile-free centers of Disneyland and Walt Disney World, and the automobile-dependent cities of Los Angeles and Orlando. Celebration is likewise dependent on Osceola County, which is "[o]ver 80 percent farmland and water" (Ross 21). The rural county separates Celebration from the old urbanism and dilapidated strip malls of Orlando (5), and its sparse population allows for some forgetfulness of the racial and economic diversity present in the real urban center. The hyperreality of New Urbanism is more easily maintained when not set directly against the complicated realities of old urbanism, when it is instead protected, like the mall, by "basic tendencies toward *self-containment* and *introversion*" (Gibian 34). Indeed, many of the setbacks faced by Celebration were caused by an inability to fully extricate the town from broader social responsibilities and realities — the question of whether to link Celebration's school to the Osceola district, for instance (Ross 188), or tension between Celebration and neighboring Old Town, a "themed attraction" described as "a seedy amusement park area" by one Celebration resident (274). Although residents were certainly not unanimously in favor of isolationism, such controversies reinforced the practical difficulties of maintaining New Urbanist aesthetics and values in the face of wider political realities.

Ross makes much of the hard materiality of the town and the ways in which residents' real experiences and political participation undermine Disney's pixie-dust exterior. At the same time, however, Disney's ethos — especially via a conception of Walt as a sort of benevolent spirit guiding the town (cf. Ross 74) — leads many residents to especially resent anything not up to the hyperreal caliber of the company's theme parks. Their real political participation is motivated by the desire to maintain Celebration's hyperreality. And New Urbanism via Duany, in privileging private governance, undermines the large-scale implications of the New Urbanist philosophy. Communities like Celebration allow those who can afford it the benefit of being cut off from the rest of the world in an isolated New Urbanist world, albeit in the midst of impoverished Osceola County, with Disney's poor minimum-wage park workers close at hand. Given the economic flexibility implicit in their ability to afford a life in Celebration, Celebrationites don't have to be devoted to New Urbanism in action — only in words. The poor resident who lives in a city where the nearest grocery store is miles away and who can't afford so much as the bus fare is still left out. If New Urbanism is about mixed income living, racial integration, and the like, the hyperreal price-increasing patronage of Disney undermines the social realities New Urbanism claims to address.

Even with irate and mischievous citizens upsetting and challenging Celebration's established status quo, the utopian expectations that are part and parcel of the Disney image — and bleed over into New Urbanist philosophy — create a hyperreal ideal for residents, visitors, and the casually interested. This ideal, combined with Celebration's relative isolation and introversion, residents' actual-but-hidden reliance on the automobile and socioeconomic/racial homogeneity, and preference for the private over the public, aligns Celebration and New Urbanism less with urban and social responsibility, and more with the mall and the suburb.

Suburban Geographies

In her essay "Enduring Proximity: The Figure of the Neighbor in Suburban America," Cuff points out that "suburb makers [like New Urbanist designers] marketed themselves as 'community builders'" (para. 11). Cuff further insists, as quoted earlier, that the postwar Levittown suburbs "democratized the Panopticon's principle of surveillance" (para. 20). In less nefarious terms, life in Levittown and many other postwar suburbs came with heavily imposed social norms and an ideology of homogeneity. Levittowners were thus simultaneously oppressed and oppressors, with their private lives squeezed into "four small rooms" and their public lives premised on maintaining and making sure the neighbors maintained a curtain of conformity (Cuff). In Celebration, however, where a premium is placed on sociability, public life, and the maintenance of property value (Ross 35), such accountability to one's neighbors is all but written into the ideology. Indeed, what Disney seems to have done, in many ways, is to embed traditional suburban life and values behind a hyperreal New Urbanist veneer. Perhaps this veiled suburbanism is best embodied in Duany's connection of the movement with "Neotraditionalism" (qtd. in Ross 27).

What Celebration invokes here is the *sub*urban: the suburbs before people sequestered themselves behind ballooning lot sizes, automobilism, and 60-hour work weeks — though any mention of work is conspicuously absent from the promotional brochures. Although New Urbanism may set itself up as a utopian counterpoint to suburbanism, Celebration has a hard time avoiding the "nonutopian residue" and habituated suburban lifestyles of its residents (Ross 9). These interstices between the suburban and the New Urban merit exploration. Although New Urbanism may advertise itself as the polar opposite of suburbanism's thoughtless sprawl, there are far more similarities than the New Urbanist cares to admit. Unveiling such similarities highlights the ways in which both suburbia and New Urbanist prototypes forward parallel hyperreal agendas.

Edward Soja describes Los Angeles as "the place where 'it all comes together,'" a "*prototopos*, a paradigmatic place" (191). Los Angeles is the city of cities, a large-scale urban site exemplifying twentieth-century social trends such as "capitalist centralization." What happens in Los Angeles, Soja suggests, hints at what is happening or will happen in all urban centers. Soon thereafter, however, he claims, "Few other places make such a definitive mockery of the standard classifications of urban, suburban, and exurban [as L.A.]" (245). The city has "deconstruct[ed] the urban into ... little more than imaginary communities and outlandish representations of urban locality." If L.A. is a paradigmatic city, it is also hardly a city at all: a place so thoroughly signified — so constructed around representation, imagination, and advertisement — that the actual city practically disappears behind a smokescreen of tropes. L.A. is exemplary because it is so fluid, multifaceted, and colossal, but these features also render it difficult to critique and theorize.

The suburbs, however, seem atomized enough to allow theorizing, and are often the individual facets Soja examines in order to make some sense of L.A. He quotes Nico Poulantzas' "description ... of the production and reproduction of capitalist spatiality" (215):

> Social atomization and splintering ... a cross-ruled, segmented and cellular space in which each fragment (individual) has its place ... separation and division in order to unify ... atomization in order to encompass; segmentation in order to totalize; closure in order to homogenize; and individualization in order to obliterate difference and otherness [qtd. in Soja 215, ellipses original].

This atomization is the "fragmentation and segregation of the labor force at the place of work and the place of residence."

Segregation at the place of residence: suburbia. The suburbs are, as Jon Teaford vehemently points out, impossible to accurately totalize: "no generalizations apply" (58). Totalizing *individual* suburbs, however, is almost precisely what Teaford's book does. Consider his description of one of Los Angeles's suburbs: "not only is Maywood 90 percent Latino but so are the nearby communities" (66). He also discusses Sun City and Sun City West, Arizona, suburbs of Phoenix "restricted to those over fifty-five, ... worlds apart where seniors can enjoy their active retirement lifestyle free from noisy, disrespectful, troublesome youth" (74). Even in his discussion of a purposefully diverse suburb such as Oak Park, Illinois, which has officially "reject[ed] the notion of race as a barrier dividing us" (qtd. in Teaford 62), diversity seems so central to the suburb's identity that diversity itself becomes a totalizing characteristic. Suburbia is so wildly diverse because individual suburbs are often so homogeneous. In the "Afterwords" of *Postmodern Geographies*, Soja writes, "Totalizing visions, attractive though they may be, can never capture all the meanings and significations of the urban when the landscape is critically read and envisioned as a fulsome geographical text" (247). "It all comes together" in L.A., it would seem, only to elude and resist unification. Suburbs, on the other hand, achieve totalization through fragmentation and separation. This is not to say urban spaces are ideally integrated — the neighborhoods and boroughs of large cities often have clearly defined borders (New York City's Long Island or San Francisco's Chinatown come to mind)—but the geographic dispersal of suburbia makes demographic isolation—e.g., a Sun City with no children—especially viable. The suburbs have, after all, made it possible for "residents to escape the heterogeneity of American life" (Teaford 11).

The very conditions of suburban life, then, lend themselves to stereotyping. In *White Diaspora: The Suburb and the Twentieth-Century American Novel*, Catherine Jurca is intrigued by the leveling of suburban difference in literature, writing, "One of my reasons for examining representations of a variety of residential environments is to draw meaningful connections between them in order to understand how and why such a generic term as 'the suburb' might have come to stand in for them all" (13). Perhaps it is easier for "such a generic term as 'the suburb' ... to stand in for" Maywood, Oak Park, and Sun City, for "bland, homogeneous" stereotypes to gain cultural weight, because the suburbs are so often meticulously segmented according to ethnicity, lifestyle, class, or other demographic categories. The immediate invisibility of other ways of living makes the suburbanite's personal lifestyle seem all the more natural, whether that lifestyle involves speaking English or Spanish at home, planting rutabagas or roses in the backyard (Teaford). Even if one's suburban surroundings do not reflect the generalized stereotypes of American suburbia writ large, one may be sequestered enough to suppose that most suburbs do. Jurca gets at this point in her discussion of Sinclair Lewis' *Babbitt*. The novel's titular protagonist typifies the banal, quietly desperate "Tired Business Man" in his suburban habitat. For the novel's suburban readers, however, "[t]he question ... asked of [*Babbitt*] was not *Am I Babbitt?* but *Are we Babbitts?* and the answer ... was *Yes, they are*" (69). Even if one's own life (at least in one's own eyes) doesn't meet the criteria of the stereotypical suburbanite, even if one's own suburb isn't the suburb as signified in literature, art, and popular culture, the suburbanite may take this as an indication that the stereotype must exist all the more truly in everyone and everywhere else.

The individual suburb, generally speaking, would seem to have no existence unto itself. In its very name it is subordinated to the city, its identity contingent on the urban center to which it is attached—thus the suburbanite, finding herself more than a few hours from home, often claims the nearest urban center and not the empty signifier of her suburb—as her hometown. Anyone from anywhere could be a suburban resident. Los Angeles, Miami, and Atlanta all have their fringe settlements, but one has meaning when identified as a Chicagoan or New Yorker.

This is not to say the suburban resident has no identity via the suburbs.

It is simply the case that the reference is to a generalized concept instead of a proper noun. It is only in dealing with a small group of comrades familiar with a particular city's satellite districts that the specific names mean anything. One is a "New Yorker" more than one is a "city dweller," but a "suburbanite" more than a "Maywoodian." The lack of established adjective forms for individual suburban place-names may be taken as an illustration. Specific referentials, as Baudrillard suggests, would seem to have been lost. The only one remaining is the insufficiently vague "suburbia."

This is a point of departure between Celebration and suburbia as a concept. Celebration certainly has a unique identity. If anything, its associations with Disney and New Urbanism render Celebration, like Los Angeles, a signified overwhelmed by signifiers, "deconstruct[ed] ... into ... outlandish representations of [New] urban locality." While Glendale may be a suburb of Los Angeles, Celebration is a (even *the*) suburb of Disney, and unique association with a company whose signifying constellation is so strong recaptures an identity for Celebration. Simultaneously, however, that identity becomes something other than the town itself.

Conclusion: Thoughts on Celebration's Public Sphere

As he concludes his investigation of Celebration, Ross writes the following paragraph:

> In my time there, I watched as some kind of provisional public sphere, built on blunt opinion, common sentiment, and the stoic pursuit of civic needs, pushed its snout into the moist Florida air. It was fresh, cranky, and fraught with all the noble virtues and sorry prejudices that contend in the republic at large. Kindled by self-interest, and fiercely mindful of the property values of the developer and residents alike, this public awareness was raised to a new pitch by the ever-present performance anxiety.... The result sometimes felt like uncharted territory for life in a democracy [314].

Ross' point here is that a very real, very political, very public sphere can emerge from even so maligned a town as Celebration. Despite the tensions and ironies of New Urbanism, Ross hopes the town can manifest an alternative to the "privacy and isolation" of suburbia (312). This public sphere, however, may not even be what Celebrationites want. |

In *Simulacra & Simulation*, Baudrillard writes, "advertising is completely in unison with the social, whose historical necessity has found itself absorbed by the pure and simple *demand* for the social: a demand that the social function like a business, a group of services" (90). This demand is the cause of Celebration's public sphere: not an interest in the public sphere for its own sake, but the public sphere as a selling point — a bullet point in a real estate listing.

As the subtitle of Ross' book suggests, Celebration residents, like Levittowners, are supremely interested in the maintenance of property values. His acknowledgements of this primarily capitalist motivation, however, are overshadowed by his romanticized, anthropomorphized description of Celebration's "provisional public sphere." He laments the lack of civic disobedience in Celebration, but civic disobedience is the sort of thing that keeps property values down and drove early suburbanites out of old urban centers. Even if Ross' hopes are based on Disney granting Celebration its independence, making the town "stand on its own to prove its authenticity" (314), the town's continued focus on property value allows a hyperreal agenda to persist. Selling real estate, after all, is a hyperreal endeavor: making properties out to be better than they are, playing up selling points and downplaying "the shoddiness of the construction work" (36), turning a two-story Dutch Colonial into the manifestation of everything its owner could want or dream of: the model "utopian ideals of the Dream Home and the Main Street town" (238)—the home as the realization of the prospective buyer's participation in the "Disney dream" and achievement of "[f]ull citizenship"—precede the real, material concerns of construction (305–306).

Indeed, ten years after the publication of Ross' book, with a decade elapsed since "Disney management took a deep, dread-lined breath, and then stepped back [from Celebration]" (Ross 314), the town still projects itself in a hyperreal manner. The image on the front page of the community web site features a row of white Celebration front porches on a sunny day, with two of the porches prominently displaying American flags. The picture suggests homogeneity via the uniform porches and the patriotism manifested by the flags. Interestingly, the image lacks one aspect of Celebration central to Ross' book: residents. There are no people in the image. A clean, sterile ideal, untroubled by the messiness of real residents, is thus set forth. Celebration transcends the real through its virtual self-presentation (*Celebration Front Porch*).

Electronic versions of the town's official newsletter, also available via its web site, likewise foreground the social as "a mode of living" rather than the actual complicated realities of community life (Baudrillard 90). The February 2009 issue of the *Celebration News* features community events such as the American Pie Festival, the Celebration Games, and the Celebration Spring Art Festival. Any evidence of civic disobedience or town politics—even the names of specific residents—is noticeably absent. The March issue features the same three events and likewise elides the names and issues of particular residents. The only nod to a specific person is a reference to a memorial buried on page 25. The memorial itself, a eulogy for a twenty-year-old resident who recently died, is titled "Remembering Our Angel." This is not to make light of what was certainly a community tragedy, but simply to highlight the way in which it is subordinated to the American Pie Festival, and quickly represented as an opportunity to remember a hyperhuman (angelic) member of the Celebration community.

The issue here is the materiality Ross privileges versus the hyperreal sociality suggested by Baudrillard and reaffirmed in *Celebration News*. Whatever might go on behind the scenes, the web site and newsletters represent the way in which Celebration chooses to present itself. The reawakening of the public sphere Ross hopes to come from New Urbanism and Celebration is counteracted by the motivation of property value and Celebration's desire to present itself in a hyperreal manner. As long as the social itself is subordinated to a commodified version of the-social-as-selling-point, the public sphere exists only instrumentally. The real concern is whether the house and neighborhood remain profitable and respectable, whether Celebration provides its residents with the opportunity to simultaneously nostalgize and participate in a hyperreal past-future hybrid—"the town your grandparents grew up in" with the added convenience of "all the newfangled, modern stuff" (Ross 25). Civic participation is driven by the attempt to maintain the imagined possibility of Walt's dream, the possibility of living in a neighborhood "at once absolutely realistic and absolutely fantastic" (Eco 43).

Celebration combines the controlled urban space of the mall with the ideals and futurist nostalgia of Disney and New Urbanism; it ideally works against the isolation, homogenization, and privatized public realm of the suburbs, but practically propagates suburbia's property-value-driven, middle-class conformist ideology. The different hyperreal models popularized by Disney, the suburbs, and shopping malls are overlaid and overlap in a dialectical process that eliminates realities and perpetuates the dream of a fully synthesized hyperreal utopia. Celebrationites, like Borges' cartographers, work to cover Celebration with a map of what it should be, erasing "the sovereign difference" between the real and the hyperreal "that constituted the charm of abstraction" (Baudrillard 1–2). If a real public sphere emerges in Celebration—and this caveat is what Ross misses by idealizing the messy, practical complexities of civic life and political participation manifested in the town—it is in the service of the hyperreal: an attempt to make the hyperreal not a destination to which one must travel, but the everyday place where one resides.

Works Cited

Baudrillard, Jean. *Simulacra and Simulation*. Trans. Sheila Faria Glaser. Ann Arbor: University of Michigan Press, 1995.

Celebration Front Porch. Celebration Joint Committee. 2008. 15 April 2009. <http://www. celebration.fl.us/>.

Celebration News. Celebration Town Hall. February 2009. 15 April 2009. <http://www.cel ebration.fl.us/celnews/200902cn.pdf>.

Celebration News. Celebration Town Hall. March 2009. 15 April 2009. <http://www.cel ebration.fl.us/celnews/200903cn.pdf>.

"Charter of the New Urbanism." *Congress for the New Urbanism*. 2007. 15 April 2009. <http://www.cnu.org/charter>.

"CNU History." *Congress for the New Urbanism*. 2007. 15 April 2009 <http://www.cnu. org/history>.

Cuff, Dana. "Enduring Proximity: The Figure of the Neighbor in Suburban America." *Postmodern Culture* 15.2 (2005): n.p. *Project Muse*. 4 February 2009.

Eco, Umberto. *Travels in Hyperreality*. Orlando, FL: Harcourt Brace, 1986.

Fotsch, Paul Mason. "The Politics of Neighbors." *American Quarterly* 52.4 (2000): 782–90. *Project Muse*. 3 February 2009.

Gibian, Peter. "The Art of Being Off-Center: Shopping Center Spaces and Spectacles." In *Signs of Life in the USA: Readings on Popular Culture for Writers*, edited by Sonia Maasik and Jack Solomon, 32–45. Boston: Bedford of St. Martin's, 1994.

Jurca, Catherine. *White Diaspora: The Suburb and the Twentieth-Century American Novel*. Princeton, NJ: Princeton University Press, 2001.

Morse, Margaret. "An Ontology of Everyday Distraction: The Freeway, the Mall, and Television." In *Virtualities: Television, Media Art, and Cyberculture*, 99–123. Bloomington: Indiana University Press, 1998.

Ross, Andrew. *The Celebration Chronicles: Life, Liberty, and the Pursuit of Property Value in Disney's New Town*. New York: Ballantine, 1999.

Schuermer, David. "Utopian Ironies." *Postmodern Culture* 10.2 (2000): n.p. *Project Muse*. 3 February 2009.

Scott, Shelly R. "Conserving, Consuming, and Improving on Nature in Disney's Animal Kingdom." *Theatre Topics* 17.2 (2007): 111–27. *Project Muse*. 4 February 2009.

Soja, Edward. *Postmodern Geographies*. London: Verso, 1989.

Teaford, Jon C. *The American Suburb: The Basics*. New York: Routledge, 2008.

"The Walt Disney Company and Affiliated Companies — Company History." Disney.com. 15 April 2009 <http://corporate.disney.go.com/corporate/complete_history_2.html>.

The Walt Disney Internet Group. "The Disney Store Online Launches with Virtual Grand Opening." 19 November 1996. 15 April 2009 <http://corporate.disney.go.com/wdig/news_release/1996/1996_11_19.html>.

Disneyland's
Influence

Theme Parks and Films — Play and Players

J. P. TELOTTE

While the theme park, as originally conceived and effectively invented by Walt Disney, had no essential connection with the movies, it has become a key component in what Paul Virilio has described as our thoroughly "cinematized" or "mediatized" contemporary cultural landscape (*Lost* 24), taking its inspiration from particular films, exploiting characters created for the movies, and even functioning after the fashion of our popular films. Walt Disney repeatedly described how he originally intended simply to fashion a place where children and their parents could simultaneously engage in pleasurable activities, a kind of "playground" where they could safely "play" together[1]— a place partly modeled on Copenhagen's famed Tivoli Gardens. However, Disneyland, as well as each of the subsequent Disney theme parks, has almost inevitably been shaped by what its founder and the The Walt Disney Company know best, the movie business, as we see demonstrated in the parks' key icons, such as Disneyland's Sleeping Beauty Castle, in a number of their signature rides, such as the *Star Wars* "Star Tours," in their cinematic approach to construction that depends on forced perspectives and carefully-controlled points of view, and perhaps most obviously in the creation of a park devoted entirely to the world of the movies — Disney's Hollywood Studios (formerly Disney–MGM Studios). That embodiment of Disney films and of the larger filmic canvas attests to the extent to which the company's conception of the theme park has been fully colonized by its film icons, as well as by our entire culture's cinematic consciousness, as a place to "play" together has become something more, a kind of set on which — or *in* which — we might collectively participate in various ways in the *filmic* experience, perhaps becoming in the postmodern tradition all the more cinematized ourselves.

Despite the playfulness that seems implicit in the description of such experiences, there is, if we follow Virilio's lead, also a sign of trouble, that implicit in the very trajectory of cinematization. He describes how "a mobile people might easily become entirely victims of the set" (*Art* 79). Of course, the Disney parks were predicated on the emergence of just such a mobile public, particularly in the cases of Disneyland and the Magic Kingdom, both of which were carefully planned with a mind to travel patterns, the development of interstate highways, and the emergence of a populace that in the postwar era had come to see travel itself as a common mode of recreation. The new Disney Vacation Club, which promises to take members on carefully planned, "safe" excursions to well-selected tourist sites throughout the world — effectively treating the world as a large-scale extension of the theme park — is just the latest extrapolation from this conception of "a mobile people." But more to the point, Virilio cautions how, in our contemporary dromoscopic (or speed-oriented) circumstances, "our habitual notions of surface, of limit and separation, have decayed, and given way to those of interface, commutation, intermittance and interruption" (*Lost* 110), leaving us feeling unanchored, sundered from a sense of reality — as if our world had no more substance, significance, or reality than any movie set and as if we were all simply *players* (i.e., actors) within those sets.

Certainly, the Disney parks with their cinematic emphasis might be seen as fostering that effect, of exploiting and profiting from the way contemporary culture seems to "interface" with a cinematic world. In fact, there are simply so many ways in which the parks' many attractions insist on their cinematic nature that our further immersion in that "set" about which Virilio cautions — and our further identification as players — would seem practically inevitable. Given Disney's early recognition and application of the power of synergistic marketing, the company has naturally sought to mine the appeal of its most successful films by basing a number of the earliest Disneyland rides on its top cartoon features: "Snow White's Adventures," "Peter Pan's Flight," "Mad Tea Party" (from *Alice in Wonderland* [1951]). More recently, a work like *Finding Nemo* (2005) has proven the inspiration for Disneyland's restored submarine ride "*Finding Nemo* Submarine Voyage," for the Epcot attractions "The Seas with Nemo and Friends" and "Turtle Talk with Crush," and for Disney's Animal Kingdom's elaborate theatrical presentation "*Finding Nemo*— The Musical." The company has also often rushed exhibits into the parks in order to capitalize on the sudden popularity of its latest releases, as the early Disneyland Davy Crockett Museum and the *20,000 Leagues Under the Sea* exhibit or the more recent Hollywood Studios' "Chronicles of Narnia" presentation attest. Following a model made popular by the 1939–40 New York World's Fair,[2] Disney has also simply created a wide variety of films specifically for the various parks, such as the *Captain EO, Body Wars,* and *Cranium Command* efforts presented over the years at Epcot; the variety of panoramic or Circle-Vision documentaries that have been offered in the national pavilions of that park's World Showcase (works like *O Canada!* and *Reflections of China*); and the special 3-D attractions it has placed in each park, including "Jim Henson's Muppet Vision 3-D" (Disney's Hollywood Studios and Disney's California Adventures), "Honey, I Shrunk the Audience" (Epcot), "It's Tough to be a BugC!" (Disney's Animal Kingdom and Disney's California Adventures), and "Mickey's PhilharMagic" (Magic Kingdom). In recent years condensed musical stage productions of Disney's hit films have also become a popular park feature, as exemplified by the theatrical versions of *Tarzan* (1999), *Beauty and the Beast* (1991), *The Little Mermaid* (1989), and *Finding Nemo*. As this brief listing begins to suggest, many visitors might even be surprised — or disappointed — to find that some attractions do *not* have such an obvious cinematic pedigree. However, in a further suggestion of just how pervasive that film heritage is, we might note how, most recently, Disney has managed to locate even in some of its more conventional "dark rides" a filmic character. Thus, following the pattern of what Henry Jenkins has termed "media convergence,"[3] the company has mined such attractions as "The Haunted Mansion" and "Pirates of the Caribbean" as film texts by recognizing that at the core of their experiences there has always been a highly cinematic nature. Yet in itself this variety of cinematic influences tells us little about the appeal of the Disney parks or helps us understand how they have over more than fifty years managed to speak so effectively to their "guests," or as I would like to frame the issue, how they allowed them to "play" without being reduced to the status of mere "players."

In his Marxist analysis of the Walt Disney World complex, Stephen Fjellman uses this filmic character to frame much of his discussion, observing that "the form that structures our experiences at WDW is the cinema" (11). He suggests that the majority of the rides there tell "cinematic metastories in which each attraction becomes a scene in a larger production" (258), as if each park were itself a film theater and the guests just moviegoers. His point is that, while each park might seem almost a fairgrounds of loosely related attractions, those varied elements betray their ideological logic when seen as parts of a larger corporate movie, unreeling in order to help sell the Disney imaginary. It is an appealingly simple perspective, one that might even lead us to think of the Disney theme parks as if they were like giant metroplexes, with guests simply shifting from one cinematic experience to the next, one short subject to another, and with the transitions made all the easier by employees who are all designated as "cast members," participants in a larger "feature" that *is* the movie world of the parks. Disney's Hollywood Studios' "The Great Movie Ride" is perhaps the ultimate embodiment of this spirit, as it takes trams of spectators — literally a "mobile people" — on a tour of scenes recreated from some of the great films in Hollywood history, led by a cast member who functions, by turns, as tour guide, as a character within one of the movie scenes, and as director of the entire "production." In the course of the ride we are effectively immersed in the world of the movies, as scenes unfold on both sides of the tram; we witness how easily one might pass through the "screen" to become a character in that world, as the highlights of the ride are two points at which the guide and an actor in one of the scenes change places; and we are ushered out "stage right," as if we were now being sent out to "act" in other elements of this film-like world, to function as players. For Fjellman, this cinematic metastory serves to build a larger corporate discourse, that of Disney's constant "hegemonic speech" which is aimed at bringing "everything associated with human life into the market and thus under control" (14), rendering us all — whether we stay "on property" or off— docile inhabitants of and players on the larger "set" that is both Disney and capitalist culture.

Fjellman's argument of "control" easily dovetails with many others that have, in recent years, sought to criticize Disney for its functioning so successfully as a capitalist enterprise; however, it does leave something to be desired, particularly from the vantage of the parks' cinematic consciousness. As several commentators have noted, Disney texts almost invariably prove rather slippery subjects of analysis. The recently reconfigured "Alien Encounter" attraction, for instance, always posed a problem for this analysis. Designed by filmmaker George Lucas and partly inspired by the film *Alien* (1979), it gradually immersed audiences in a demonstration of the latest technology produced by the X-S Tech Corporation. In preparation, viewers watched a film in which Chairman Clench described how his company wished to provide the "less fortunate" peoples throughout the galaxy with the latest technological wonders, such as his new teleportation device, and he noted that the resulting corporate profit from such endeavors "is simply a by-product we have learned to live with." Since in Tomorrowland, the site of the attraction, Disney too offers its guests the latest technological experiences, promises to transport them if not across the galaxy at least to other "worlds" and "kingdoms," and is also renowned for its emphasis on the "by-product" of profits, the introduction inevitably has a self-referential ring — an effect only underscored when, by way of demonstration, a fluffy alien creature is teleported from one side of a room to the other, emerging singed, in some pain, and clearly unwilling to repeat this soon-to-be-offered to the masses technological boon. But in projecting its reputation in this way, in translating it into a presentation that is mindful of the company's exploitation of cute animal figures, and in employing this comically reflexive mode, the attraction also effectively disarms its audience, allows them to, as it were, *knowingly* buy into the narrative that is being constructed and in which they would soon take a role. More broadly, it reminds us of a point made by Eleanor Byrne and Martin McQuillan who have wrestled with this question. Arguing, much like Fjellman, that the typical Disney text is "synonymous with a certain conservative, patriarchal, heterosexual ideology" and with a powerful "American cultural imperialism" (1–2), they also recognize that it is almost "self-evidently" so, in fact, that there is a certain "blatantness of Disney" that "makes it so resistant to the challenge of ideological exposure" (3), as "contradictory and unstable ideological codes" (5) surface at almost every turn in the Disney worlds.

While this "blatantness," as Byrne and McQuillan put it, presents a problem in trying to understand the obvious popularity of the Disney attractions, it also offers an interesting insight into those Disney texts, particularly since it corresponds so neatly to that other element of self-consciousness we have observed, the parks' emphasis on — and constant evocation of— the movies as a pervasive context. For the movies are both part of a stratagem of blatantness — they too constantly show themselves, even show their very showiness — and a clue as to one of the key appeals of the parks. By way of exploring this connection further, we might consider several exemplary "cinematic" attractions, selected for their different natures, their own levels of blatantness, and their popularity.

For one case study, I want to turn to one of the Disney's Animal Kingdom's most popular rides, "Dinosaur: Countdown to Extinction." Based on the Disney animated film *Dinosaur* (2000) and employing the same motion-simulator technology as another movie-based ride, Disneyland's "Indiana Jones Adventure," it involves guests in time travel to the end of the Dinosaur era where they help retrieve a young specimen for "The Disney Institute," the putative foundation for paleontological research that houses the ride and that is supported, as a sign notes, by "a generous grant" from the McDonald's Corporation — which provides the burgers and fries at the "Restaurantosaurus" restaurant located opposite the ride. These obvious capitalist resonances recall the similar emphases noted in the "Alien Encounter" attraction, and they find an echo in another filmic element here, the videos that riders must see in the "Orientation Room" prior to boarding their time machines. In the first of these films we learn that the Institute's technology, designed for direct observation of the past, will make traditional history study obsolete — or as the Director of the Disney Institute tells us, "the future of history is the past." It is a comment that, while sounding clever, also hints at an unsettling attitude, a belittling of traditional historical study in favor of a technological or mediatized solution. And that attitude is made all the clearer in the following video, wherein our "tour guide" reveals that we will be involved in an "unscheduled" activity; we shall not simply *view* the past as if it were a 3-D movie, but help to retrieve a dinosaur specimen — the young Iguanodon of the Disney film — that we are told might subsequently be displayed — or sold, or starred in a movie (like *Dinosaur*), or perhaps even turned into Dinoburgers at Restaurantosaurus. The attitudes displayed here and the questionable use to which this new technology is being put only underscore the corporate profiteering that is one of this ride's key subtexts and one of its own most blatant bits of reflexivity.

Of course, the sense that guests are involved in a conspiratorial activity, along with the dangers that an impending meteor shower and the presence of meat-eating dinosaurs lend to the enterprise, helps motivate the thrill portion of the ride. But what is also significant is our gradual immersion in that world — an immersion that begins with the building housing the ride that looks and, with its carefully-crafted exhibits, even functions just like a real paleontological museum. It is a key to achieving the attraction's overall effect. For we are step-by-step and via a series of short films recruited into this movie-like world and its relatively familiar action-adventure narrative: asked to buy into its ideology, to embrace its technological attitude, to play along with its hidden profiteering agenda. And we do so not because we share the ideology, prefer technology, or champion unfettered capitalism. Rather, it is because we like the sort of safe thrills that the movie-like world offers us, the sense that we *can* pass through and immerse ourselves in that experience — but also pass back, *play* at playing along. Mark Dery in his discussion of the Disney theme parks' major predecessor, Coney Island, notes that a number of its attractions seemed to create a kind of "permeable membrane between fact and fiction, actual and virtual" (30), an effect that he sees as a persistent character of postmodern technological culture. I would suggest that this "permeable membrane" effect is fundamental to the "Dinosaur" ride, as its "blatant" elements, its various "shows," invite us to step through into this world, to relish its adventure, even as we remain secure in our own identities — or in this case, in our own time and place, even our own values.

It is a similar permeability that we see performed in the various movie-focused stunt shows that have become another staple of the Disney parks, as well as those run by its competitor Universal Studios. Disney's Hollywood Studios park hosts two such attractions, the "Lights. Motors. Action! Extreme Stunt Show" (also at Disneyland Paris) and the "Indiana Jones Epic Stunt Spectacular!" although there are several other rides that, appropriately for this park, take a similarly behind-the-scenes focus on the movies, perhaps most notably Hollywood Studios' "Backlot Tour."[4] While "Dinosaur" first established its reflexive pattern and then immersed guests into its thrill experience, the "Indiana Jones Epic Stunt Spectacular!" begins with an exciting, live-action event, a highly atmospheric, near-recreation of the opening scene of *Raiders of the Lost Ark* (1981), wherein Indiana Jones negotiates a series of ancient traps in order to steal a golden idol. At the conclusion of the thrilling scene, a voice shouts "cut," the lights come up, stage hands appear, and props are put back in place in case another "take" might be needed. And at this point the blatant dimension comes to the fore, as the "second-unit director" appears, introducing the stunt double we have seen in action, playing at Harrison Ford playing Indiana Jones, explaining that the "crew" will be "shooting" other scenes connected to the film, and proposing to show us how these and other exciting effects are typically achieved. It is a sudden shift, underscoring how easily the movies can draw us into their world, and how movie audiences are manipulated by the medium's mechanisms. And the promise to demystify the movies, by providing guests with an insider's knowledge of how they typically work — and work *on us* — suggests the possibility of gaining a certain power over them, effectively reversing that pattern of "control" that Fjellman notes. However, we have to recognize that the very appeal of this attraction depends largely on its exploitation of the cinematic illusion, thanks to the very magnitude of the sets, the manifest skill of the personnel involved, and the elaborate coordination of pyrotechnics and action involved in the various scenes.

Moreover, we implicitly understand that, despite the presence of cameras, microphone booms, various "production personnel," and even the "stunt doubles" for Harrison Ford and Karen Allen, no scenes are actually being shot here; guests are not witnessing a movie's production. But we buy into — or simply enjoy — the show partly because it is such an impressive cognate of the movies, and also because it literally invites us in, in fact, recruits guests as players in the show, where they effectively stand-in for the rest of us, as also occurs in a ride like "Backlot Tour." At the start, a "casting director" seeks out volunteers to play various "roles" in the upcoming shoot, allowing them to identify themselves before the rest of the audience, giving them comic bits to perform (and for those not selected to relish and applaud), and sending them off "to wardrobe" for appropriate costuming. When they subsequently reappear in the show, forming a crowd of "native" onlookers in a Cairo street scene, they not only help justify our own easy fascination with the movies' illusory world, but they also suggest the possibility for crossing over that "permeable membrane," for seeing that world, and the world of the theme parks, as an extension of our own. When it is later revealed that one of these volunteers who has clearly been singled out for various humorous indignities is not actually one of us, but rather a "plant," a trained stuntman, we recognize that there is another level of playing along going on here, another dimension of audience manipulation. But that additional revelation only more blatantly renders the movies in this and the other similarly functioning behind-the-scenes attractions as fake, as constructed worlds, and as manipulative mechanisms of the first order, while also helping to reassure us that we can indeed recognize their characteristics, even conspire in their power through our own playing along with the illusion.

In the cases of both "Dinosaur: Countdown to Extinction" and the "Indiana Jones Epic Stunt Spectacular!" we thus see an interesting paradox at work: a blatantness or rendering transparent that works hand in hand with our immersion in the attractions' worlds. To add further dimension to this dynamic, I want to briefly examine another sort of ride that has a rather less conventional link to the world of the movies. Grounded in an old amusement park tradition of the "dark ride," "Pirates of the Caribbean" remains one of the Disney parks' signature and most popular attractions. It employs a great number of the company's signature Audio-Animatronics robots, its Caribbean sets are elaborate and convincingly realized (if also done on the reduced scale and with the forced perspective found throughout the parks), and its "fun" atmosphere is keyed by one of the Disney parks' most memorable theme songs, "Yo Ho, Yo Ho, a Pirate's Life for Me." Of course, its overt concerns — murder, pillaging, torture — do seem an ill fit for Disney's family reputation; as Fjellman understates the case, "masked by the fun, the story told is not so pleasant" (228). Yet that issue of fit may be precisely the point here, the blatantness at work in this ride, as it foregrounds the avarice and power some would associate with Disney, while also readily acknowledging what in early discussions of Disney productions has often been glossed over, that is, that transgressing the boundaries of culture or propriety, that *playing* at being a pirate, can be fun, as the attractions centered on such other popular culture transgressors as Tom Sawyer ("Tom Sawyer Island"), Peter Pan ("Peter Pan's Flight"), and Mr. Toad ("Mr. Toad's Wild Ride) all readily illustrate.

And while "Pirates" is not based on any specific film, it too has a cinematic background, as its scenes freely quote from a number of classics of the genre, most notably *Captain Blood* (1935), *The Spanish Main* (1945), *The Crimson*

Pirate (1952), and *The Buccaneer* (1938, 1958). Perhaps more to the point, it, like many other rides at the parks, draws heavily on a cinematic model for its structure, particularly that of classical film narrative with its emphasis on an objective point of view, readily identifiable central characters, cause-effect logic, the linear arrangement of events, and narrative closure. As Bordwell, Staiger, and Thompson describe this model, it also relies upon a mindfulness of the audience's relation to the text, for classical narration typically "places a spectator within or on the edge of the narrative space," even extending "that space out toward" the audience's position in order to create "a more three-dimensional narrative space" and thus enhance the possibility for our sense of involvement (158). To bring us into this historical world, the ride thus begins with various atmospheric tableaux, a warning about entering into this world, delivered (in the current version of the ride) by the figure of Davy Jones, projected onto a sheet of mist, and then a watery plunge into the initial scene of an attack on a Caribbean port. These various spatial markers not only build a foreboding yet exciting context for what is to follow, but they effectively reach "out toward" us, literalizing that sense of a dividing "membrane" through the misty curtain and waterfall we have to traverse, while also providing us with the sort of knowledge or sense of complicity — of playing along — that we have noted in the other attractions.

It is another component of classical film narrative, though, that qualifies this sense of participation and underscores the real thrust of this attraction. Certainly, the pirates we watch are manifestly enjoying themselves, but with the exception of the recently added figure of Captain Jack Sparrow, drawn from the three movie versions of this ride, they are all fashioned as grotesques, and the original closure for this ride, with a group of drunken pirates sitting atop kegs of gunpowder while firing pistols and rifles at each other, promises a volatile and appropriate end to their chaotic reign. Classical narrative, of course, usually offered not only closure, but closure of a particular sort: an ending in which wrong-doing is punished, justice served, order restored. With that implied explosive punishment — or in the most recent updating of the ride,[5] the implication that the pirates will simply be outsmarted by Captain Jack Sparrow and thwarted in their quest for riches — that classical pattern is served and guests are freed to rise out of this netherworld, as they do when their boats literally ride *up* another waterfall at the ride's conclusion.

The fact that "Pirates" has inspired a trio of Disney's most popular live-action films, *Pirates of the Caribbean: Curse of the Black Pearl* (2003), *Pirates of the Caribbean: Dead Man's Chest* (2006), and *Pirates of the Caribbean: At World's End* (2007) suggests a further possible gloss on this attraction, another dimension of "media convergence." For as the comments on Captain Jack

Sparrow indicate, the films have also influenced the latest version of their ride inspiration, making it more cinematically self-consciousness, while eliminating some of its violent implications — such as the explosive ending — and suggesting that the very term "pirate" might be open to different interpretations. This is the point that Elizabeth Swan, the governor's daughter in the movies, comes to recognize, as she sees that "pirate" might simply be a term to describe someone like her who wants freedom from society's dictates — including the freedom not to wear a corset. And as the gruesome opening of *Pirates of the Caribbean: At World's End* suggests, with its seemingly endless line of men, women, and children all condemned to the public gallows, it could well refer to all those who do not abide a government's repressive actions. Seen in the light of the films and their emendations, the ride thus becomes a show of alternatives between two types of piracy, the bloodthirsty and amoral sort associated with Captain Barbossa and the attack on the town that remains the attraction's centerpiece, and the freedom-loving sort embodied in Captain Jack and his constant efforts — now inserted into most of the ride's scenes — to escape capture by all sides. And it is he with whom we identify in the new "Pirates" ride, as we play at spotting Captain Jack in the various scenes, even as he repeatedly avoids the notice of the other pirates all around him. At risk of suggesting a somewhat less than blatant dimension to this attraction, we might read what follows our watery descent into this world as the playing out of a kind of moral struggle between these alternatives, while our almost improbable ascent points up our own freedom, a freedom from the lure of the "set" in which we just been immersed, in fact, our ability to play with these cinematic sets and Audio-Animatronics players, much like Captain Jack does.

On this note we have obviously returned to that caution from Paul Virilio with which this essay began. His warning about becoming "cinematized," about becoming "victims of the set," must seem, at least on one level, quite appropriate for those who enter the Disney parks. For the signs of the cinema, as we have seen, are there at every turn — or turnstile. The elements of film fakery — even the fakes of that fakery, as in the case of the "Indiana Jones Stunt Spectacular!" the "Backlot Tour," and the "Lights. Motors. Action! Extreme Stunt Show" — are central attractions. And the structures of film subtly construct much of our park experience, even our walk down the quaint Disney Main Street. Yet for the most part, as we have also noted, these effects are overt, obvious, blatant, as is, increasingly, Disney's own reputation mocking. The show is almost always showing itself, and showing too how easily we might step in *and out* of its precincts, across the filmic "membrane," while retaining our own "control."

Perhaps it is only natural that in constructing a postmodern space in which to "play," Disney would have looked to and depended upon an earlier model of industrialized pleasure, that of the movies and movie theaters. However, what we see and experience in the parks are not just the movies; they are the movies-as-rides, attractions that do invite us to play roles, even "sell" that participation, while also reminding us of how those movies typically play *us*— manipulating and controlling us both within and outside of their precincts. And as the immense popularity of the various Disney parks throughout the world attests, people are interested in "buying" that full sensibility, including the level of knowledge or awareness that is offered. But through such experiences — and in a variety of modes — Disney offers not just an illusion or pleasant fantasy, but ultimately a different awareness, actually a kind of *play* or playfulness. Disney does not simply fool us or immerse us in the sort of reality illusion that has always been the film industry's stock-in-trade, but rather it winks at us and gets us to acknowledge our own complicity with the technologically mediated world — which is Disney's complicity as well — and all that it so attractively promises to deliver.

Of course, being able to craft that sort of paradox is an interesting accomplishment in itself. Yet more important is the payoff that is involved. For the Disney parks — as it seems Walt Disney early on realized — ultimately provide their guests with far more than a site of play or a "magic kingdom." And as I have tried to suggest, they are more too than just movie-like mechanisms of control, treating guests as players in their movies. Through the complex, movie-modeled structures of their attractions, and through their ability to speak the universal language of the movies, they also help us negotiate our own difficulties with a reality that has become somewhat less reliably real as our world itself becomes ever more cinematized or mediatized. One of the appeals of the parks, then, is that they offer more than just escape from a dreary contemporary culture or "flight from public space and social responsibility," as Mark Dery has recently suggested (172). Rather, they let us explore the "sets" of our world, the sets that, as Virilio reminds, threaten to victimize us, to make our lives less real, and in doing so, in playing in these precincts, we can, if only briefly, reverse the control a cinematized world would wield over us.

Notes

1. For background on Walt Disney's initial conception of the theme park, see Thomas' *Walt Disney: An American Original,* pp. 241–47, and Neal Gabler's *Walt Disney: The Triumph of the American Imagination,* pp. 484–85. I draw my motif of "play" here in part

from a brochure Walt Disney created to accompany his planning sketches as he sought funding for the theme park project. In that brochure, Disney pointedly described the proposed Disneyland as "a playground" (246–47).

2. It is worth noting that during the two-year run of the New York World's Fair, more than 500 different films were screened on the grounds. For a brief commentary on these films, see Kihlstedt's "Utopia Realized," pp. 110–11.

3. "Media convergence," as Jenkins describes it, actually refers to a variety of effects that he sees occurring in our contemporary, highly mediated culture: "the flow of media across multiple media platforms, the cooperation between multiple media industries, and the migratory behavior of media audiences" (2). All of these practices can easily be observed in the interactions between Disney's theme parks and its films.

4. Disney has recognized the attraction and, quite naturally, the profitability that attaches to such behind-the-scenes shows and has created special guided tours that effectively treat the parks themselves as large-scale movies — or shows — providing guests with access to normally off-limits sections of the parks, with explanations of how certain effects are achieved, and with historical background on the various attractions. Among these special offerings, we might note Epcot's "Behind the Seeds" and the Magic Kingdom's "Keys to the Kingdom" tours.

5. The recently revised version of "Pirates of the Caribbean" offers a slightly altered conclusion, one in which we see the figure of Captain Jack enjoying the treasure that the pirates, under the direction of Captain Barbossa, have been seeking. The new focus of the ride is on the pirates' effort to capture Captain Jack and gain a map to hidden treasure. His ability to avoid capture, combined with the new implication that the treasure is not that of the town, but rather pirate gold, lends a new thrust to the ride's narrative and also suggests that a new sort of justice has been achieved by the end of our trip.

Works Cited

Bordwell, David, Janet Staiger, and Kristin Thompson. *The Classical Hollywood Cinema: Film Style and Mode of Production to 1960*. New York: Columbia University Press, 1985.

Byrne, Eleanor, and Martin McQuillan. *Deconstructing Disney*. London: Pluto, 1999.

Dery, Mark. *The Pyrotechnic Insanitarium: American Culture on the Brink*. New York: Grove, 1999.

Fjellman, Stephen J. *Vinyl Leaves: Walt Disney World and America*. Boulder: Westview, 1992.

Gabler, Neal. *Walt Disney: The Triumph of the American Imagination*. New York: Knopf, 2006.

Jenkins, Henry. *Convergence Culture: Where Old and New Media Collide*. New York: New York University Press, 2006.

Kihlstedt, Folke T. "Utopia Realized: The World's Fairs of the 1930s." *History, Technology, and the American Future*, edited by Joseph J. Corn, 97–118. Cambridge: MIT Press, 1986.

Thomas, Bob. *Walt Disney: An American Original*. New York: Hyperion, 1994.

Virilio, Paul. *Art and Fear*. Trans. Julie Rose. London: Continuum, 2003.

_____. *The Lost Dimension*. Trans. Daniel Moshenberg. New York: Semiotext(e), 1991.

Of Theme Parks and Television
Walt Disney, Rod Serling,
and the Politics of Nostalgia

DOUGLAS BRODE

Though Walt Disney and his company would emerge between 1955 and the present as one of the top (if not the top) suppliers of T.V. product in that medium's history, the man who ran Buena Vista until his passing in 1966 had resisted prior opportunities to work in television on a weekly basis. Disney did participate in event programs, first hosting "One Hour in Wonderland" (December 25, 1950), then participating in a special edition of CBS's *Toast of the Town* (February 8, 1953) with Ed Sullivan. Though brief clips from Disney classics were included, such rare TV outings were designed to promote then-current film projects (*Alice in Wonderland, Peter Pan*). Earlier, Disney said "no" to NBC and CBS (then competing for the status of leading network) as to what seemed a natural: regularly running the backlog of Disney product. So why did he at last agree to do weekly T.V.? More intriguing, why on the third (a low third at that!) place network which, during the four seasons that the Nielsen ratings had been in effect, scored only one Top Twenty hit, *The Lone Ranger*?

The larger/prestigious networks were still interested, but not on Disney's terms. He knew full well that if all he desired was a once-a-year opportunity to hype a new film, he could continue with the in-place syndrome. What captivated Disney's imagination then was Disneyland, the planned park. This explains why, for its first four years, the TV program was called *Disneyland*, that title eventually dropped in favor of others, beginning with *Walt Disney Presents* in the 1959-60 season, changed again to *Walt Disney's Wonderful World of Color* when the series switched to NBC. There it would remain for a full two decades, until 1981. Other temporary titles included *Disney's Wonderful World*, that one providing P.R. for the second park, located in Florida. The first had been chosen because Disneyland, and not feature films, was primarily to be hyped and as often as possible. During the first season, "Operation Undersea" (December 8, 1954), a behind-the-scenes peek at the upcoming epic *20,000 Leagues Under the Sea* (released on December 23, 1954), was the only hour-long program to preview a theatrical project. There would, however, be four (three Wednesday night hour-long filmed installments plus a 90 min. live weekend afternoon special) designed to "educate" the public as to the park's existence.

The first installment of *Disneyland* (October 27, 1954) was titled "The Disneyland Story," referring to the upcoming place. Though that evening's fare did feature scenes from what would be offered during the first season on the air, notably the three-part *Davy Crockett* mini-series, as well as a trio of Mickey Mouse cartoons, most of the running time served to explain the park's stages of conception and the reality even then being built in Anaheim. Here then is the key as to why Disney, despite his high profile, accepted a deal from the then low-status network. Already successful, NBC and CBS would have welcomed the Disney product. Neither was about to allow their airtime to openly be used for such a calculated purpose. ABC had no choice; to entice the Disney brand into an association with their venue (ABC drew to a closer third in the overall ratings and, in time, full parity), they'd let Disney dictate the rules.

On that premiere night, Disney at once revealed a map showing four various lands and the entranceway, Main Street, U.S.A. All but the latter had been identified for viewers in the animated opening credits, which would remain in use for four years: Tinker Bell, flying about from one area to the other, employing pixie-dust as she highlighted each. Though in later years this division of stories into a quartet of anthologies would be dropped, and while even in those early seasons unique episodes had to be shoe-horned into one or the other sub-division, the implication had to be obvious: *Disneyland* the show and Disneyland the park were one and the same. If there was a single running theme to *Disneyland*'s first year on the air, it was the park's gestation period.

The second such episode, filling viewers in as to what had transpired during the past four months, was suitably titled "A Progress Report" (February 9, 1955). Host Disney offered precisely that for a half an hour, followed by the True-Life Adventure "Nature's Half Acre." Such an openly commercial approach, rendered acceptable by Disney's appealing onscreen image, allowed audiences to feel as if they had a personal stake in the park's success. TV's intimate nature at that time of small screens playing to entire families, added to this sensation. When in due time the "Pre-Opening Report" aired (July 13, 1955), viewers felt as if the long, hard process amounted to a personal victory for *them*; this half hour update was followed by reruns of the same Mickey shorts offered on the opening show. This sense of congruity between Disneyland the park and *Disneyland* the show, if not already absolute in anyone's mind, would be forever cemented the following Sunday. As the park opened for its first day of business, "Dateline Disneyland" presented a live projection of the festivities as they unfolded. Official hosts Art Linkletter and Bob Cummings and guest host Ronald Reagan did their best to play down opening day malfunctions, duly reported elsewhere, even as they, Disney, and other luminaries somehow maintained a happy face.

If TV had been employed to make the park a part of the public imagination before it opened, this moment set the icing on the cake. Viewers of the still relatively new medium felt as if they were a part of the happening while wondering if a family trip to Disneyland might someday serve as the ultimate vacation. After all, hadn't they, thanks to the magic of television, been involved in its creation? Bob Hope and other celebrities had chosen not to invest in Walt's seemingly impossible dream (the cost originally estimated at a then-inconceivable $6,000,000) for fear that the concept might not work. Later, they would admit that they had missed out on a sure thing, wondering how they could have been so wrong-headed. The possibility remains that, if Disney had not been so sharp in his analysis of how nearly a year of TV promotion would make the difference between a failed venture and a successful one, they might have been proven right. In addition to episodes listed above, endless references to the coming park were slipped into the host's opening remarks, a *Crockett* adventure a good bet for a subliminal reference to Frontierland.

Without such promotion, the park might have remained virtually unknown outside of Southern California. TV, in the hands of a master, made all the difference. If Disney were something of a late comer to television, he defined the very nature of the medium which the public was then coming to accept as our most basic form of viewed-entertainment even as Disney, with his park, redefined the American vacation.

In the past, joy rides were merely possible sidelights; at once, they became the arbiter of potential destinations. What child could possibly watch *Davy Crockett and the River Pirates* (December 14, 1955) and not dream of riding downriver on the keelboat that Davy (Fess Parker) learned to navigate? That TV-created dream, Disney assured his audience, could soon be incarnated in reality: just such a keelboat awaited holiday season customers on the park's

"Rivers of America." Some day, every viewer decided, I've got to go there and, like the hero of this show, step on board; live out an adventure I know I'll love because I've already seen it on TV.

One avid viewer of the show and, in short time, fan of the park was a thirty-year-old writer named Rod Serling. Like Disney, Serling always remained a small-town boy at heart; the former hailed from Marceline, Missouri, the latter from Binghamton, New York. Just as Disney had left his journeyman work in Kansas City and traveled to California in 1923 to break into the still-evolving film business, so did Serling in 1951 move from Cincinnati to New York to find employment in the brave new world of live television. But the era of *Playhouse 90* and *Studio One* drew to an end as Rod provided them with several classics (*Patterns*, January 12, 1955; *Requiem for a Heavyweight*, January 11, 1956). Disney's success on ABC caused the networks to determine that live broadcasting ought to be retained only for talk, game, variety and news. At this juncture Rod Serling moved to L.A., where TV had to be headquartered now that the transition was all but complete. He set to work developing *The Twilight Zone* (CBS, 1959–64), for the next five years struggling to convey serious messages while appearing to produce escapist fantasy.

On *Zone*, Serling would also slip in autobiographical material of the sort that had previously surfaced in his realistic work. Most notably, in *The Velvet Alley* (January 22, 1959), among Serling's final non-fantasy pieces for *Playhouse 90*, a once idealistic TV writer and Serling surrogate discovers that, in the medium's new paradigm, creativity too often gives way to calculated commercialism. Flawed protagonist "Ernie Pandish" wails: "They give you $1,000 a week and keep giving you $1,000 a week until that's what you need to live on. Then... You (exist) in a nightmare for fear that they'll take it away from you." Without ever naming his upcoming show Serling referenced *Zone*. CBS wanted sci-fi with some nifty scares; he hoped to create a commentary on the emptiness of the Eisenhower-era. Rod's daily struggle to keep the upcoming series "his," despite CBS's constant efforts to make it "theirs," left him exhausted, fearing that he had "optioned his soul." One weekend afternoon, distressed over the fear that he might "give up a little more" come Monday, Rod hopped into his car and wheeled away from his home, wishing more than anything that he could return to some earlier and, in his now erratic state of mind, kinder/gentler point in life.

Months later, the first overtly autobiographical *Zone* episode to be telecast began with a fantastical extension of precisely that flight from Serling's all-too-real situation. "Walking Distance" (October 30, 1959) opens as "Martin Sloan" (Gig Young) wildly drives up to an out-of-the-way gas station, fleeing from his intolerable upscale lifestyle. "This is not just a Sunday drive," Serling explained in his voice-over; "he is looking for an Exodus." Realizing he's inadvertently come close to the small town where he grew up, Sloan wanders into "Homewood." To Sloan's amazement, the village has not changed in twenty-five years. Or so it seems. Sloan is the first of many *Zone* visitors to segue back in time to the way things were. Or, perhaps more correctly, the way he — and we — wish they had been.

Importantly, the Homewood scenes were not filmed in an actual small-town, either Serling's beloved Binghamton in upstate New York or something similar in California; rather, on the MGM back-lot, a standing set once used for those enduring/endearing Andy Hardy films, which idealized small town America as only the 1930s Hollywood Dream Factory could. Those images continued to prevail when such films were endlessly viewed and re-viewed on television, even as the actual small towns that such sets had romanticized were transformed over the years. Organically developed downtowns were after World War II replaced by cookie cutter shopping malls; haphazard neighborhoods gave way to formulized tracts. With little comparison now possible, the TV viewing public came to believe that a lovely lie had once been actuality. At that moment, the nostalgia craze began. As critic Richard Schickel noted in *The Disney Version*, our national longing, during those postwar years, was for "an imagined past"; a fantasy that, with each successive year of removal of the postwar people from an ever-diminishing real thing, small-town America was mentally reconfigured into a golden age (31).

At that point the dramatic thrust of "Walking Distance" shifts from the village to an amusement pier just beyond the town limits. Here, Sloan discovers a humble precursor to the large-scale theme parks then in the process of replacing them. On a carrousel, Sloan confronts the child (Michael Montgomery) he once was, informing him that "this is a wonderful time of life for you. Don't let any of it go by without enjoying it." Grasping that he and his child-self cannot long remain in the same sphere, the man leaves, accepting that "there's only one summer to every customer." Or, as Thomas Wolfe put it, You Can't Go Home Again. Still, the episode ends on a cautiously optimistic note. Sloan's father (Frank Overton), realizing that this dark stranger is indeed a grown-up projection of his son, softly insists: "Maybe when you go back you'll find there *are* merry-go-rounds and band concerts." Perhaps the problem is not that they no longer exist, only that Sloan hasn't been searching in the right places.

Shortly before writing "Walking Distance," Rod had taken his wife, Carol, and their daughters, Jodie and Nan, to Disneyland. One might expect that the man even then creating the greatest science-fiction series in TV history would head directly for Tomorrowland. Yet Carol most vividly recalled Rod's joy while riding on the immense Carrousel in the heart of Fantasyland, listening to a band concert on Main Street, U.S.A., then traveling by raft over to Tom Sawyer Island. The carrousel specifically reminded Rod of the one he, as a child, rode in Binghamton. The Mark Twain attraction recalled a still earlier era, one Serling had missed and, as such, seemed even more golden than the recalled joys of his own actual childhood.

Serling has always been perceived as a political liberal and Democrat, Disney a conservative Republican. Still, Serling's unbridled delight at what he discovered at Disney's park suggests a link between the two that cuts through any easy, simplistic notions of party loyalty.

If Walt "had any politics at all," Schickel notes, "it was the politics of nostalgia" (37). By 1959, the public at large already grasped what eluded Martin Sloan, if not the writer who created him: one only had to visit Disneyland to re-experience the good ol' days. Here, it's necessary to note Disney's inspiration for the park that, in his own words, incarnated "the happiest place on earth." Like Serling, Disney had two daughters, Diane Marie (with wife Lilly) and Sharon Mae (adopted). Also like Serling, Disney decided one afternoon, if several years earlier, to escape the stress in his own life by taking the girls to the sort of amusement park he recalled from his youth. As every Disney biographer has noted, Walt instead encountered a sleazy remnant of what had once been. Rusty rides, their paint long since peeled away, did not appear safe. The charm was gone, what remained but a bitter foil for a once agreeable sanctuary. As he left, Disney rightly guessed that most other parents felt the same way. Being Disney, he decided to do something about it. What he originally conceived as some small rides near his Burbank studio, plus picnic tables, gradually grew into an ever more ambitious conception.

So! As far apart as they might currently be posited in the annals of American popular culture — one soothed us into sweet dreams, the other inspired nightmares — Disney and Serling are in truth considerably less than polar. Lest we forget, *Snow White and the Seven Dwarfs* (1937) had been refused a General Admission status in England owing to a fear that its dark images might permanently scar children; likewise the Snow White attraction in Fantasyland had to be toned down when Disney Imagineers realized that kids were devastated by the wicked Witch and simulated winds. On the other hand, such comedic Serling scripts as "Mr. Dingle, the Strong" (March 3, 1961), Burgess Meredith playing a sad little fellow blessed with remarkable power by a pair of easygoing Martians, could as easily have been broadcast on *Disneyland* as on *Zone*. Indeed, anyone tuning in that night in hopes of a fright could only come away disappointed by the overall pleasantness of the episode's tone.

Serling and Disney, properly understood, are united by an instinctive subscription to what Schickel described as a growing hunger for "an imagined past that informed much of the new popular culture," which developed while *Disneyland* and *The Twilight Zone* were both first run on TV (42). Disneyland the park meanwhile allowed Serling and others, disappointed by the domestic conformity within suburbia's sprawl, to rediscover not only carrousels and calliopes but a vivid and believable if simplified and idealized equivalent of the small-towns that once contained them. If Homewood evoked Disneyland's Main Street, U.S.A, the village in Serling's "A Stop at Willoughby" (May 6, 1960) offered a carbon copy of what Disney insisted must be the first area any visitor to his park experienced. Fantasy, our old Frontier, International adventure and the brave new world of Tomorrow awaited. Your choice! First though *everyone* had to experience Marceline, Missouri as Disney now recalled it. However quaint Homewood appeared to Martin Sloan, no calliope played on its main street. That's the first thing "Gart Williams" (James Daly) notices about the title place in "Willoughby."

A passenger on a commuter train from Manhattan to his upscale hell in Connecticut, Gart — Serling's second alter-ego — falls asleep and dreams that the train (converted to a turn of the century model, just like the one Disneyland visitors, Serling one of them, could board at the park's entrance) has halted in a kind of quaint turn-of-the-century Shangri-La. There, Twain's Tom Sawyer and Huckleberry Finn return from a day of fishing on the river; though we don't get to see it, doubtless their island appears identical to the one Serling visited at Disneyland. The calliope Williams listens to looks precisely like the one Rod adored on Main Street, U.S.A, even located adjacent to a gazebo pretty much identical to the one that Walt lovingly placed on his Main Street. Marceline, Missouri in the 1920s; Binghamton, New York, the 1930s. For that matter any hometown *any* American alive, if not well, living in the postwar world longed for.

In Serling's "Willoughby," Gart pays the ultimate price for his trip: dying as, lost in his dream, he leaps off the moving train. This figure had his counterparts in "serious" literature of the era. The confused hero in John Cheever's "The Swimmer" loses his sense of self and embarks on a doomed odyssey, diving into one neighbor's pool after another in a furtive attempt to navigate his way back to something he lost along the way; the characters in J.D. Salinger's "Uncle Wiggly in Connecticut" cry about the bygone innocence of a dimly recalled youth, symbolized in that story by a children's literature second-cousin to many characters created by Disney. Perhaps the problem for these fictional well-to-do Americans is that they hadn't tuned into *Disneyland* on Wednesday evenings and learned about the escape valve offered by Disneyland. Had they, like so many actual Americans, they would have grasped that anyone could now stroll down Main Street, U.S.A., stop for a ride on the carrousel, then head off to Tom Sawyer Island without risk.

Not that Walt Disney World Resort in Florida, its California predecessor, or any of the international incarnations — Disney Paris, Tokyo DisneySea — continue to be confined to such sweet-spirited mini-journeys of the type that once seduced visitors into experiencing first hand the fable-fantasies of yore. Most of the once-loved attractions on Main Street have disappeared, notably the country-style restaurant where early-arriving guests enjoyed a leisurely breakfast. Later, they often took their time riding on a horse-drawn streetcars, a horseless carriage, the old red fire engine, or the large Omnibus to the avenue's end. Most people today rush past Main Street's flower stands or barber shop, eager to get to the modern thrill rides awaiting them in the park's other sectors. Storybook Land, the lyrical boat ride that leisurely swept guests past recreations of simple fairytale fun in '54, wouldn't be recreated in Florida's Walt Disney World when that location came into fruition some fifteen years after the first park opened its gates. The Haunted Mansion, with its palpable scares, would be. It's thrill-aspect had long since replaced softer attractions.

Everything exists in context; what frightened our collective consciousness in, say, 1959 attains with the passing of years its own aura of nostalgia. When created in '69, The Haunted Mansion may well have seemed the ultimate avatar of intense excitement in what remained, at heart, a family-oriented park. A quarter — century later, with tacit understanding that the public had by now experienced the *Halloween* and *Friday the Thirteenth* movies, something more kicky was required. The volume had to be pumped up. Again! Not that there would be attractions relating to those films; they were still too edgy, though at some point in the future ... but by the early nineties what was considered edgy way back in '59 had come to seem tame, charming even; Rod's *Zone* now recalled as much a beloved part of that era as Disney's *land*. With that in mind how could the two *not* come together?

On July 22, 1994, "The Twilight Zone Tower of Terror" premiered at Disney–MGM Studios in Florida. Its success led to similar attractions at the California (2004), Tokyo (2006), and French (2008) properties. An elevator-drop thrill ride, the original Tower — stretching 199 ft. high — enticed brave souls eager to enjoy Grand Guignol frissons to que up before a lightning-scarred hotel. By this point in time, Florida's ever more extensive "world" already included such non–Disney film–based features as Star Tours (inspired by the George Lucas's *Star Wars* film for 20th Century–Fox) and The Indiana Jones Stunt Spectacular (Lucas and Spielberg's *Raiders of the Lost Ark* for Paramount). Such an inclusionary attitude had been initiated with the appearance of the Florida studio-park, titled Disney–MGM Studios for no other reason than that The Walt Disney Company wanted to include what may be the finest non–Disney family film of all time, *The Wizard of Oz* (1939), in The Great Movie Ride, and permission to do so legally bound them to let MGM share top-billing.

A sense of completeness, if not outright closure, occurred as not only artistic descendants of Disney and Serling, but Serling himself found a place in the "lands" and "worlds" that outlived both key creators.

The Tower of Terror initially transports guests to October 31, 1939, that juncture in Hollywood history when *The Wizard of Oz* was released. Also, in the view of most film historians, 1939 was at once the greatest single year for the Old Studio system (*Gone with the Wind*; *Goodbye Mr. Chips*; *Stagecoach*; etc.) and the final moment in which such dreams-by-daylight sufficed: just before the release of *Citizen Kane* (1941) and our simultaneous entrance into World War II forever destroyed any sense of American innocence, actual or imagined, leading directly to that postwar period when television would replace film as the public's number one source of filmed escapism. How appropriate, then, that even as visitors to the Tower hear a bolt of lightning crack, they are transported two decades into the future. The year 1939 gives way to 1959; an old fashioned (new-fangled, of course, in its time) TV set lights up. There is Rod, with that strange smile which enchanted America as much as Walt's sweeter one did, explaining that each gathered guest will momentarily "ascend directly into your very own episode of *The Twilight Zone*." They will actualize (or more correctly approximate) the experience at a theme park that previously could only be glimpsed, thus indirectly enjoyed, on TV.

Even as in 1959 Rod Serling physically, emotionally, perhaps intellectually lived out his nostalgic memory of an idealized small town of the sort just then ceasing to be, so could today's nouveau-nostalgists now likewise actualize (approximate) the '59 that Rod had wanted to run away from, that era perceived now as being as charming as the 1930s — which of truth had been the era of the Dust Bowl and the Great Depression — seemed to Serling and Disney. Today's Disney-park traveler to Serling's *Zone* then experiences the starry-starry-night that opened every episode. In its time, the image conveyed to the masses what Van Gogh's painting had to the art gallery elite: a fearful sense that, as Kurt Weill once put it, we were all lost in the stars. Little stars. Big stars. Now, that image enchants both people who watched *Zone* on its initial release and those younger fans who know it from endless reruns on the TV's Sci-Fi Channel.

Then, as those stars fade, they briefly (the duration is so short most visitors don't notice) form an image (icon might be a better term) of Mickey

The Twilight Zone Tower of Terror ride at Disneyland and other Walt Disney theme parks allows for a creative collapsing of one popular 1950s TV icon into another, seemingly antithetical one (Wikimedia Commons).

Mouse. Throughout the ride, visitors witness the set of icons so basic to Rod's series: an opening door, a ticking clock, a mannequin, a shattering window, a giant eye, E=MC2. Yet they also are allowed glimpses of the park itself, the Disney vision that might once have seemed oppositional to Serling's.

The politics of nostalgia are simple to comprehend: Any golden age is the one that now no longer exists. Camelot is what came before, ever more dimly (and ever less accurately) recalled today by those who lived through what were then hard times as The Good Old Days. Yet what once sufficed no longer does. People used to be satisfied with an afternoon on Main Street, U.S.A. Now, they want to live there. And they more or less can, if they take up residence in one of the homes or apartments in Disney Celebration, where the illusion of a prettier past becomes an everyday reality for residents. Here then is the ultimate: a theme park not offered as escape from reality but an alternative reality. For them, Wolfe has at last been proven wrong: You *can* go home, if not to the reality of the way things actually were then at least to a fantasy of how they ought to have been.

And to a degree how they were, if not in life then in the movies. There is something of Leo Bloom, that frustrated dreamer in Mel Brooks's *The*

Producers, in each of us; when asked by his corrupter Max what Leo will do with the money they're going to make, he leaps up and in mad glee darts about, screaming: "I want ... I want ... everything ... I've ever seen in *The Movies*." So do we all! For most Americans, though, it isn't the grandeur of some chateau or a chic beach resort, however appealing they might briefly seem. What we want is to be teenager Mickey

Next to Main Street, U.S.A., Rod Serling's favorite attraction at Disneyland, was the boat ride to a lost world out of Mark Twain; here, James Daly sits in for Mr. Serling as both Tom and Huckleberry Finn greet him and extend an invitation to "go fishin'" the following day.

Rooney, gracious mom Fay Holden, stern but sweet dad Lewis Stone, or coming of age big-sis Cecilia Parker in a Carvel, California, of the American imagination. In the end, the great American Dream is not to be Jay Gatsby but Jimmy Gatz, on the edge of that big river, dreaming of riches and luxuries he was about to achieve, not grasping that the good life lay behind him.

Scott Fitzgerald knew that. So did Walt Disney and Rod Serling. Both apparently believed in '59 that the best times were gone and as a result we moderns suffered from acute melancholia. Today, the 1950s provide a mythic golden era for those unfulfilled by the present as vividly, if perhaps with unconscious irony, as the 1930s did then. Ultimately, *all* of American popular culture derives from the politics of nostalgia; any true understanding of jazz or The Western genre derives from precisely that conclusion. And what is "culture" but those fashions and fads which, unlike myriad others they competed with for our passing attention, pass the test of time? That rule holds true for entertainment mediums as diverse as television and the theme park.

In the mid–1950s, *Disneyland* and *The Twilight Zone* were perceived as polar opposites by home viewers, providing brightly lit and darkly shadowed video alternatives as to what life was like at that time, in that place. The idea that Serling's horrific way of seeing everyday life could ever be collapsed into Disney's genial conception would have been laughable then. Today, variations on The Twilight Zone Tower of Terror sit comfortably within the context of each Disney theme park worldwide. Yes, King Arthur's Carrousel awaits us moments after we have passed through Main Street, U.S.A., the turrets of Cinderella Castle shining in the sun as we enjoy our ride. Yet when our time on the merry-go-round is over, it is but a brief stroll to the Rod Serling's own little enclave in the park. No one might have believed it in '59 but today, Rod and Walt comfortably exist in tandem. The happiest place on earth can in the twenty-first century accommodate what in the twentieth represented the pure and abject horror that people fled to Disneyland to escape from.

Works Cited

Schickel, Richard. *The Disney Version: The Life, Times, and Commerce of Walt Disney.* 3d ed. Chicago: Ivan R. Dee, 2007.

Vacation in Historyland

KATHERINE HOWE

In a television viewing market suffused with disturbing examples of human self-debasement marketed as "reality," public television wins praise for elevating the genre of reality television through several examples of living history programming. Beginning with *1900 House* in 1999, continuing in 2001's *Frontier House*, and extending through *Colonial House*, PBS borrows the attractive casts and near-constant surveillance common to its network cousins, but replaces manipulated contemporary living arrangements (a bugged house in Los Angeles, a set of Amish roommates) with manipulated historical living arrangements, and prize money with something less tangible-pride, perhaps, or the opportunity for a deeper grasp on national identity. In doing so, these seemingly novel programs represent yet another entry in the vast catalogue of visual culture treatments of distant time periods, from history painting through epic films, relying on historical tropes to explore contemporary questions of culture, morality, and power.

The use of "history" with a capital H as source material is intended to bring a sense of gravity to these proceedings. The apparent democracy of the television medium invites high-minded proposals for the use of entertainment for the education, and perhaps improvement, of potential viewers. It could be argued that the PBS *House* series seeks to bring the study of history out of the academy and into the living room, rendering it more accessible. Furthermore, the two American-produced series focus on periods of American history which have been credited, both academically and popularly, as fundamental moments of some essential American character — the frontier, and the colonization of New England. These programs have little to do with history per se, and everything to do with contemporary tensions filtered through the lens of historiography. They presume that bringing contemporary people into contact with these supposedly foundational periods will clarify some ineffable truth about American identity. At every turn, the programs imagine that something important has been lost to contemporary America, whether that is meaningful labor, or intimacy, or self-reliance, varies among the participants (and, one suspects, the producers). This nostalgic approach to history assumes the nuclear family unit as the central social organizing system, that the individual is a transhistorical construct, and most importantly, that encounters with the physical reality and material culture of a given period will sufficiently simulate the total experience of that period. PBS, however, does not represent the first attempt to merge American history, the built environment, edification, and nationalist identity-building in the ubiquitous plane of television; in fact, *Frontier House* and *Colonial House* fit neatly in a continuum that begins, oddly enough, in Walt Disney's back yard.

Disneyland: History as Theme Park

By the late 1940s, Walt Disney was already fantasizing about building a place that interwove fables of American history with American popular entertainment. He operated a small scale recreational train ("The Carolwood-Pacific Railroad") at his house, and his ideas for a studio back lot tour brought to life with places and characters from his films began to coalesce upon his visit to the Chicago Railroad Fair of 1948, a hobbyist convention organized along regional themes that Disney would later borrow (Marling 100, 102). He envisioned combining recreational railroad technology (itself an increasingly nostalgic exercise as the real railroad was displaced by air travel and the expanding network of interstate highways) with lively exhibits on the highlights of American history as seen through the Hollywood cinema. His tour would include stops in the Wild West, the Gay Nineties, and visions of America's future. Disney's conservative nationalism and amateur railroading culminated in the 1955 opening of Disneyland in Anaheim, a family theme park organized under the headings of Tomorrowland, Fantasyland, Adventureland, Main Street, U.S.A., and, most importantly for our purposes, Frontierland, a grouping of shopping opportunities and meek rides which celebrated the westward march of American settlement (Marling 87). A 1954 newspaper article described the coming Disneyland as an "ambitious amusement center and living museum of Americana" (Pryor, "Land" 86). Significantly, Disney's Mecca of Americana appeared in California, notable both for being the origin of Hollywood mythmaking and the terminus of the westward flow of empire.

Disney expressed his idealized vision of American history not solely through the physical plant of Disneyland itself, but also through the televised *Disneyland* program which aired on ABC beginning in 1954, and continued under various guises until 1983. The park represented the first intersection point between Hollywood studio production, television, and architectural space; Frontierland as a physical attraction corresponded with the televised adventures of Davy Crockett at the Alamo, or "The Saga of Andy Burnett," a serial about a pioneer traveling from Pittsburgh to the Rockies (Pryor, "Disney" 24).[1] The *Disneyland* program served not merely as a widely disseminated advertisement for the theme park, but also as a forum for historical storytelling aimed at children, always with an emphasis on celebratory myth over analysis. As one newspaper reported in 1954, "Disneyland was designed to combine entertainment and instruction for young and old alike. 'It will be a place for parents and children to share pleasant times in one another's company: a place for teacher and pupil to discover greater ways of understanding and education,' Mr. Disney declared" (Pryor "Land" 24). Although the article was talking about Disneyland the theme park, it could just as easily been talking about the television program: *Disneyland* on TV created a visual space for entertainment-as-education, with emphasis on moral content over historical accuracy.[2] Also, the physical creation of an American frontier that could be visited on a car trip and purchased in the form of Davy Crockett hats and memorabilia meant that children watching the historical tales on *Disneyland* could persuade their parents to travel west on vacation, so that they too could go back in time (albeit back in time on a steamboat named "Mark Twain").

In particular, both the theme park and its televised counterpart used historical narratives to represent wholesome mid–twentieth-century American values of consumerism, family "togetherness," moral rectitude, and patriotism (Marling 96). Disney thought that these ideals could be mined from American history, and then built upon to create an appropriately American future (thus, the twin emphases on past history and future technology in both Disneylands). Disney envisioned his historyland as a place where "the older generation can recapture the nostalgia of days gone by, and the younger generation can savor the challenge of the future.... [Disneyland] will be based upon and dedicated to the ideals, the dreams, and *hard facts* [emphasis mine] that created America. And it will be uniquely equipped to dramatize these dreams and facts and send them forth as a sort of courage and inspiration to all the world" (qtd. in Pryor, "Land" 86).[3] Clearly Disney's ideological motivation owed much to the virulently anticommunist political climate of the late 1950s. The ideological underpinnings of both the physical and televisual Disneyland drew attention from outside the country as well; on his widely televised visit to the United States, Soviet Prime Minister Nikita Khrushchev suggested a visit to

Disneyland, though security concerns caused the State Department to veto the suggestion (Barnouw 252).

Like Disney history, *Frontier House* and *Colonial House* emphasize specific, supposedly foundational, periods of American history over others, aesthetic qualities of history over systematic analysis, and largely middle class conceptions of family togetherness, community, and morality that are rooted in mid- to late-twentieth century cultural ideologies. The casts of the PBS series travel to remote places that have been built to simulate another period in time, and they do this explicitly as a departure from their work and home lives; their sojourn in PBS's historyland resembles, though to a much more detailed degree, the mid-century family car vacation to explore Disney's version of history. Analysis of the two PBS programs' respective reenactments of history reveals less about the periods ostensibly under discussion and more about the uses to which history can be put in the present. The programs are, at heart, an interpretive enterprise, as loaded with contemporary baggage as Disney's own vision of American history, and through the medium of television (plus accompanying web sites), as widely disseminated.[4]

Structural Constraint on the Frontier

Frontier House and *Colonial House* take similar approaches to their representations of American history. Each attempts to simulate a given period by bringing contemporary family groups into contact with the material culture of the time, and to a lesser extent with basic instruction in the ideologies of the period as well. Both take for granted that the nuclear family should serve as the foundation for society. Both also assume that engagement with the material culture of the period will reproduce the social relationships of an earlier era; *Frontier House* and *Colonial House* both assume a transhistorical subject who is merely constrained by technology. Each project has a stated goal, loosely based on the requirements of physical survival and economic success. Each series emphasizes the totalizing quality of the experience for the participants by alluding to "time travel," terminology which simultaneously admits to the contemporary mindsets of the cast while insisting on the complete transformation of their bodies. For this reason, the selected periods also posit a degree of isolation for the family groups, in part to make removal from the contemporary era complete for the participants (cameras and jeans-clad camera crews notwithstanding), but also to reinforce the sense of robust individualism and self-reliance that forms such a major theme in popular narratives of the American "character." The program participants all travel to an isolated, controlled, physical space in which they will perform a total immersion version of history tourism, like a minutely detailed translation of Frontierland.

The *House* series are most effective at addressing the quotidian details of everyday life in the past, details which in many respects form the cornerstone of public interest in the programming. Both projects depict in loving detail the uses of material culture for domestic work and the hassles inherent in supplying creature comforts for oneself and one's family; introductory material of *Frontier House* in particular emphasizes the challenges of homemaking with limited tools in stark contrast to the comforts of a postindustrial house. Who among us has not imagined the pre-modern colonial period of the nineteenth century west and wondered, not about the larger problems of politics and culture, economics and religion, but about menstrual periods, broken toes, leaky roofs, rotting food, and other mundane problems of everyday existence that likely absorbed much of the attention of people living at the time. It is precisely these details which are lost in the "great man" style of history telling. However, the series still privilege individual experience over systematic analysis — the fetishization of objects in the *House* series overlooks the fact that these objects existed only within larger systems of class, gender, and economics.

To satisfy this time-traveler curiosity about history, participants in *Frontier House* and *Colonial House* receive intensive training in period-accurate cooking, house maintenance, day labor, limited technology, and scratchily uncomfortable clothing. Additionally, each project supplies the participants with a book of rules, which sketches out the social codes and practices to which the participants are expected to adhere. However, if most of the initial cast (and audience) interest focuses on mastery of these everyday details, very soon tensions materialize around bigger, more difficult to define issues.

Both *Frontier House* and *Colonial House* face the difficulty of recreating social structure, reaching a limit in the possibility of reenactment. Legitimate social power, whether it is in the form of force of social constructs such as "competition" or "fair play" is necessary for the maintenance of norms within a given community. For both *House* programs the stated "norm" was historical accuracy, both material and social. However, both programs faced problems upholding that norm. If the cultural relationships original to the periods cannot be recreated, then the programs must come up with a system that will serve as a proxy. The social rule books in each program serve this function, but incompletely. The cast members may have assumed that they joined the project to recapture the experience of their forbears; in fact, the programs illustrate tensions more central to turn of the twenty-first century life. In both programs, issues about class, gender, community, and morality supercede any pretenses that the programs may have had to historical accuracy, showing definitively how historical narrative can be bent to accommodate contemporary political discourse.

Both projects suffered under the weight of their own goal-setting. For instance, *Frontier House* instructed its participants that they would be judged based on their ability to survive the coming winter. Because real physical survival was assured by the safety net of contemporary life waiting on the other side of the camera, the only way to enforce compliance with this goal was for the project to evolve into a competition between family groups. The desire to "win" proved necessary for adherence to the rules. Also at stake was the translation of hours of video and film into a coherent eight-hour miniseries, complete with character development and narrative arcs. Therefore when one family was caught smuggling in beauty products and trading with people off-project, program producers elected to keep them in the cast for dramatic purposes (Oldenwald n.p.). In world where survival is assured and law unenforceable, the only means to ensure compliance with a set of rules is to transform the experience into a game. The competition between families on *Frontier House*, though not intended by the producers, had the paradoxical effect of ensuring some modicum of compliance with historical accuracy; the project transformed from merely a well documented encounter with late nineteenth material culture to a challenge to see who could encounter that culture more authentically.

However, the larger historical goals set by each project foundered as well. In response to the divisiveness on *Frontier House*, producers of *Colonial House* decreed the project's major goal to be the establishment of a functioning community. "Functioning" in this sense came to mean both the economic viability of the colonial enterprise but also the ability (or lack thereof) of the participants to simulate the existential world of colonial America. Here the project confronted a nearly insurmountable problem: the impossibility of the rule of law, both figurative (in the form of illegal exodus to the modern world and the struggle over gender roles and sexual identity) and literal (swearing, Sabbath breaking). Vacation in historyland being ultimately a simulation, the systems of power that would have maintained control within the real colonial world — corporal punishment, public humiliation, death — have no meaning. Instead, like on *Frontier House*, the challenge boiled down to competing interpretations within the cast of what community actions will result in the most accurate (or right-minded) representation of colonial life. Open competition is ruled out, as the community-building mandate does not allow for it, and so the only enforcing mechanism in place for the participants is their own willful interpretations of the colonial period's meaning.

Already *Colonial House*'s community building mandate raises questions about the function of historical memory within the projects. Landscape historian Joseph S. Wood, for example, has argued persuasively that the contemporary image of the New England colonial village as a collection of cottages grouped together, surrounded by farmland, containing a meetinghouse, actually reflects early nineteenth century New England village plans. Colonial settlements, though called villages, in reality consisted of widely dispersed individual homesteads, which encouraged private landholding. As rural New England began to transform into an urbanizing, industrial economy in the early nineteenth century, Romantic elites created an imagined agrarian past of proper puritan houses surrounding an idyllic village green — a lost community ideal that they could mourn. Landscape, Wood argues, can become imbued with meaning, with the past continually being remade in the present's image. The colonial village was a nineteenth century invention which persists in contemporary suburban housing developments — and on public television.[5]

History as Cipher

It is not fruitful to nitpick about whether the materials and physical aspects of each program were sufficiently historically accurate. What is important, however, is to illustrate that the performance of history, and in particular the televised performance of history as visual culture, has next to nothing to do with history itself, and everything to do with the way that our contemporary, early twenty-first century culture uses popular history to define itself. Just as Disney brought the frontier to Anaheim for the profitable enrichment of countless children, and televised it for countless more, so too do the American *House* series bend historical narrative to their own ideological ends. Early in *Frontier House* one cast member remarks that the program is like "Hollywood comes to the frontier" ("Promised Land"). He was referring to the contrasting economic and class outlooks represented among the cast members, but he could just as easily have been talking about the application of historical memory to contemporary cultural anxieties.

One of the most central contemporary anxieties articulated in *Frontier House* is socioeconomic class tension. Two family groups, one lower-middle-class and one lower-upper-class, cite differing notions of fairness in their interpretations of the parameters of the project. The wealthy family disregards the producers' rules against trade with the modern world, stating that there is no cheating as long as they work in the interests of the family. They claim that survivalism and unwillingness to compromise more closely align with the

"Frontier mentality"— in keeping with their bourgeois class outlook, the only rule is success at any cost. Contrast their approach with the lower middle class family's avowed commitment to hard work, fairness, and following the rules; the family claims that there is no point in doing any activity if you are not going to play fair. In this view, the rules exist to define the parameters of the project, and therefore breaking the rules renders the project invalid. Their interpretation of the frontier project stresses verisimilitude of physical experience over frame of mind. The language used by each family to judge the other implicitly refers to class tensions — particularly the contention that knowing how to work hard and economize puts one in closer contact with the frontier experience.[6] This reference to economic lessons imported from twenty-first century life implies a moral dimension to historical performance, that a rich California family is morally suspect both because of their real-life success, but also because of their results-oriented approach to the project. Each group used their respective readings of the nineteenth century American life and moral systems to justify their own actions and choices, each group believes that they are performing the "real" version of frontier life, though their visions of that life could not be more different.

Colonizing History — *Colonial House*

Colonial House dealt less explicitly with class tensions than it dealt with cultural differences. Because there were more participants from more backgrounds, more issues were at stake, generally having to do less with economic status in their real lives than with moral (and, by extension, religious) positions. Two dominant takes on theocracy emerged, each laying claim to a greater access to the authentic experience of the colonial period. The colony's governor, a Texan Baptist minister, saw his Protestant fundamentalism as a direct descendant of seventeenth-century Puritanism, without necessarily positioning himself (that we see) within a larger continuum that includes the Second Great Awakening, or what some historians have started calling the Third Great Awakening, a spread of religiosity and fervency in the mid- to late-twentieth century that includes not only Christian fundamentalism, but also the New Age and Western investigations of Eastern thought (Schulman 80). Even the colony's chosen minister, a professor who brings liberal intellectualism to his religious leadership, nevertheless incorporates twenty-first century religiosity into his approach to the project. Misgivings aside, he backs up the governor's articulation of the "City Upon a Hill" as his persona goal for the simulation, while overlooking the economic and fledgling capitalist reasoning that played an arguably larger role in the settling of the early colonies.

Contrast the governing council's religious approach to the project, which set the specific goal as tracing the contemporary United States' roots in colonial theocracy, with the rebellious position taken by the non-religious Massachusetts family. Their justifications for their position, while rooted in twenty-first century personal beliefs, also relied on narratives of individualism and dissent as foundational traits of the American character to argue for their non-participation in religious activities. The religion debate fueled much, if not all, or the dramatic tension depicted in *Colonial House*, again illustrating that mastery of the material culture of a given historical period comes much more easily than does mastery of a far-distant form of thought or belief. Technological fetishism holds that understanding of a given period's materials will result in knowledge of the period — to know the weapons of war is to know the war. *Colonial House* makes clear that this model of reenactment does not hold, for without the social stricture that bounded the use of those materials, the culture itself remains opaque. Both sides of the debate approached religion as a personal issue, rather than as a social or a legal issue. Underlying the tensions around religion on the program was the assumption that religion was a matter of choice, a line of reasoning that would have been inconceivable to a seventeenth century New England colonist. Seventeenth century colonial religion bound the community together with a fervor that was forged by years of civil war, exile, and the transatlantic crossing, relocating to the edge of an unknown world — individual belief would have had next to no place in such a social system.

Dissent occurred both historically and on the program. However, the mechanisms that would have addressed that dissent in the seventeenth century — whipping, burning, exile — as well as those that address dissent in the twenty-first century — debate, tolerance, consensus building — were both unavailable to the show's participants. This leaves the program's social system oddly placeless, lacking comprehension of the available social categories. One young man on *Colonial House* makes the brave decision to come out of his community, and remarks that such a thing would not have been possible in the seventeenth century because he would have been killed. This is only partly true — it would have been impossible to come out in the colonies because the category of "gay" is a twentieth-century discursive construct. His coming out reflects the belief that the individual transcends history; in wondering "what would have happened to me?" the young man overlooks the fact that the individual is constituted within the society in which he exists. Individual beliefs, be they identity-based or religious, would have been inconsequential in the face of community power and cohesion. However, each faction in the program's religious debate and other conflicts around gender roles and sexuality brought their own sets of twenty-first century political beliefs to bear on their interpretation, and performance, of the colonial period.

Endgame — The Struggle for Meaning

The moral and social debates that surfaced in *Frontier House* and *Colonial House* reflect a desire on the part of the participants to invest the projects with real meaning, elevating the *House* series to a seemingly more sophisticated level of discourse than can be found on *Survivor* or *The Complex: Malibu.* The presence of this desire also interrogates the uses to which the study of history itself is put in popular visual culture. In each case the meaning that is sought, by participants and viewers alike, has less to do with the historical periods under discussion, and everything to do with the reinforcement of abstract, even nationalist, concepts of "American-ness," community, and discipline that are under debate in the twenty-first century. Current political discourse clashes over fundamental qualities of American culture: Is it religion? Is it the nuclear family" Is it a capitalist economy" Is it the sovereign individual? What lies at a core of American identity? In that sense the *House* series borrow heavily from the precedent set by early Disney history programming in the cold war, which televised fictional stories of American history with an eye towards education and uplift, rendering the material appropriate for family consumption, During times when America seems beset from external threats, defining who *we* are becomes more important. Looking to historical narratives for that definition is somehow safer, more family friendly, than is the divisive political approach. Treating "history" as a subject for popular entertainment also applies a gloss of the highbrow, fun to watch but also *worth something* as though the *House* series were something other than "just" reality television.

This means that the educational and class signifiers under debate within the programs' casts bleed out of the screen to touch the means of the programs' consumption as well. Take for example an advertisement for TiVo, the television program recording system, that appeared in an issue of *People* magazine. The ad appeared interleaved between numerous other advertisements for the upcoming network television season's programs. The ad contains a picture of a television screen with a list of TiVo-ed viewing options, or programs that have been programmed in to save and be watched later. The screen lists *Frontier House* and *Colonial House* among the options to indicate the recording device's potential for educational, productive, family viewing — TiVo, because of the access that it can provide not only to public television in general, but to the popular *House* programs in particular, becomes not merely a tool for increasing the already prodigious amount of time that leisured Americans can devote to television viewing.[7] It becomes a tool for educational enrichment that is particularly family-friendly. Even the voice of the advertisement, with copy written in a child's crayon-scrawl and using the advertising industry's imagination of a childlike vernacular, underscores the importance of the *House* programs to signify worthwhile, meaningful family viewing (*People* 145).

Ultimately, *Frontier House* and *Colonial House*, like *Disneyland* before them, sit at the intersection point between history, material culture, visual culture, built environment, and nostalgia. All three programs rely on a fictionalized historical narrative to address contemporary cultural tensions, under the guise of popularly accessible entertainment with educational heft. All three also subscribe to tenets of American exceptionalism–produced in periods when the country appears threatened by uncontrollable outside ideologies, each program resorts to the reinforcement of a common narrative of American history, which they see as resulting in a common American character. The only problem being, no one can agree on what that common character is. In this sense, perhaps the programs do achieve something culturally meaningful, though not what they originally set out to do — by illustrating the wide variety of popular thinking about American history, rooted in varying class, religious, and gender consciousnesses, they affirm that the United States' very uniqueness as an idea lies in its total pluralism. This is perhaps not what Bob's Red Mill Natural Foods had in mind when they agreed to underwrite the PBS *House* series, and certainly the last thing on Mrs. Disney's mind as she swept the deck of the riverboat *Mark Twain* in Frontierland before an anniversary party several days before Disneyland opened to the public, but is indicative of the sometimes unexpected power to be found in popular visual culture (Marling 87).

Notes

1. See also the online "Classic TV Archive," a privately run archival project: http://aa. lasphost.com/CTVA/US/Western/Disney_SagaOfAndy Burnett.htm.
2. Disney versions of American history also appeared in film form, most notoriously in the live action and animation version of Joel Chandler Harris' Uncle Remus stories. *Song of the South*, which recounted animal parables within a framing device of a young boy's plantation life in the antebellum South, saw theatrical release to wide acclaim in 1946; it was re-released as recently as 1986. The film has since been withdrawn from distribution, not even appearing for the home video market in the United States because of its objectionable treatment of slavery in American history.
3. This is the same visit during which Khrushchev and Richard Nixon engaged in their Kitchen Debates comparing American and Soviet domestic technology and consumerism.
4. A newspaper column from 1955 devoted to general interest topics in television pro-

gramming poignantly illustrates how thoroughly grounded even Disney's reading of history must be in its own period of production. News of the rebroadcast of previously aired "Disneyland" episodes, as well as announcements of an upcoming series of episodes from the Fantasyland theme area of the park, appears in the same column with news of upcoming televised nuclear bomb testing by the Atomic Energy Commission. See Val Adams, "TV, Radio to Cover April Atomic Test," *New York Times*, March 15, 1955, 37.

5. For a complete discussion of the creation of the colonial village as a nostalgic landscape, see Joseph S. Wood, *The New England Village* (Baltimore: The Johns Hopkins University Press, 1997).

6. The mother of the family from Tennessee goes on at length to the camera about her ability to economize honed by years of living on a budget in her real life. She unpacks her food stores for the cameras to see, citing as an example her ability to make honey last longer by adding hot water. Throughout, her tone is difficult to parse; she seems simultaneously disgusted at the California family for their lack of foresight, yet pleased to discover that her economizing is a real talent, rather than an unremarkable skill that everyone possesses.

7. Also worth noting, both *Frontier House* and *Colonial House* include detailed sections on their websites devoted to incorporating the programming into secondary school classrooms, including suggested lesson plans and reading lists.

Works Cited

Erik Barnouw. *Tube of Plenty: The Evolution of American Television.* New York: Oxford University Press, 1990.

Marling, Karal Ann. *As Seen on TV: The Visual Culture of Everyday Life in the 1950s.* Cambridge, MA: Harvard University Press, 1994.

Oldenwald, Dan. "Back to These Old Houses: Time Travel Lures Millions to Living History." *Current* 21 (April 2003): n.p.

People. vol. 62, no. 12 (20 September 2004): 145.

"The Promised Land." *Frontier House.* Episode 2. PBS, 2001. 29 April 2002.

Pryor, Thomas M. "Disney to Enter TV Field in Fall: Allies His Studio with ABC Network in Deal to Produce Weekly One-Hour Shows." *New York Times*, 30 March 1954, 24.

_____. "Land of Fantasia Is Rising on Coast: Disneyland, Dedicated to the American Ideal and Youth, Will Grow on 160 Acres." *New York Times*, 2 May 1954, 86.

Schulman, Bruce. The Seventies. New York: Free, 2001.

Autographs for Tots
The Marketing of Stars to Children

KATHY MERLOCK JACKSON

Walt Disney World Resort in central Florida — comprised of four theme parks, the Magic Kingdom, Epcot, Disney's Hollywood Studios, and Disney's Animal Kingdom — is the largest amusement resort in the world. In 2007 over seventeen million people visited the Magic Kingdom, the most visited park in the world, with approximately ten million each visiting the other three theme parks ("TEA/ERA"). Another Disney theme park, Disneyland Park in Anaheim, California, has the distinction of being the most attended resort in the world, having drawn over five hundred million people since it opened in 1955 ("TEA/ERA"). All told, over 115 million guests visited a Disney theme park in 2007 ("Disney Does It"). According to Leslie Bays, seminar facilitator for Disney University, those planning trips to the Disney theme parks have three major requirements: that the parks be clean, friendly, and fun (Bays "Service — Disney Style"). The number one concern of children, though, can be summed up in just two words: Mickey Mouse. As one little girl insisted, (I don't just want to see Mickey Mouse. I want to hug Mickey Mouse" (Bays, "Service — Disney Style"). She is not alone. Disney theme parks attract children fascinated with Disney characters, and, by so doing, they cultivate one of children's earliest experiences with star culture. An analysis of how and why Disney does this sheds light on the celebrity-driven character of American society as well as on the values and mind-sets of young children.

In *The Nature of the Child*, the seminal work of Harvard developmental psychologist Jerome Kagan, he describes how preschool-age children identify with admired individuals. According to Kagan, by their fourth year, children understand their own psychological characteristics and begin to identify with others, believing that others' distinctive qualities belong to them as well (139). The object of their identification can be a family member, a friend, or a fictional character (139). Between the ages of four and seven, children tend to identify with role models who are nurturing, kind, competent and powerful (139–140) — qualities that they, as well, presumably, as their parents, value. Kagan notes that by the age of four, children "have established an attachment to their parents and are aware of and practice many of the standards their families promote" (264). Also by this age, children delight in fantasy and imaginative play, practices that help them to learn ways of coping with and solving life's problems (Smart 100–101).

Attractions at Disney theme parks capitalize on young children's tendency to embrace fantasy role models, particularly those sanctioned by parents, many of whom espouse the virtues of Disney movies and television, traveling great distances at considerable expense to bring their youngsters to the theme parks. It is worth noting, for example, that approximately forty percent of Walt Disney World Resort guests come from the Northeast, with New York being the state most represented, many drive rather than fly, and most stay an average of five days (Bays, "Service — Disney Style"). Thus, upon their arrival at Walt Disney World, children are often anxious and excited, and many of the attractions — such as Dumbo, the Flying Elephant, and Snow White's Adventure — incite enthusiasm by featuring characters in a larger-than-life form. In this frame of mind and with this backdrop, children first encounter their favorite Disney characters in person and learn behaviors suggestive of star adoration.

Let me offer a personal case in point, derived from my son's first experience with a Disney theme park. One summer, my husband Joe, my son Nick, and I spent five days at Walt Disney World. Although this was not our first trip to the Disney theme parks, it immediately took a new direction: Nick had just turned five and was familiar with many Disney characters. On our first evening at Walt Disney World, my husband asked Nick if he knew what an autograph book was. When Nick did not, Joe explained and bought him one. This marked the beginning of a quest. For the next five days Nick was intent on getting as many characters' autographs as he could. We went nowhere without the autograph book. Dutifully, we read the guidebooks and learned Mickey Mouse and his friends' routines. In the Magic Kingdom, they would be at City Hall in Town Square, at Adventureland near Pirates of the Caribbean and, during inclement weather, at Disneyana Collectibles; at Disney–MGM Studios, Greet the Characters sessions were held intermittently from 11:00 A.M. to 5:30 P.M. daily on Mickey Avenue. Continuing the search, we also talked to anyone who offered information as to where we might see the less predictable characters — such as Captain Hook or the Beast — and planned our schedule accordingly. Star watching became a game, perhaps even an obsession, connecting us to others at the park as well as to the characters whose autographs we sought (Gamson 137).

As our vacation ensued, I became aware of the many carefully orchestrated ways in which Disney theme parks promote fandom among children. In order to be assured of seeing Mickey, Minnie, Donald, and Goofy (and getting their autographs), we attended a pricey character breakfast upon an enormous, docked river boat called the *Empress Lilly*, one of the ten character meals available at the resort. Others included Mickey's Tropical Luau, Minnie's Menehune Breakfast, Breakfast with Mary Poppins and Friends, Breakfast with Admiral Goofy and Crew, Breakfast with Winnie the Pooh and Tigger, Too, Breakfast with Aladdin, and Buffet Dinner with Chip 'n' Dale as TV's "Rescue Rangers." Our Breakfast à la Disney, reinforced by a myriad of Disney character images, such as Mickey Mouse–shaped waffles and character buttons, was meticulously planned so that Mickey, Minnie, Donald, and Goofy entered individually, creating four distinct moments of excitement. Each character then made a personal appearance at every table, lingering just long enough for a hug, an autograph, or a photograph.

Throughout the parks, countless other photo opportunities ensued, leading to the startling — but not entirely surprising — fact that in the mid 1990s, before digital cameras became popular, five percent of all Kodak film developed was shot in Disney theme parks (Bays, "Service — Disney Style"). Upon our check-in at our Walt Disney World Resort hotel, we received a coupon for a free family photograph. When we arrived at the studio for the picture, Mickey was there to greet us and be a part of our "family" for about thirty seconds, just long enough for a portrait.

Another guaranteed opportunity to be photographed with Mickey Mouse occurred in the Magic Kingdom Fantasyland attraction called Mickey's Starland, touted as "the magical home of Mickey and his friends." There we visited Mickey's Hollywood Theater, listed in the "Walt Disney World Magic Kingdom Guidebook" with the following description: "Personally greet Mickey Mouse backstage in his dressing room. He loves to pose for pictures and sign autographs" ("Guidebook" 18). Just nearby was Mickey's House and Starland Show, accompanied in the "Guidebook" by an account designed to elicit reverence for stars' presence as well as for the everyday objects that they touch. It read as follows:

Visiting Mickey's house is like stepping into your favorite comic book or cartoon.

See Mickey's car, furniture and personal memorabilia from his unmatched career as a star. Follow the path out the back door past other famous homes. Next a collection of memorable Disney song videos begin the fun of Mickey's Starland Show. Then onstage, you'll see the TV superstars of "The Disney Afternoon"—performing live in a high-energy musical comedy [18].

The celebrity culture surrounding Disney characters, much of it designed for and embraced by very young children, is perpetuated at Walt Disney World in other ways. Daily parades, both in daylight hours as well as spectacularly lit at night, feature personal appearances by hundreds of Disney characters. Shops such as Disneyana Collectibles and Mickey's Starland Tent in the Magic Kingdom and Mickey's Character Shop at Disney's Village Resort display Disney memorabilia and collectibles that function as artifacts of star worship. Similar items also abounded at the Disney's Hollywood Studios, where the guidebook read, "Would you like a shirt worn by a famous star in a movie? You could find it at Sid Cahuenga's One-of-a-Kind, where props and personal possessions of the stars are for sale" ("Disney Resort Guest Planning Guide" 21).

In addition to promoting the Disney stable of characters, Disney theme parks feature personal appearances and autograph sessions by other licensed characters contracted by Disney and idolized by youngsters. At the Disney's Hollywood Studios, Nick excitedly dragged Joe and me through a huge crowd of people assembling to see Mirage Studios' Teenage Mutant Ninja Turtles, the then hottest item among the preschool set. Of this occasion the guidebook read, "Meet those bodacious crime fighters in person on New York Street, for autographs, photos, and some gnarly practice moves" ("Walt Disney World Disney–MGM Studios Guidemap"). And Barbie, America's most popular doll, appeared in the flesh and signed autographs at Epcot and Toys Fantastic at Disney's Village Resort, the result of an ongoing agreement between Disney and Barbie's manufacturer, Mattel Toys.

Given these experiences, by the time we left Walt Disney World, Nick had become a star watcher, a participant in a celebrity-driven culture. A five-year old expert in public relations, he knew the meaning of personal appearances, photo opportunities, and autograph sessions. Through touching, hugging, photographing, and receiving the autographs of his favorite characters, he had made meaningful contact.

But why was it meaningful and, perhaps more importantly, what did it mean? Daniel Boorstin addresses questions such as these in his classic work *The Image: A Guide to Pseudo-Events in America*. In this often quoted book, he characterizes stars as "the celebrities of the entertainment world. Like other celebrities they were to be distinguished by their well-knownness more than by any other quality" (154). In the case of Mickey Mouse, the most coveted star at Walt Disney World, this definition seems to apply. The Mickey Mouse series of films ended with "The Simple Things" in 1953, and Mickey has made only a few film appearances since then. Still, because of his role as the corporate symbol of The Walt Disney Company and the host of the theme parks, he remains the most recognizable — and arguably the most loved — animated character in the world.

Perhaps, though, there is a bit more to Mickey Mouse's appeal than his "well-knownness." Nick liked Mickey Mouse, whose image graced his first quilted blanket, which became faded and tattered as he clung to it from infancy through preschool. When I asked him about Mickey's stardom, his answer was telling: "When I grow up," he said, "I want to be a star like Mickey because if I'm a star, everybody will like me. Stars are just like you and me, except everybody knows them." Expressing the sociological approach to stardom, Elisabeth Weis writes that "our stars tell us a lot about ourselves and the national self-image" (Weis x). If we admire stars because they embody the qualities that we value most, Nick's comment makes sense. They reflect the most elemental concern of young children confronting their earliest experiences in a school setting: they want — most of all — to be liked, to fit in. Thus, the characteristic of Mickey that Nick admired and identified with most was, quite simply, his being liked. Akin to this, however, is the power that comes from being popular. Young children, because they are small and powerless, are attracted to personalities they see as in control. Mickey, because he is so well liked, fits this image.

Nick's observation that stars are just like us also underscores another aspect of our star culture. According to Joshua Gamson in *Claims to Fame: Celebrity in Contemporary America*, by the 1940s fan magazines typically reported on the day-to-day elements of stars' lives: their routines, tastes, likes, and dislikes (Gamson 28), in short, characteristics that do not differ that much from the average person. According to Gamson, "Such ordinariness promoted a greater sense of connection and intimacy between the famous and their admirers" (Gamson 29). For Nick and other children, seeing Mickey's modest house and personal effects seemed to serve this function.

There is no question that the success of Disney theme parks depends upon children's acceptance of their star culture, and this begins long before a child ever sets foot in a Disney theme park. What attracts children to the theme parks, guaranteeing their appeal, is the popularization of Disney characters through other sources: films, videos and DVDs, television, computer games, and an extensive line of toys, clothing, school supplies, home decorations, and other articles bearing the image of Disney-licensed characters. Such character merchandising is crucial for Disney. In *Sold Separately: Parents and Children in Consumer Culture*, Ellen Seiter characterizes Walt Disney as one of the first and most aggressive proponents of product licensing. Calling

Disney's licenses (the longest-lived and most successful in the toy industry,"
Seiter notes how (the Disney organization devotes considerable time and
money to the project of igniting interest in its characters among successive
generations of children and parents" (Seiter 198–199). This leads to a typical
scenario: A parent who, as a youngster, loved Goofy is likely to take his or
her own child to the new Goofy movie, decorate the child's room with Goofy
bedding and curtains, and buy the child a Goofy stuffed toy, thus promoting — even celebrating — the child's participation in fandom (Seiter 227).
Children's acquiring such licensed products and developing a greater awareness
of brand-name items encourage other children to do the same, thus contributing to a shared Disney culture. As children strive to be accepted and fit
in, this becomes a useful strategy.

But where does it lead? By adolescence, children who have been primed
to be star followers abandon their animated heroes for figures they regard as
desirable and less childish, such as today Miley Cyrus, the Jonas Brothers,
Paris Hilton, Nicole Richie, Britney Spears, Jessica Simpson, or Lindsay
Lohan. In some cases, youths become intent on seeking out role models that
are *not* parentally sanctioned, such as rebellious movie or recording stars or
sexy celebrities. And in adulthood, star worship continues. Stars in America
occupy in the popular imagination a role similar to that of royalty, and it is
not inaccurate to say that Americans are obsessed with stardom. According
to *Psychology Today* writer Carlin Flora, "fascination with celebrity is a symp-
tom of a larger obsession with the three A's: affluence, attractiveness and
achievement" (qtd. in Worgul E3). It also reflects the need for ritualized worship in an increasingly secular society (Worgul E3). As psychologist James
Houran comments, "Nonreligious people tend to be more interested in
celebrity culture. For them, celebrity fills some of the same roles the church
fills for believers, like the desire to fit into a community of people with shared
values" (qtd. in Worgul E3). Television presentation of the film industry's
Academy Award ceremony typically reaches over thirty million homes, easily
making it the week's most watched program. People tune in not so much to
learn the winners of the coveted awards but rather to see their favorite movie
stars. Among magazines, *People*, dedicated to following the lives of stars, is
second only to *T.V. Guide*, itself a star vehicle, in total revenues (Black 135).
Finally, supermarket tabloids — which have sales figures in the stratosphere —
trace, or fabricate, stories of stars' every move. The *National Enquirer*, for
example, sells four and a half million copies a week and claims to have "the
largest circulation of any paper in America" (Merrill 113). Parents who enjoy
star gazing themselves are likely to set examples and facilitate their children's
desires to join in the practice.

In the twenty-first century — with twenty-four hour cable channels, reality programming, game shows such as the overwhelmingly popular *American Idol*, youtube.com and other Internet sites, and celebrity labels reaching nearly fifteen percent of clothing industry sales — star culture has become easily accessible, with more individuals intent on not only following stars but becoming famous themselves (Halpern xv). This fascination with celebrity begins in childhood. It is brought about by clever marketers, such as Disney, who use stardom to sell images and products to children, priming them to be star worshipers in a celebrity-oriented culture, and by parents, themselves products of the same culture, who sanction the practice. Walt Disney himself no doubt realized this. Near the end of his life, he reflected upon the vastness of his character-generated empire, saying, "it all started with a mouse" (qtd. in Jackson 77). Perhaps the same can be said today of young children's participation in the star-driven culture of America.

Works Cited

Bays, Leslie. "Service-Disney Style." Disney University Seminar presented at Virginia Beach Community Quality Day, March 16, 1995, Virginia Beach, VA.

Black, Jay, and Jennings Bryant. *Introduction to Media Communication*. Madison, WI: Brown and Benchmark, 1995.

Boorstin, Daniel J. *The Image: A Guide to Pseudo-Events in America*. New York: Atheneum, 1972.

Davis, Daphne. *Stars!* New York: Simon and Schuster, 1983.

"Disney Does It Again: The World's Most Popular Theme Parks Revealed." *Parkworld-Online* 21 April 2008, 20 January 2009 http://parkworld-online.com/news/fullstory.php/aid/762/Disney_does_it_ again!.html.

Gamson, Joshua. *Claims to Fame: Celebrity in Contemporary America*. Berkeley: University of California Press, 1994.

Halpern, Jake. *Fame Junkies: The Hidden Truths Behind America's Favorite Addiction*. Boston: Houghton Mifflin, 2007.

Jackson, Kathy Merlock. *Walt Disney: A Bio-Bibliography*. Westport, CT: Greenwood, 1993.

Kagan, Jerome. *The Nature of the Child*. New York: Basic, 1984.

Konner, Melvin. *Childhood*. Boston: Little, Brown, 1991.

Merrill, John C., John Lee, and Edward Jay Friedlander. *Modern Mass Media*. New York: Harper and Row, 1990.

Piaget, Jean, Barbel Inhelder. *The Psychology of the Child*. New York: Basic, 1969.

Seiter, Ellen. *Parents and Children in Consumer Culture*. New Brunswick, NJ: Rutgers University Press, 1993.

"Selling to Children." *Consumer Reports* (August 1990): 518–21.

Smart, Mollie S., and Russell C. Smart. *Preschool Children: Development and Relationships*. New York: Macmillan, 1978.

"TEA/ERA Theme Park Attendance Report 2007." *Park World*. 14 March 2008. 20 January 2009 http://www.themeit.com.

Walt Disney Company. "Disney Resort Guest Planning Guide."

_____. "Walt Disney World Disney–MGM Studios Guidemap."

_____. "Walt Disney World Magic Kingdom Guidebook."

Walt Disney World. "Walt Disney World Epcot '94 Guidemap."

Worgul, Doug "Seeing Right Through Celebrity." *The Virginian-Pilot*, 30 May 2006, E3.

Weis, Elisabeth, ed. *The National Society of Film Critics on the Movie Star.* New York: Penguin, 1981.

Forget the Prozac,
Give Me a Dose of Disney

CATHY SCIBELLI

In early 2000, Doug Todd spent $9,100 on an eBay auction in order to give his wife a special surprise birthday gift — he bought her a temporary position as "Honorary Cast Member" at the Walt Disney World Resort. In other words, he spent nearly $10,000 to give his wife the privilege of working as an unpaid employee at a theme park. Suzanne Todd described her gift in the *Walt Disney Insider* magazine: "To be able to step in to put on a costume, say the words, live the life of a cast member — this was a once in a lifetime event!" (*Walt Disney Insider* 6). During a five-day stay at the Disney resort, Suzanne drove the monorail, played the part of a scary cast member at the Haunted Mansion, and acted as hostess for the Jungle Cruise ride, where her husband was allowed to fulfill his own "lifelong dream" to become the skipper of a Jungle Cruise boat.

What could cause affluent people to develop such a mania for Disney theme parks that they view the opportunity to pay dearly to work for free in a menial service position as a "once in a lifetime event?" Further, what about the millions of Americans who return year after year to the Disney theme parks for vacations, or who save for years so that their children can experience a pilgrimage to meet Mickey Mouse? Why do they long for a vacation experience that requires waiting in long lines, dealing with tired and cranky children, and paying an outrageous price for a hot dog?

I have been among them and wondered. Several years ago while on a trip to Walt Disney World Resort in Florida, I was caught in a typical tropical thunderstorm. Standing under the shelter of a porch awning on a Frontierland shop building, I marveled at the sight of dozens of tourists in rain slickers assembled in the downpour in order to secure their front row vantage points for the upcoming parade, which was still two hours from starting. As I watched these Disney enthusiasts getting drenched, risking life and limb as thunder crashed and lightning lit the sky, I sought to find out what is so special about the Disney theme park experience that it wields such power. First-hand research led me to the conclusion that the Disney theme park provides a reassuring dose of vicarious Prozac for stressed-out modern Americans. The original Disneyland Park in Anaheim illustrates this point.

Within the attractions at the original Disneyland Park, one "theme" surfaces again and again, the desire for visitors to temporarily escape their everyday lives in the modern world. Steven Watts writes: "From the mid–1950s on, travel sections in dozens of newspapers all over the United States promoted trips to Anaheim, extolling the park's pleasures for 'people who are seeking release from the cares and concerns of today's tense times'" (394). The former ruler of the Disney empire, Michael Eisner, described the impression the park made on him and his wife on their very first visit: "Jane and I stepped from the chill and gloom of an Eastern winter into the sunny glow of Main Street, a place so clean that it seemed we could eat right off the sidewalk, a place where our cares and concerns couldn't get past the gate" (Bright, *Foreward* 17). Consider some of the specific aspects of modern life that visitors want to leave outside the gates, and see how the Disneyland Park offers an illusory antidote.

In the late nineteenth and early twentieth centuries, post-industrial life brought sweeping changes that often occurred so rapidly it was difficult for humans to adjust. Small cities turned into large urban metropolises seemingly overnight; new building growth edged out or competed with older architectural styles. Immigrants mixed with recent arrivals from small towns, resulting in a sometimes confusing blend of cultures. Furthermore, as the twentieth century progressed, technology moved into the home at a dizzying pace, altering every aspect of life from domestic duties to family entertainment. In place of the former customary cycle of life, where there seemed to be an overriding sense of order and control governing the universe, the only constant now was change. Modern life thus was often characterized by its sense of chaos.

Disneyland provided the atmosphere of order and control that was missing from everyday modern life. As soon as the visitor stepped through the gates, he or she was greeted by the reassuring specter of an idyllic Main Street where all the architecture blended in one uniform pattern and nothing jarred one's vision. Disney's Main Street, U.S.A. is a recreation of the small town Main Street that has nearly vanished from the American landscape.

The architectural styles of the commercial buildings on Disney's Main

Street are soothing in their similarity, as the facades of the stores are all representative of late Victorian architecture. Exteriors are painted in bright colors with decorative embellishments, and none of the buildings are taller than two or three stories. All is clean, neat and inviting. As Richard Francaviglia describes it: "In Disney's Main Street, U.S.A., architecture becomes the facade that creates the impression that all was right with the world in the small town at the turn of the century; it implies that commerce (and merchants) thrive along Main Street, and that society and a community are working together in harmony" (156). And in this harmonious setting the darker side of life is conspicuously absent — on this Main Street there is no funeral parlor, no police station, no seedy theaters or bars.

Moreover, the street gives the impression of being frozen in time, as if modernity had passed it by. The geometric layout of the buildings on Main Street, featuring long straight rows of stores tied together visually by connecting walkways and similar architectural styles, flanked on either end by public squares, contributes to the visitor's sense that here is a place reassuring in its static conformity. No winds of change blow down these avenues, no bulldozers wait in the wings to demolish this community and replace it with another strip mall or office complex.

To add to this feeling of stability and order, Disneyland maintained rules of decorum that were slowly being shunted aside in the modern world outside the park. Dress codes for workers and guests were enforced, and the park itself was spotlessly maintained. Guests waited patiently in lines obeying orders not to eat or drink until they exited the attraction. The line system itself, as Richard Shickel describes, was designed to soothe:

> The "Imagineers" have broken the usual single line into many short lines by an arrangement of railings that neatly ... divide the patrons into small groups who are then kept moving through a sort of maze until they reach their destination... The whole thing is a marvel of technology applied to mass psychology. People simply feel better if the line they are in is short and if it is constantly moving [321].

Although the various themed lands contained widely disparate architecture and attractions, Disney's Imagineers used a trick learned from filmmaking, the principle of the cross-dissolve to maintain a sense of order: "A stroll from Main Street to Adventureland is a relatively short distance, but one experiences an enormous change in theme and story. For the transition to be a smooth one, there is a gradual blending of themed foliage, color, sound, music and architecture" (Imagineers 90).

To the typical modern visitor to Disneyland in the 1950s, who may have crossed the threshold of this Magic Kingdom seeking a vacation from the cacophony and confusion of daily life battling traffic, pushing through crowded streets lined with a garish mixture of building styles in order to compete in a business world that demanded constant reinvention, the obsessive order of Disneyland must indeed have seemed a welcome relief. In Karal Marling's words:

> Disneyland is about mild contentment and the overarching reassurance that there is an order governing the disposition of things. A detectable order that will take the visitor by the hand and lead him through an astonishingly varied array of ersatz places, back to the Main Street from whence he began [105].

Along with a comfortable feeling of order and control, the Disneyland theme park offered predictability and the assurance of safety to visitors seeking a safe haven from the often scary reality of the Cold War world. Older guests to Disneyland in the 1950s had seen the horrors of modern warfare and understood the threat posed by atomic energy if it fell into the wrong hands. They also lived in an unpredictable everyday world where machinery broke down, jobs were not always secure, and family and friends disappeared from their lives through death and the increasing mobility of the population.

In Disneyland things generally ran smoothly, and everyone smiled and felt safe. The pack mules in Frontierland might occasionally balk, and now and then a car might come off the track in the Autopia, but these were minor glitches; one could travel through the jungles of the world, rocket to the moon, experience a train trip through America's natural wonders and fly over London with Peter Pan without a thought as to safety and comfort while doing so. According to historian Katherine W. Rinne: "Disneyland was a means of shutting out the realities of life and entering a city perfectly balanced between the safety of the past and the hope of the future" (qtd. in Dunlop 41).

The Disneyland theme park also provided a sense of community, a characteristic of society that had been slowly eroding from American life during the twentieth century. Before World War II, people used to gather on Main Street for festivals and parades; they would do most of their shopping in the stores along this main road where they not only knew the merchants but also most of their fellow customers. A trip into town thus provided an opportunity for socializing. Disneyland recreated this community atmosphere with its daily parade down Main Street and with shows and attractions that encouraged interaction among visitors.

Part of the reason for the popularity of earlier amusement parks near large cities, such as New York's Coney Island, had been to give lonely individuals and displaced immigrants a common meeting ground similar to the community activities of earlier times. According to David Nasaw,

> The crowd was a necessary constituent of the amusement park experience. The park was, in this regard at least, a twentieth-century adaptation of nineteenth-century fes-

tivals, fetes, and holiday celebrations, where revelers took over the streets, the parks, and the waterfronts to have a good time publicly and collectively. On entering the park, one surrendered one's individual standing in the outside world and merged into a temporary play community which coexisted with one's visit and dissolved immediately thereafter [94].

One drawback to the "community" of these earlier parks was that it was not exactly family-oriented. Although families did patronize these parks, many of the rides and attractions were designed with the interests of a young single crowd in mind. Typical rides, such as the Barrel of Fun at Steeplechase Park in New York, literally tossed visitors on top of each other; most slower rides through scenery involved at least a partially dark section, encouraging illicit snuggling. Risque vaudeville acts featuring scantily clad dancers were also a staple entertainment. Walt Disney decried the sleazy, carnival atmosphere of these parks and was determined that his creation would differ: "It [Disneyland] will be a place for parents and children to share pleasant times in one another's company" (qtd. in Smith 56).

The price of admission to the Disneyland park also guaranteed that the vicarious "citizens" roaming along its Main Street would mostly be from a similar economic class, those who could afford the steep admission to this fantasy community. Thus, families could mingle along Main Street in a community of their peers; they could gather for parades and festivals similar to the rites enjoyed by homogenous small-town communities years earlier. As the narrator of Disneyland's tenth anniversary telecast observes, "it's tradition that every event at Disneyland has a parade down Main Street."

And all the citizens of Disney's world are reassured of having a special status in this community through a sharp marketing strategy developed in the early years of the twentieth century by corporations competing for consumer dollars in a market flooded with similar products. William Leach recounts the strategy:

> To make customers feel welcome, merchants trained workers to treat them as "special people" and as "guests." ...Salespeople were grilled everywhere in the formulas of proper decorum — to be "gracious" at all times and neat in appearance, unobtrusive but accessible, careful to "emphasize the value of the merchandise," and equipped with the right questions [131, 133].

In an era of shopping malls, supermarkets and increasingly impersonal service, the visitor to Disneyland no doubt found this throwback to an earlier era of customer service novel and very welcoming, according him or her a sense of status. (I once inquired at a shop on Main Street about the mouse-eared confetti that was tossed from floats during the afternoon parade. A store clerk who was not familiar with this product called a manager, who phoned someone in Disney marketing who informed her that this product wasn't yet available for sale to the general public but that if I really wanted a sample they would provide one free of charge.) This is the sort of fantasy shopping experience that in modern American society could only happen to the richest or most famous among us outside the Disney park.

Finally, Disneyland offered an antidote to the uncertainty over where humanity was headed in the twentieth century. Two devastating wars had not, after all, made the world safe. Material progress seemed to be creating as many problems as it solved. Disney answered the anxieties of mid-century Americans with a resounding promotion of the benefits of corporate capitalism, a reassurance that, indeed, everyone was heading toward a better future after all. In writing on the Disney park in general, Alan Bryman perfectly captures this positive message of Disneyland:

> In its depiction of science and technology and of the future, the reigning message is one of progress and more particularly of the capacity of scientific progress to continue to deliver a constant stream of consumer goods for our enjoyment. The downside of scientific and technological advance — pollution, deforestation, depletion of scarce resources, and so on — is concealed from view or reserved for upbeat treatments in specific locations [106].

The corporate showcase exhibits in Tomorrowland, such as the Monsanto House of the Future with its array of dazzling technological wonders and the Kaiser Aluminum Hall of Fame, were obvious promotions of this image of the good life brought through the benevolence of the American corporation. Some of the futuristic consumer goods displayed in the Monsanto House included picture telephones, microwave ovens, electric toothbrushes and atomic food preservation. Several of the inventions presented still seem futuristic in the twenty-first century, such as ultrasonic dishwashers and plastic sinks with adjustable heights for each family member. Corporate sponsorship of other attractions throughout the park also reinforced a positive corporate image. As Steven Watts asserts,

> Disneyland became a showcase for thriving corporate capitalism as well, proudly featuring an imposing array of big-business entities that underwrote its consumer paradise... [Disneyland] assured potential visitors that they could expect (to choose just a few examples) the finest food products from Carnation, Swift, and Frito; quality clothing from Pendleton Woolen Mills; and efficient services from Gibson Greeting Cards, the Bank of America, and Eastman Kodak ... Trans-World Airline's presentation of the Rocket to the Moon, Richfield Oil's fueling of miniature autos in the Autopia ride, ... and the Golden Horseshoe dance hall, sponsored by Pepsi-Cola, all earned space in Disney publicity [394].

At least within the confines of the Disneyland park, American corporate capitalism meant fun times, excellent quality and service, and a bright future filled with exciting new products that would bring a life of leisure to all.

It is perhaps ironic that Americans today share many of the same fears and concerns as those living in the middle of the twentieth century. The Cold War with Russia has ended, but it has been replaced by a new nuclear threat from former Third World countries such as North Korea and Iran; in addition, terrorism poses a constant threat. E-mail, cell phones, and pagers have added to the chaotic pace of our modern lives. We work longer hours and have less time for community events in "communities" that are turning increasingly into gated fortresses. At the same time, those "benevolent" corporations lay off American workers and transfer operations to foreign countries where labor and production costs are cheaper. As Susan Strasser opines,

> ... a belief in progress is more difficult to sustain in the face of environmental destruction, of market segmentation that codifies increasing class distinctions, and of a consumer culture that itself breeds constant discontent, depending always on individuals wanting more. Despite shopping malls full of things to buy, we are denied satisfactions that we identify — and romanticize — in our own past and in the activities of other human cultures: a sense of community, meaningful work, and time not consumed by getting and spending [290].

From this viewpoint, it is not hard to understand the pull that the Disney theme park still has for American psyches. We still crave that perfect fantasy of a neat, safe, friendly world where things can only improve. One man in Illinois has taken this desire to an extreme, recreating his own version of Main Street, U.S.A. in his basement. As a feature on Home and Garden Television reported,

> John Scapes of Schaumburg, Ill., has been working for three decades on a very intricate creation in his basement. The retired mechanical engineer has brought an incredible attention to detail to his project, building a full-scale replica of a turn-of-the-century Main Street...
> Everything looks authentic, down to the last detail. The street is paved with faux cobblestones, the streetlight actually works and carefully placed mirrors make the street appear to curve. Scapes' little piece of Americana includes a barbershop, hat shop and a photo shop. The general store's shelves are stocked and the store includes a post office and a working hand-cranked phone.
> The double doors of the sawmill open to reveal the pristine workshop where Scapes crafted his nostalgic world. Other neat features include storefronts that open to reveal storage space, a mirrored saloon and a milk wagon in the corner that conceals plumbing [Home and Garden Television Channel].

Perhaps the "Disneyfication" of our society in the last half century has come about precisely because so many of us, like John Scapes, want some part of the fantasy world it promises. In a eulogy for Walt Disney in 1966, Eric Sevareid offers the following insight:

> By the conventional wisdom, mighty mice, flying elephants, Snow White and Happy, Grumpy, Sneezy and Dopey — all these were fantasy, escapism from reality. It's a question of whether they are any less real, any more fantastic than intercontinental missiles, poisoned air, defoliated forests, and scraps from the moon. This is the age of

fantasy, however you look at it, but Disney's fantasy wasn't lethal [*Disneyland: The First Quarter Century* 83].

The last statement sums up the continued popularity of the Disney theme park: in a world where fantasy often turns lethal, many of us still need that dose of corny Disney optimism, that opportunity to retreat to a childlike world where everything is magical and safe — even though we realize intellectually that much of what we are swallowing is simply another corporate promotional gimmick. In a world where our daily lives are filled with reports of terrorism, war, financial crises, natural disasters, and a host of other unsettling news, we remember the prophetic words of Walt Disney: "The most important thing ... is the recognition that amusement, recreation, mass diversion is no longer a dispensable luxury" (qtd. in Smith 147).

Works Cited

Bright, Randy. *Disneyland: Inside Story*. New York: Harry N. Abrams, 1987.

Bryman, Alan. "Theme Parks and McDonaldization." In *Resisting McDonaldization*, edited by Barry Smart, 101–115. London: Sage, 1999.

Disneyland: The First Quarter Century. N.p.: Walt Disney Productions, 1979.

Disneyland USA: Special Historical Broadcasts. 2 DVDs. Buena Vista Home Entertainment, 2000.

Dunlop, Beth. *Building a Dream: The Art of Disney Architecture*. New York: Harry N. Abrams, 1996.

Francaviglia, Richard V. *Main Street Revisited*. Iowa City: University of Iowa Press, 1996.

Home and Garden Television Channel. Home and Garden Television. 24 September 2003. <http://www.hgtv.com/hgtv/re-Modeling/article/0,1797,HGTV_3659_2036860,00. Html>.

Imagineers, The. *Walt Disney Imagineering: A Behind the Dreams Look at Making the Magic Real*. New York: Hyperion, 1996.

Leach, William. *Land of Desire: Merchants, Power and the Rise of a New American Culture*. New York: Random House, 1993.

Marling, Karal Ann. "Imagineering the Disney Theme Parks." In *Designing Disney's Theme Parks: The Architecture of Reassurance*, edited by Karal Ann Marling, 29–177. New York: Flammarion, 1997.

Nasaw, David. *Going Out: The Rise and Fall of Public Amusements*. 1993. Cambridge: Harvard University Press, 1999.

Schickel, Richard. *The Disney Version*. 1968. Chicago: Ivan R. Dee, 1997.

Smith, Dave, comp. *The Quotable Walt Disney*. New York: Disney, 2001.

Strasser, Susan. *Satisfaction Guaranteed: The Making of the American Mass Market*. Washington: Smithsonian, 1989.

Watts, Steven. *The Magic Kingdom: Walt Disney and the American Way of Life*. Boston: Houghton Mifflin, 1997.

"Who Wants to Be a Cast Member?" *Walt Disney World Insider*. Fall 2000: 6.

The Disney Effect
Fifty Years After Theme Park Design

MARGARET J. KING

"A triumph of historical imagination."
Richard Snow, editor
American Heritage Magazine
about Disney's Main Street, U.S.A.

The theme park can be defined as a "social artwork designed as a four-dimensional symbolic landscape, evoking impressions of places and times, real and imaginary" (King 837). The essence of the theme park is its value as cultural invention, channeled by the highly evocative art of thematics (context-based), unlike the kinetic experiences of amusement parks (effects-based).

As the original theme park, Disneyland was born at the convergence of several social and technological developments after World War II: the expansion of the middle class, California development, the baby boom, the national highway system and automobile ownership, and the rise of television as a universal household medium.

Disneyland recreated the park idea as a middle-class destination reachable mainly by automobile rather than public transportation, and to appeal across generations of "guests," from young children to older adults, conceived by Walt Disney as "a family park where parents and children could have fun — together" (qtd. in Walt Disney Corporation 30). As the Los Angeles area grew in population and diversity, the park became engulfed by the city, creating a more accessible venue. In contrast, Walt Disney World Resort in Florida, surrounded by a green belt, featuring multiple parks necessitating a multi-day stay at on-property hotels, remains a "total destination resort."

After over fifty years of operation and billions of visitors, Disneyland has influence as a high-profile cultural institution that pervades every aspect of the built environment as a mainstay of the "experience economy." According to Peter Blake, for design applications, Disneyland acts as an "urban lab" (437) for the testing of design and building technologies. The theme park is now considered an idealized urban center "unattainable" by ordinary design strategies, a "very serious, very creative experiment in urban design" (426).

As the engine of theme park design, thematics is a compendium of techniques borrowed from animation and filmmaking rather than architecture: the familiar storyline, identifiable archetypal style that architect Phillip Johnson terms "organization of procession" (qtd. in Goldberger 95), stagecraft, iconography, special effects, audio-animatronics (3-D animation), and color palette coordination. These features are all led by the concept of "story," "show," and "enhanced reality" (Hench 2, 56), tightly focused to evoke specific times and places with strong cultural resonance. These distillations — from musical cueing and food to landscaping, lighting, scaling, signage, sounds, surfaces, textures, and smells — play off perception and collective memory to create "instant moods."

These are achieved by high-profile motifs, layered detail, and multi-sensory environmental designs, favoring images over signage to tell stories and give direction. Inherent in themeing's sense of place as theater is the legacy of style revival or nostalgia in latter-twentieth-century design, and the multi-media assemblage of art forms and styles from many eras, traversing the range from crafts to high-tech (as in filmmaking). Overall, these techniques serve to convey an integrated pastiche of collective memory and American shared values. In Disney's words, "Disneyland would be a world of Americans, past and present, seen through the eyes of my imagination" (qtd. in Walt Disney Corp. 29).

The adaptive use of technology to solve human problems in the built environment made Disneyland, according to architect James Rouse, "the outstanding piece of urban design in the U.S." (qtd. in Jackson 101) to exert broad and lasting effects on the American city. The Disney Effect can be seen in towns of "authentic" American design: Celebration, Florida, Reston, Virginia, and Columbia, Maryland, recreate the small-town ideal as showcased by Walt Disney in Main Street, U.S.A.

In the theme parks, Disney's Imagineering design team pioneered the total-control governance of utilities and building process; integrated design, and computer-controlled information, communications, and operations (a byproduct of the space program), prefabricated modular construction, sequestered infrastructure, and ecology-minded development. Disney also organized crowd behavior in the form of switchback lines to minimize the feel of waiting in line, the pedestrian mall and the psychology of way-finding, multilevel, multiform mass transit (favoring rapid transit over the automobile), and the concept of "guests" rather than visitors or customers. The techniques perfected at Disneyland are featured in banks (line theory), food courts (themeing), airports (people movers), museums (total immersion exhibits), and customer service ("guestology" training).

Most important, the mind of Imagineering sees every component within a bordered system (the park itself is a recap of the animation art form), with synergistic subsystems. "The one thing I learned from Disneyland," Disney said, "was to control the environment" (qtd. in Walker 10). Accordingly, Disney's famous "integrated marketing" links built space with the formats and content of film, television, video, and merchandising. Although Disney is famous primarily for his animated characters, it is the theme park that is his greatest contribution to public life.

Even the National Trust's adoption of main streets across the country as "sacred spaces" was inspired by archetypal Main Street, U.S.A., according to historian Richard Snow, who was inspired by his visits there to make the past his profession (22–24). Out of the distilled imagination of American history Disney created a townscape in Main Street, U.S.A., possibly the most important 4D artwork ever created. It is a streetscape instantly recognizable by its stylized and distilled iconography. At the opposite end of the time scale, Tomorrowland's prefabricated all-plastic Monsanto House of the Future (1957–1967) was like nothing ever seen before — yet instantly recognizable to all as a "Futuristic" dwelling.

A half century after Disneyland's inception, it is safe to say that few urban spaces remain untouched by the Disney Effect. This effect constitutes a radical shift from one type of design and design vision to another: from effects-based (materials, physics, engineering) to context-based (human perception and values).

The Disney parks' enormous success is based on the way they operate as a "national trust" of mainstream cultural values. For this reason alone they must be considered a category completely distinct from amusement or thrill parks, whose value is in the immediate gratification of successfully challenging physical and mental limits. The power of the themed environment lies in embodying critical shared cultural values as embedded in history, innovation, adventure, and fantasy. This is "entertainment" in its original meaning: that which engages the attention.

As a master communicator in image and symbol, Walt Disney did what all great artists do: he made the invisible and abstract concrete, in a form that can be experienced directly. Disneyland made the popular imagination visible in a way that few other landscapes, including Greenfield Village — Ford's pastiche of the American past — have been able to do. For that reason, it is not hard to understand why Walt Disney World Resort, the amplified, expanded version of the Disneyland prototype, is the world's leading tourist destination.

In this sense, the Disney theme parks offer a ready-made index to American culture. The historic draw of Disney parks lies within the themes and stories from many times and places, recreated as based on core American values. As such they are tangible expressions of the folktale as defined by Joseph Campbell: "told and retold, losing here a detail, gaining there a new hero, disintegrating gradually in outline, but re-created occasionally by some narrator. It is a democratic art — an art on which the whole community of mankind has worked" (qtd. in Schickel 208).

Theme parks are remarkable and even unique in their ability to resolve the inherent conflict between individual and shared values and create an art form — the "art of the show," as Imagineering puts it, as a platform for shared experience across generations and subcultures. This is why amusement parks, to raise their cultural stock, have escalated their category title to include "theme," even for the most obvious Six Flags coaster-based thrill park, and the current "theme" designation now covers many hybrid parks operating outside the pure Disney form. Thrill and amusement parks, including the Six Flags chain, Universal Studios, SeaWorld, and Busch Gardens all identify themselves as "theme parks" to fit into the Disney model (and create cachet for themselves), but they operate as far more traditional forms.

Works Cited

Blake, Peter. "The Lessons of the Parks." In *The Art of Walt Disney* by Christopher Finch, 423–449. New York: Harry Abrams, 1973.

Goldberger, Paul. "Mickey Mouse Teaches the Architects" *New York Times Magazine,* 22 October 1972: 40–41, 92–99.

Hench, John. *Designing Disney: Imagineering and the Art of the Show.* New York: Disney, 2003.

Jackson, Kathy Merlock. *Walt Disney: A Bio-Bibliography.* Westport, CT: Greenwood, 1993.

King, Margaret. "The Theme Park." In *The Guide to United States Popular Culture,* edited by Ray B. Browne and Pat Browne, 837–839. Bowling Green, OH: Bowling Green State University Popular Press, 2001.

Schickel, Richard. *The Disney Version.* New York: Simon and Schuster, 1968.

Snow, Richard. "Disney Coast to Coast." *American Heritage* 38:2 (February-March 1987): 22.

Walker, Derek. *Los Angeles (Architectural Digest Profile).* New York: St. Martin's, 1982.

Walt Disney Corporation. *Walt Disney: Famous Quotes.* Lake Buena Vista, FL: Walt Disney, 1994.

About the Contributors

Douglas Brode is a novelist, screenwriter, playwright, and multi-award winning journalist. He teaches courses in popular culture at Syracuse University's Newhouse School of Public Communications, Television-Radio-Film Department. His more than thirty books include two on Walt Disney (*From Walt to Woodstock* and *Multiculturalism and the Mouse*) and one on Rod Serling (*Rod Serling and the Twilight Zone: The 50th Anniversary Tribute*, co-authored by Carol Serling).

Eric Detweiler holds an MA in English from the University of Louisville and a BA in English from Belmont University. He has written and presented on the concept of hyperreality irony in popular culture, Southern culture and identity, writing center theory, and existential philosophy. He lives and teaches composition in Nashville, Tennessee.

Richard Francaviglia is a cartographic historian and historical geographer. He is a professor emeritus (University of Texas at Arlington) and lives in Salem, Oregon, where he operates his consulting firm Geo-Graphic Designs. He is especially interested in how the American landscape has changed over time and how this change is depicted in maps, art, film, and literature.

Derham Groves is a senior lecturer in architecture at the University of Melbourne in Australia and the author of the book *Feng-Shui and Western Building Ceremonies* (1991) and the article "Walt Disney's Backyard" (1994). His latest book is *There's No Place Like Holmes: Exploring Sense of Place Through Crime Fiction* (2008).

Katherine Howe is completing a PhD in American and New England studies at Boston University. She is the author of the *New York Times* bestselling novel *The Physick Book of Deliverance Dane*, a historical thriller about the Salem witch trials.

Kathy Merlock Jackson is a professor and coordinator of communications at Virginia Wesleyan College, where she specializes in media studies and children's culture. She has written *Images of Children in American Film: A Socio-Cultural Analysis*; *Walt Disney: A Bio-Bibliography*; *Rituals and Patterns in Children's Lives*; and *Walt Disney: Conversations*; and many articles. She edits *The Journal of American Culture* and is a former president of the American Culture Association.

Margaret J. King received the first graduate degree ever granted in popular culture and her PhD in American studies from the East-West Center at the University of Hawaii. As director of the Center for Cultural Studies and Analysis she researches and reports on the cultural archetypes, values, and themes that inform and drive the values and behavior of groups, organizations, and societies.

Robert Neuman is a professor of art history at Florida State University, where he teaches courses on early modern European art as well as the class Walt Disney and the American Century.

J. G. O'Boyle is a cultural analyst with the Center for Cultural Studies and Analysis, a Philadelphia-based think tank that studies the unconscious assumptions that drive group decision-making.

Suzanne Rahn is the author of *Rediscoveries in Children's Literature* (1995) and *The Wizard of Oz: Shaping an Imaginary World* (1998) and co-editor (with Susan R. Gannon and Ruth Anne Thompson) of *St. Nicholas and Mary Mapes Dodge* (2004).

Christian Renaut graduated from English University in Rennes, France, and became an English teacher. He interviewed 100 Disney artists for his book *From Snow White to Hercules*. He continues to write articles for the French press and participates in radio and television programs.

Cathy Scibelli is a freelance writer and editor living in East Norwich, New York. Her master's thesis at Excelsior College analyzed how Walt Disney created idealized environments that express the deep and often unarticulated hopes, dreams, fantasies, and beliefs of our culture. Her thesis can be accessed by contacting the Disney Archives in California.

Craig Svonkin is an assistant professor of English at Metropolitan State College of Denver. His areas of interest include children's literature, American poetry, Melville, film studies, and the Museum of Jurassic Technology in Culver City, California.

J. P. Telotte is a professor of film studies and chair of the School of Literature, Communication, and Culture at Georgia Institute of Technology. Co-editor of the journal *Post Script*, he has published widely on film and media studies. Among his books are *Disney TV*, *The Mouse Machine: Disney and Technology*, and *Animating Space*.

Mark I. West is a professor of English at the University of North Carolina at Charlotte, where he teaches courses on children's and young adult literature. He has written or edited a dozen books, including *The Japanification of Children's Popular Culture: From Godzilla to Miyazaki; A Children's Literature Tour of Great Britain; Psychoanalytic Responses to Children's Literature* (with Lucy Rollin); *Roald Dahl; Trust Your Children: Voices Against Censorship in Children's Literature*; and *Children, Culture and Controversy*.

Index

229